Justice and World Order

Justice and World Order

A Philosophical Inquiry

Janna Thompson

London and New York

First published 1992
by Routledge
11 New Fetter Lane, London EC4P 4EE

Simultaneously published in the USA and Canada
by Routledge
a division of Routledge, Chapman and Hall, Inc.
29 West 35th Street, New York, NY 10001

Set in 10/12pt Bembo by Witwell Ltd, Southport
Printed and bound in Great Britain by Clays Ltd, St Ives plc

British Library Cataloguing in Publication Data

Thompson, Janna,
  Justice and world order: a philosophical inquiry.
  I. Title
  341.552

Library of Congress Cataloging in Publication Data

Thompson, Janna
    Justice and world order: a philosophical inquiry/Janna
  Thompson.
        p. cm.
    Includes bibliographical references (p.   ) and index.
  1. Justice. 2. Justice and politics. 3. International relations.
I. Title.
JC578.T48   1992   91–30985
320′.01′1––dc20   CIP

ISBN 0–415–07033–3
ISBN 0–415–07034–1 pbk

Contents

Acknowledgements

I wish to thank all of the people who gave me help and encouragement, especially Professor H.J. McCloskey, Robert Young, John Campbell, Marion Tapper, Kim Lycos, Graeme Marshall, Mary Mulroney.

An earlier version of Chapter 6 was published as 'A rational world order: Hegel on international relations' in *International Journal of Moral and Social Studies* 2, 2: 105–18 (1987).

An earlier version of the Introduction was published as 'Towards a theory of international justice' in *Interdisciplinary Peace Research* 2, 2: 3–22 (1990).

Introduction – the problems of international justice: a survey

Now that the stalemate caused in world affairs by the Cold War has ended and problems of environmental degradation and resource distribution loom so large, the time has come, so it seems, to make the establishment of a just international world order into a political priority. The way in which a philosopher can contribute to the achievement of this objective seems obvious. What is needed is a well-grounded, universally acceptable conception of international justice. There are, however, a number of serious difficulties which stand in the way of performing this task, or even beginning it. Two forms of scepticism come to the surface as soon as the topic of international justice is introduced. The first is a doubt about whether international justice is possible at all, whether any conception of justice, however well grounded, could have much or any influence on world politics. The second is a doubt about whether the philosopher, or anyone else, will ever be able to come up with an acceptable answer to the question: what is international justice? I will explore in this section what these doubts mean and why they exist.

A strong current of pessimism runs through many accounts of world affairs, fuelled by reports of crises, conflicts, threats, repression and war. World politics presents us with a spectacle of greed, cruelty and conflict of the most destructive kinds. Since justice seems to have little to do with how leaders generally act, observers are inclined to conclude that appeals to principles of justice are forever doomed to be made in vain. The obvious response to this pessimistic view of the world is to point out that the mere fact that injustice is rife in world affairs does not give us reason to believe that a just international world is impossible. Optimists are able to point to small signs of progress, less well-publicised but positive developments in peace-making, international law or international co-operation. Why shouldn't it be reasonable to hope that the end of the Cold War and the ideological divisions it created will make a just world more easy to achieve?

However, the pessimism which people so often express about the possibility of a just world is nourished by roots that go deeper than mere observation. It is based on a conception of the 'necessities' governing the behaviour of agents in international affairs or on ideas about politics and human nature which seem to rule out the achievement of a truly just international order.

There are a number of starting places for this theoretically based pessimism. The first, and probably most familiar, is the set of positions commonly described as 'realist'.[1] The world, according to the realists, is an arena of conflict. Each state, pursuing its own interests in world affairs, will inevitably find itself in competition with others, for resources, allies, territory, influence. Since there is no authority, whether world government or dominant power, which can reliably force recalcitrant parties to obey a law, reach a settlement or keep the peace, each has to be prepared to defend its interests by force or the threat of force, and leaders must be concerned above all to maintain and enhance the power of their state. Given that the very survival of their society may be at stake, these leaders cannot afford to make justice their priority. States do what states must, and short of a radical and unlikely change in world politics international relations cannot be expected to be just.

This general statement of the realist position leaves open the question of whether appeals to justice mean anything at all in the international world. Some realists have denied this. In a famous passage the ancient Greek historian, Thucydides, concludes his account of the Athenian invasion of Melos by drawing the lesson that 'they that have odds of power exact as much as they can, and the weak yield to such conditions as they can get'. If every action that an international agent performs is rightly perceived by others as a threat or a sign of weakness, as the speech that he puts in the mouths of the Athenian generals suggests, then there is no room at all for the exercise of justice. A state willing to act justly would make itself vulnerable to the power of others – with unpleasant and possibly fatal consequences.

Michael Walzer in *Just and Unjust Wars* points out that this account of the 'necessities' of international politics ignores the political decision-making process in which matters of war and foreign policy are debated. In parliaments and councils acts of war are treated not as matters of necessity but matters of choice. There will always be reasons for and against courses of action. The Athenians were not compelled to engage in an act of aggression, and there were those who argued against this course. Where there is choice, Walzer says, moral considerations become relevant and political acts cannot be presented as if they were necessitated (1980a: 5).

Critics of Thucydides' version of realism also point out that the international world is not an arena in which everyone is continually threatening everyone else. Between most states of the world most of the time relations are friendly, or at least respectful, and for the most part leaders of states are prepared to keep their agreements, act according to international law and according to the informal rules for conducting relationships which they have built up over time. Moral opinion, including ideas about justice, do have some effect on how these leaders behave – though not to the degree that moralists desire (Cohen 1984).

What these objections against realism establish is that it is generally not true that leaders of states are compelled by their situation to ignore all other considerations but the pursuit of power. But how much room there is for the pursuit of justice depends upon the alternatives from which parliaments and councils have to choose. Though Walzer strongly advocates the pursuit of justice in international affairs, he admits that if the stakes are high enough, if the very survival of a state is in question, then there is no real choice but to meet power with power and to do whatever is necessary in self-defence, even if this means violating generally accepted moral principles. He gives the fight against Germany in World War II as an example of a 'supreme emergency', in which it was justifiable to do what had to be done in order to defeat the enemy (1977). In the age of nuclear weapons, he says, 'supreme emergency has become a permanent condition':

> Deterrence is a way of coping with that condition, and though it is a bad way, there may well be no other that is practical in a world of sovereign and suspicious states.

> (1980a: 274)

Thus Walzer, and many others, reject extreme statements of the realist position, such as that of Thucydides, but accept what is basic to the realist view of the world. Since laws can always be violated and agreements broken, the threat of aggression and violence always hovers in the background of international relations even in periods of relative peace. How much room there is for pursuing justice will depend upon how overt, persistent and serious these threats become. What separates Thucydides' world from Walzer's world are mere contingencies. If, in the future, states come into mortal conflict over non-renewable resources or land for a growing population – as some environmentalists fear – then parliaments and councils of states will be forced more and more frequently to make a choice between evils, and who will be surprised if they choose to do what they must to ensure the survival of their own society?

For many people the truth of the realist view of the world is a matter of commonsense which gains its plausibility from the dilemmas which sometimes face even the best-intentioned of leaders. The history of realism stretches back to the ancient world. Its more recent popularity among post-World War II academics, strategists and politicians stems, in part, from what people have taken to be the lesson taught to us by the rise of fascism and Nazi aggression: that it is necessary to meet power with power, and appeasement is an invitation to aggressors. Those who are in the grip of a realist view of the world are likely to regard the present abatement of hostilities between the great powers as a temporary lull, a vacuum in world power politics which will soon be filled by anarchic struggles between smaller states or by a resumption of conflict between the USA and USSR or between another constel-lation of big powers.[2] The best we can hope for, they say, is that there will be a more or less stable balance of power and room within its framework to act justly on most occasions. But we cannot reasonably hope that justice will ever become a dominant or over-riding consider-ation in world politics. Those who try to make it such are doomed to frustration or worse.

However, the realist lesson is not the only lesson which people have derived from history. After the experience of World War I, many thoughtful people concluded that war is caused by the preparation for it, and that power struggles between nations should be replaced by compromise and conciliation. It could be argued that in an age when threat and counter-threat between dominant powers could lead to nuclear war, this lesson is the one most relevant to us. If leaders and citizens have practical as well as moral reasons for wanting a peaceful and just world, then why can't they manage to achieve it? What are the 'necessities' of world politics which are supposed to make this impossible or unlikely? Before we can determine to what extent, if any, the international world can be just, we must look more closely at the assumptions realists make about agents in international affairs, their motivations and the situations in which they act.

In the last decades the realist view of international politics has been under attack by those who believe that interdependence, particularly economic interdependence, has changed the nature of international relations. Keohane and Nye argue that international relations, as a result of interdependence, have become more and more like domestic politics: issues other than power and security have become more and more predominant; agents other than states now play a significant role in international affairs; and the domestic affairs of states and domestic agents have an increasing effect on international developments, and vice versa. These changes to the international scene, they claim, are not compatible with the realist understanding of how international politics works (1977: Chs 1, 2).

Whether the nature of international politics is changing in a significant way is a matter of debate among experts on international relations. What those concerned with justice must also consider is what opportunities or difficulties interdependence (to the extent it exists or will exist) presents for the pursuit of justice in the international world. Some people are inclined to believe that the consequences will be favourable. Liberals of the nineteenth century used to argue that an interdependent world economy creates mutual prosperity and encourages peace, harmony and just relations: 'It is commerce which is rapidly rendering war obsolete', claimed John Stuart Mill, 'by strengthening and multiplying the personal interests which are in natural opposition to it' (1885: 582). His ideas about the future of the world were, to say the least, premature. But can we hope that these predictions are now coming true? Or is it more likely that present world economic and political developments will lead to greater injustice and more conflict?

Realism is not the only position from which optimistic hopes for a just world order can be contested. According to Marxists, capitalism – a system based upon private ownership and market relations – generates exploitation, conflict, revolution, war. If this position is true, then Mill and other advocates of world commerce are seriously wrong about the course of world developments and the possibility of justice and peace. If Marxists are right, we can expect that as capitalist and commercial relations spread over the world and come to dominate the relationships between societies and between people in most societies, injustice and conflict will become even more prevalent. The unavoidability of this result, short of revolutionary change, is at the heart of the Marxist view of international affairs, though in responding to the events of their times Marxists have presented different views about what form the exploitation and the resulting conflict will take.

Because the struggles and revolutions which Marxists predicted for advanced capitalist countries have not occurred, Marxist theory on social affairs is often dismissed as implausible. But even if it is, it still deserves serious consideration as a view about international developments. For if it is the welfare and economic management policies of national governments which have curbed the worst effects of capitalist competition (as Marxists and others sometimes argue), then in the international world, where these checks do not exist to any great extent, the war-like tendencies of the system should become manifest.

What separates Marxism from realism is its account of what forces drive international relations. Realism is a view about the logic of international politics. For Marxists, politics is wholly or largely epiphenomenal, and the significant developments of world society are the product of economic relationships. But what Marxist views about world affairs have in common with realism is the idea that conflict, injustice, threats of war are embedded in the very structure of relationships in the international world, and that so long as these relationships remain, the peaceful and just world which so many people have worked for or longed for will be impossible to achieve. Both views imply that only radical restructuring of world affairs would significantly alter this situation: for realists, the institution of world government or a world empire capable of making and enforcing a law; for Marxists, a world socialist revolution. If some version of either realism or Marxism is true, this would have profound implications for any attempt to bring about, or even envision, a just future world. I will therefore discuss these views at some length.

Pessimism about world affairs is not confined to those who have realist or Marxist views about social and political 'realities'. People may also believe that attempts to achieve universal justice are likely to fail, not because the structure of international society makes a just world impossible, but simply because there are tendencies in present policies of some states or propensities in human beings themselves which encourage war-like conflict and injustice. The unfortunate result, these pessimists think, is avoidable short of a revolutionary reorganisation of the world, but it is not likely to be avoided.

The roots of conflict and injustice are found, some people are inclined to believe, in human nature itself. We are by nature, they say, emotional and aggressive creatures who endlessly strive for dominance over each other and are not easily dissuaded from destructive behaviour by either reason or morality. Armed aggression, dominance of one state over another, are simply expressions on an international scale of our propensity towards violence or of an innate will to power (Morgenthau 1946). We cannot expect that the wickedness and perversity of human nature will be curbed by any conception of justice, however well supported by reason or moral considerations.

This conception of human nature – with its roots in the theological conception of original sin – has been one of the starting places for post-World War II American realism. But there have also been attempts to ground scientifically the idea that the roots of war and injustice are found in our basic biological or psychological make-up. Konrad Lorenz, an ethologist, argues in *On Aggression* (1966: Ch. 13) that the instinct of aggression, found throughout the animal kingdom, drives human beings towards war and attempts to dominate or destroy others. The sociobiologist E.O. Wilson claims that group hostilities, and the atrocities these groups sometimes commit, spring from an inclination, programmed into us by our genes, to defend and sacrifice ourselves for the sake of those who share our genes (1978: Ch. 7). Freud in 'Why war?' suggests that behind the atrocities of histories and the cruelties of everyday life is a death instinct, an aggressive drive, which stands in the way of the achievement of a truly civilised and peaceful world (1933: 209). Neither the ethologists and sociobiologists nor Freud are claiming that a just and peaceful world society is impossible. Lorenz thinks that people can be moral if they are determined enough to resist their instinctive impulses, and Freud hopes that enlightened, rational leaders can direct group instincts into harmless channels. But on the whole their conception of human nature leaves us with the impression that the prospect for a peaceful and just world is not favourable.

Lorenz and the sociobiologists have been frequently criticised for putting forward views that are conceptually confused or inadequately supported by evidence. In any case, even those who share their approach do not invariably agree with them about the sources of human conflict and injustice. Eibl-Eibesfeldt (1979) suggests, for example, that human beings have a natural tendency to settle their differences with minimum conflict, and that the extreme violence prevalent in the modern world has to be explained in terms of culture rather than nature. Freud's psychological theory is similarly controversial, and those who are Freudians do not all accept his postulation of an aggressive drive. Wilhelm Reich (1970) argues, for example, that aggressive and exploitative behaviour is best explained and treated in a Freudian framework as the consequence of sexual repression suffered by members of the patriarchal family. However, what makes theories about the biological or psychological basis of human aggression and domination perennially attractive, in spite of their questionable scientific basis and their controversial nature, is the persistence not only of conflict and injustice, but of what can only be described as irrational hatred, blind ambition, ideological madness; and nowhere is human perversity more prominently displayed than in international affairs. Whether or not there is any truth to biological theories about human behaviour, the facts that they are trying to explain are bound to be a worry to anyone concerned about international justice.

The same point can be made about another set of hypotheses which lead people to make pessimistic prognoses about the future of the world. Liberals and Marxists of the nineteenth and twentieth centuries have sometimes worried about what they describe as the 'militarist' tendencies in their society. This term is generally used to describe a state of affairs in which political rights and freedoms are undermined by the requirements of the military establishment, military aims come to dictate both domestic and foreign policy, and commitments to peace and international justice are forgotten. That modern societies, east and west, north and south, have become or are becoming increasingly militarist remains a popular hypothesis for explaining the behaviour of political and military elites, as well as the ideological commitments of populations.[3]

E.P. Thompson argues in 'Notes on exterminism' that in both the USSR and the USA, economic, technological and political factors are creating an 'inertia', an 'internal dynamic' which encourages an arms race and military confrontation.

> There is an internal dynamic and reciprocal logic here which requires a new category for its analysis. If 'the hand-mill gives you society with the feudal lord; the steam-mill, society with the industrial capitalist' what are we given by those Satanic mills which are now at work, grinding out the means of human extermination?
>
> (1980: 7)

The category we need, he says, in order to describe contemporary tendencies is 'exterminism'. If exterminism does indeed result in extermination it will not be because of a logic of international affairs or any necessities within capitalism, he thinks, but because of tendencies internal to both the United States and the Soviet Union: the militarisation of their economies and scientific institutions, the technological developments generated by these institutions, and the influence of military elites and military agendas on political affairs. Thompson does not believe that the forces which create 'exterminism' are irresistible, but by describing them as constituting an 'internal dynamic' he is suggesting that we will be fortunate indeed if they are successfully resisted.

The ending of the Cold War and the subsequent willingness of the USSR and the USA to get rid of some of their armaments suggest that Thompson was overly pessimistic about the political processes and economic tendencies in these countries. But the exterminism hypothesis is by no means dead. It remains to be seen whether the interests of arms manufacturers and the military establishments can be subordinated to the process of bringing about peace; it remains to be seen whether the arms race will really come to an end. In any case, the increasing traffic in arms to developing countries and the build-up of military might in some areas (Klare 1990) give us reason to fear that militarism in one form or another will continue to have a devastating effect on the world.

In this book I will not attempt to refute the 'exterminism' hypothesis; nor will I discuss theories about the biological origins of aggression and hatred, and thus even those who agree with what I have to say about international justice may remain deeply pessimistic about the future of the world. But though I do not try to show how all of the barriers which may stand in the way of a just world order can be eliminated, central to the approach I take is the idea that a theory of justice ought to be practical. This means, first of all, that it should provide a plausible account of the social, political, psychological conditions in which people are likely to satisfy the requirements of the theory. Not everyone can be expected to be just, and perhaps no one is likely to be just all of the time. But if a social order is to count as just, then compliance with just laws or procedures must be fairly widespread (however this is achieved). Second, we must have reason to believe that this state of social, political, psychological affairs can actually be achieved (if it has not been achieved already). The usefulness of a theory of justice obviously depends upon these conditions being satisfied. People are not so likely to strive to bring into existence a world order if they do not think this world order can actually be realised or if they do not think that its maintenance is humanly possible. But more important, the validity of a theory of justice – whether it can be regarded as true – and its practicality are intimately related.

A theory of justice tells us how individuals and groups with their different and sometimes conflicting interests and needs can resolve their disputes, adjudicate their claims and define their entitlements in accordance with their conceptions of what is rational and moral. A necessary condition of a theory being acceptable, then, is that people who count as rational and moral be in the end willing and able to comply with its judgments. If these people do not accept its consequences, and cannot be persuaded by argument and moral appeals to do so, then we have good reason to regard the theory as unsound. If they are not generally in a position to act according to its judgments, and they either cannot, or do not want to, make the changes to their objectives or their political arrangements which would be required in order to put the theory into practice, then however appealing in other ways, it is not a theory appropriate for their use, and for that reason will have to be rejected. If, on the other hand, they are prepared to accept it and abide by it, then there is also a good chance that they will be able to overcome the difficulties, whether inherent in human nature or embedded in social institutions, which stand in the way of a peaceful and just resolution of disputes.

A theory of justice, so understood, always has a context. It has to be appropriate to the interests and objectives of individuals and groups in the political-social environment in which these interests are formed and expressed – either the environment which already exists or one which they can be persuaded would be desirable and possible to create.[4] To be practical, a theory of justice must either presuppose or propound a view about social organisation – about what a just social order would be like – and a view about the interests and motivations of those who are supposed to live according to its principles and procedures. In the case of a theory of international justice this requirement poses a problem: the international world is in flux and even experts disagree about what outcomes are possible or desirable. Thus we cannot take for granted a fixed or generally accepted political and social background from which to theorise. What distinguishes my approach to international justice from many others is that I take as central the question of world organisation. My concern is not primarily to come up with principles of international justice but to try to work out what a just world would be like, what forms of political authority it would contain, what social relations and motivations it would encourage.

What political and social arrangements are possible or likely in the international world is not a matter on which a philosopher can definitively pronounce. Nevertheless, philosophers too can have their opinions, and indeed all theories of justice contain, explicitly or implicitly, ideas about social organisation, as well as assumptions about the interests of individuals and groups. So it seems important to bring these ideas out into the open, subject them to criticism, and consider alternatives. This is my principal task. If in the course of carrying it out I venture onto the plane of social theory, I am doing no more than what other philosophers have done and must do.

For a theory of justice to be acceptable – for it to count as true – it is not enough that people be persuaded or induced to accept it. It must be accepted for the right reasons. The principles, procedures, ideals which it contains must be in accordance with the considered judgments about matters of justice of rational, morally sensitive people, or at least it must be something about which these agents can reach a mutually satisfactory compromise. What makes many people sceptical about the very idea of a theory of international justice is that they have doubts about whether agreement or compromise over principles or procedures of justice is possible.

The problem is once again not merely that people as a matter of fact disagree about what justice is and what actions and situations are just. There are deeper difficulties which lie in wait for any attempt to theorise about international justice. These problems are created or aggravated by the nature of social and political relations in the international world and the allegiances and ideals which are an intrinsic part of this world. The first is the difficulty of reconciling the entitlements which states are generally assumed to possess with demands that are often made in the name of justice – that human rights be protected, that individual needs be fulfilled, that past wrongs be righted, that economic justice be done – demands which challenge or threaten the international status quo. The second is the difficulty of justifying, or even propounding, a universal moral theory in a world in which moral differences of opinion are profound and in which the very criteria of moral justification are in dispute.

The first difficulty becomes evident as soon as we begin to examine existing theories of international justice. Among philosophers and other political theorists there have been two basic approaches to international justice. The first builds on the body of doctrine called Just War Theory, deriving an account of international obligations from commonly held assumptions about the rights associated with national sovereignty. The second attempts to apply theories of domestic justice to international society by focusing on individuals and their entitle- ments. Both of these approaches are problematic.

Just War Theory in both its traditional and more contemporary versions defines what counts as a justified war (as well as setting out the rules for conducting war in a just fashion), and in doing so it both defines what acts are just and unjust in world society and indicates what must be the case if peace is to prevail in the world. When John Rawls, in a short discussion of international justice in *A Theory of Justice*, considers what representatives of states, if they were forced to be impartial, would accept as principles of justice, he arrives at the fundamental idea accepted in most modern versions of Just War Theory: that each state has an equal right of self-determination, and thus each has an entitlement to defend its sovereignty against outside intervention, by war if necessary, with the proviso that war be conducted in a just fashion (1980a: 378–9). Michael Walzer in *Just and Unjust Wars* begins by defining 'the crime of aggression', the paradigm case of which is armed invasion of the territory of a state by the armed forces of another, and argues that not only do states have an entitlement to defend themselves against aggression, but that it is the responsibility of agents in world society to counter aggression and punish aggressors (1980a: 51ff.).

Behind the insistence that aggression is a violation of 'rights to which we attach enormous importance' (Walzer 1980a: 53) is the assumption that the citizens of a state through their institutions and leaders are entitled to exercise political sovereignty over the territory they occupy, determining for themselves their laws, their way of life, their political system. Justice in international society for proponents of Just War Theory consists in people recognising and respecting the sovereignty exercised by others unless there are very good reasons for intervention.

One of the problems with this common conception of international justice is that what counts as aggression, or more generally, unjustified intervention, is notoriously difficult to define. A theory which concentrates on condemning armed aggression is clearly insufficient. For in a world becoming more interdependent, states can interfere, intentionally or unintentionally, in each other's affairs in many different ways: through tariff and trade policies, economic incentives and disincentives, political pressure, clandestine activities, etc. The way in which the people of one country develop their industries may have detrimental environmental and economic effects on the people of another. It seems reasonable to require that a theory of international justice have something to say about these different kinds of interferences: what constitutes an injustice and what should be done about it.

An equally serious problem with a conception of international justice based on the rights of national sovereignty is that it takes no account of social inequalities – of divisions in the world between rich and poor. This is a serious failing, first of all because this inequality is widely perceived to be unfair: why should we tolerate a situation in which some people are born to misery and starvation and others have far more than they need for a decent life? Moreover, once we acknowledge that our activities can be responsible, directly or indirectly, for the plight of others, then it is difficult to deny that we have a duty of justice to alleviate the suffering we cause and ensure that the harm will not continue.

> In an interdependent world, confining principles of social justice to domestic societies has the effect of taxing poor nations so that others may benefit from living in 'just' societies.
>
> (Beitz 1979: 150)

It seems reasonable to require that a theory of international justice deal with problems of resource distribution.

A further reason for being dissatisfied with a theory of international justice based on the entitlement of states is that it is inherently conservative. It assumes that the international world is and should be a system of states, and that the states which happen to exist have in general a right to exist. This conservatism means, first of all, that it cannot adequately take into account the existence and operations of international agents which, according to Keohane and Nye (1977), have an increasing impact on world affairs, e.g. transnational companies, international regulatory bodies, financial institutions, etc. It seems reasonable to expect a theory of international justice to have something to say about the activities of these organisations.

Furthermore, a theory which assumes the legitimacy of the international status quo cannot adequately deal with challenges to this status quo – challenges which come from those who believe that some presently existing states have no entitlement to existence or to the territory they presently occupy, or from those who believe that a state system of any kind is inherently unjust or unable to cope with our existing problems. An adequate theory of international justice should provide a basis for justifying or criticising existing or alternative conceptions of world political organisation.

In short, a theory of justice based on the entitlements of sovereign states seems inadequate to deal with the questions of justice which inevitably arise in world affairs, especially in a world becoming increasingly interdependent. For this reason Charles Beitz in *Political Theory and International Relations* (1979) argues that in our present situation a more demanding theory is required, one similar to what has been proposed for domestic societies.[5] The approach to international justice that Beitz favours relies upon the method adopted by John Rawls for arriving at principles of justice. In *A Theory of Justice* Rawls argues that individuals, however diverse and contrary their interests and objectives, would arrive at mutually acceptable basic principles for governing the social affairs of their society if they made their choice in the 'original position'. In the original position individuals are assumed to be rational, to have a sense of justice and to know all the relevant facts about their society, including theories about social and economic affairs. But they are constrained to make their choice of principles behind the 'veil of ignorance' where no one knows what class he/she belongs to, or what race or sex; no one knows what position he/she occupies in society or what idea of the good he/she ascribes to.

Given that individuals behind the veil of ignorance are forced to be completely objective, Rawls believes that they will agree on two basic principles of justice: they will agree that the freedom of individuals to pursue their own ends is fundamental to a just society, and will thus insist that each person is entitled to have an equal right to the most extensive basic liberty compatible with a similar liberty for others (what Rawls calls the 'equal liberty principle'). Each individual will also wish to ensure that the resources and benefits of his/her society will be distributed in a way that will not be disadvantageous – whatever his/her interests or position in society turn out to be. Rawls argues that rational individuals will want to minimise the bad effects they might suffer if they find themselves in the worst-off position in society, and will thus choose a principle that requires that whatever social and economic inequalities are allowed to exist work to create the greatest possible advantage to the least advantaged – with the proviso that offices and positions be open to all under conditions of fair equality of opportunity. This is what Rawls calls the 'difference principle'.

Rawls assumes that he is constructing a theory of justice for a national society. But since his argument is that any rational individual behind the veil of ignorance will choose the equal liberty principle and the difference principle to govern social affairs, Beitz sees no reason why this result cannot be further generalised. If we stick everyone in the world in the original position, if these individuals are assumed to be ignorant of their nationality, as well as of their race, class, etc., if they are, on the other hand, fully aware of the way in which, in an interdependent world society, they create benefits and burdens for each other, then it is likely, Beitz argues, that they will arrive at the same two principles of justice for international society. They will acknowledge that 'persons of diverse citizenship have distributive obligations to one another analogous to those of citizens of the same state' (1979: 128).

What is attractive about this approach is that it seems able to deal with the problems that an international theory of justice ought to be able to address. It makes no apparent assumptions about the desirability of a political status quo. It appeals directly to the needs of all the individuals who make up world society. The interests and activities of states, transnational companies and other bodies, their very existence, can thus be criticised in the name of justice. Moreover, it has something to say about how the resources of the world ought to be distributed given the needs of individuals.

On the other hand, it is not at all clear how his theory can be applied to the international world. There is, for one thing, no world political body capable of taxing rich individuals for the sake of the least well-off; no world body capable of ensuring that resources actually benefit needy individuals. To make this theory practical it seems that we need, at the very least, an organisation capable of administering and enforcing a universal system of social distribution. But if such a political initiative seems unfeasible or undesirable, then the theory of justice which makes it a requirement begins to look irrelevant or dubious. Beitz argues that his theory should be regarded as an ideal to which individuals and states ought to aspire. The question remains how we can regard something as an ideal without seriously considering what political and social changes are required in order to realise it and whether these changes would be possible and desirable. Beitz has to persuade us that his theory is practical.

Another related difficulty for Beitz's approach is that there is not likely to be any agreement among individuals in world society about what the difference principle actually requires: what social inequalities are relevant, what resources worst-off individuals can reasonably demand. Rawls' theory assumes that individuals of a society will be able to agree on a list of basic goods, and in his later writings he is prepared to admit that this list contains items which are only likely to be valued by people in a liberal democratic society – things like liberty, wealth, freedom of movement and free choice of occupation (1988: 257). Even so, he has been criticised for making assumptions which are far from universal within democratic, pluralist societies. The problem becomes more pronounced when the theory is applied to a world in which not all societies are liberal or democratic, or have the same prevailing idea of what goods are most important.

Whether a theory of justice similar to Rawls' theory could in practice be applied to world society thus remains in doubt. However, Beitz's theory of international justice encounters a more serious challenge: that the difference principle, however interpreted, is likely to be regarded by many rational, moral agents as inappropriate for international society. This is indeed assumed by Rawls himself. The representatives of states whom he puts in the 'original position' accept an equivalent of the equal liberty principle, but not an equivalent of the difference principle. Why this is so is not difficult to understand. Rawls' theory of justice is a contract theory. It makes assumptions about the nature of the social relations which people have with each other and the social life they want to achieve and maintain. In a liberal pluralist society, he supposes, people not only have co-operative relationships but are sufficiently committed to maintaining them, and sufficiently value the principles and institutions on which they are founded, to be willing to accept the idea that some of the fruits of their labours and talents should be distributed to others within their community.[6] The question remains what should be distributed and how, but in a community where people have developed the kind of relations which encourage them to take responsibility for each other, the difference principle is, at least, an appropriate result of the contract-making process. But outside this community, a commitment to maintaining co-operative relationships cannot be assumed to exist, let alone the values of a liberal pluralist society. Rawls, like many others, thus assumes that in international society, where there are no strong universal bonds, where people in general are not inclined to recognise a duty to care for each other, where leaders and citizens of states are inclined to place their own interests above those of foreigners and to object to outside interference, principles of justice will have to be based on mutual tolerance and a respect for the rights of sovereign states. It is this perception which makes the Just War approach intuitively appealing in spite of its obvious drawbacks.

Beitz suggests, however, that our intuitions about what is fair or unfair in world society are unreliable. The nature of international society is changing so fast that our ideas about social relationships and our moral attitudes are undoubtedly outmoded and inadequate. This is presumably the reason why he ignores presently existing social bonds, our feelings about them, and our resulting ideas about what is fair, and why he insists on basing his conception of justice on the 'reality' of economic interdependence. Obligations of justice, he says, are not created by sentiment but by the existence of co-operation and interdependence. If applicability of principles of justice did depend upon sympathy and solidarity, he argues, then people within a family, a local community, would be justified in keeping their resources to themselves. As citizens of national states, we do not regard this kind of selfishness as justifiable. Why then should we think that national sentiments are an acceptable reason for people of nations to refuse to recognise international principles of distributive justice (1979: 155ff.)?

However, obligations are not created by interdependence any more than they are by sentiment. This is particularly so when these relations are perceived to be burdensome and exploitative (as is the case sometimes even within states). Interdependence and co-operation are not the same thing. But even if everyone in the world did benefit from economic interdependence this would not be enough to lay the foundations for the application of a difference principle. For this principle presupposes, for one thing, that people not only have mutually beneficial relationships but that they desire to maintain them. Within states this presupposition is generally fulfilled (though not always). However, in international society where relations of interdependence are not always chosen or welcomed, it cannot be regarded as surprising if people refuse to acknowledge the obligations which Beitz tries to thrust upon them, especially if these duties require further disruption or dissolution of those social bonds, national or local, which they regard as important. This consideration raises the question of why increasing economic interdependence should be taken as given. In some states leaders and citizens attempt to deal with the problems caused by the international economy by asserting national control over economic affairs: by imposing tariffs, limiting the entry of foreign capital, nationalising industries and financial institutions, providing subsidies to local industry, establishing marketing boards, etc. This reaction to increasing interdependence, though difficult to carry through effectively, is not obviously irrational or immoral. Indeed those who attempt it often do so because they believe that they will only be able to preserve their culture and determine their own political destiny if they are independent enough to control their economic affairs.

We can now see that Beitz's approach to international justice makes assumptions which are just as questionable as the assumptions made by the Just War approach. Just War Theory takes the entitlements of sovereignty for granted and closes off attempts to criticise these entitlements. Beitz's theory takes for granted world economic interdependence and closes off criticisms of the way in which world economic affairs are presently developing. Nevertheless, the inadequacies of Beitz's approach leave us with a problem: inequalities in world society, doubts about entitlements of sovereignty and about the legitimacy of the present international status quo suggest that a more robust theory of international justice is needed than that provided by the Just War approach. On the other hand, my criticism of Beitz suggests that existing loyalties, social commitments or political ideals are likely to make any more robust theory unacceptable as well as impractical. The search for a theory of international justice thus seems to lead to an impasse. One of my objectives in this book is to find a way out of this predicament.

There is another reason for fearing that the search for a theory of international justice is a hopeless and questionable activity: prescriptions about international justice, it might be argued, presuppose the existence of a moral standpoint which transcends the ethical traditions of particular cultures, and are thus subject to post-modernist criticisms of transcendentalism and 'totalising' theories or to communitarian complaints about individualist approaches to ethical justification. These critics of 'universalist' or cosmopolitan morality argue that there is no adequate foundation for theories which attempt to justify actions or policies by reference to individual rights or interests, the desirability of universal liberation, eternal peace or human progress. Neither appeals to rationality, nor the transcendentalism of Kant, nor the original position of Rawls and Beitz can ground universal ideals or principles of justice. For all of these starting points presuppose questionable views about individuals, their needs, interests and objectives, and their way of reasoning – questionable either because they assume things about individuals which are not universally true or because the very conception of the individual on which justification rests is incoherent or inadequate.

Jean-François Lyotard insists that the supposedly impartial, rational stance of the moral philosopher, who pontificates about what we ought to do, turns out to be inadequately grounded and partial. The attempt to legislate for everyone, which universalistic appeals to human progress, social justice, human emancipation, etc. inevitably involve, contributes, he thinks, to the marginalisation, subordination and oppression of those who do not satisfy the 'standards' set by moral theory for being rational, moral or impartial. The post-modern, he says, is 'incredulity toward meta-narratives', a recognition and acceptance of heterogeneity and incommensurability (1984: xxiv, v).

Communitarian critics of universalistic morality argue that the concept of the impartial moral agent, the transcendental ego of Kantian philosophers, or even the self who chooses principles of justice in Rawls' original position, is incoherent, and thus the moral principles or ethical standpoint which this self is supposed to validate are meaningless or inadequately grounded. The self, says Richard Rorty, is a continually changing network of beliefs, desires, emotions, which is always located historically and socially. It is not capable of the transcendence and impartiality which Kant or Rawls requires of it (1983: 585–6). The self, says Michael Sandel, is embedded in the social relations of a community. Our membership of a community shapes our self-identity, and thus affects what we regard as morally meaningful. We cannot regard ourselves as autonomous subjects capable of constructing a moral standpoint for ourselves (1982: 179).

From these criticisms of the transcendent, impartial self and the impartial perspective comes a moral standpoint which is tied to a local discourse, a particular community or historical tradition. Morality from this point of view arises out of the particular loyalties and relationships which people have developed with each other, and there is no way of appealing beyond these traditions to some universal or transcendental ideal or principle. A tradition-independent standard of judgment, says MacIntyre, is impossible (1988: 353).

These post-modernist and communitarian criticisms seem to place an insurmountable barrier in the way of any attempt to formulate an international theory of justice. For such a theory has to appeal in some way beyond the traditions of particular communities in order to provide a basis for resolving disputes between them, and it is this appeal which the critics seem to be suggesting is impossible or pernicious. Moreover, a theory of international justice, whether it comes from a transcendental standpoint or somewhere more mundane, seems to require general consensus, which, given the way in which moral agents are tied to their communities and the incommensurability of their traditions or discourses, is not likely to be forthcoming.

However, post-modern and communitarian critics need some account of how communities, or people with different language games or traditions, are supposed to relate to each other and resolve conflicts, and in fact these critics generally appeal explicitly or implicitly to a principle or ideal of tolerance. Lyotard recommends that we should learn to live with difference and incommensurability. This, he suggests, is a requirement of justice in a world of difference (1984: 66). Presumably the 'principle of tolerance' implies that traditions or communities which are belligerent, aggressive and intolerant to others are acting unjustly. We can, it seems, sometimes criticise communities from the 'outside'. If nation-states count as communities, as Rorty and others seem to assume, then the post-modern or communitarian standpoint seems to imply a conception of international justice similar to that of Just War Theory.

Post-modernists and communitarians do not want to abandon all universal ideas of justice; nor do they want to imply that individuals cannot be critical of their communities and traditions or are not entitled to criticise them. Are critics of cosmopolitanism and individualism being inconsistent – denying the possibility of universal moral principles and yet relying on them? The answer to this question depends upon what exactly communitarians or post-modernists mean by insisting that individuals as moral agents are constituted by their membership of a community and that communities or traditions are incommensurable. If the moral standpoint of individuals is entirely determined by their community, and if there is no way in which they can find a standpoint from which relations in the community can be judged, then a theory of inter-community justice, however minimal, is impossible. For no moral basis would exist for condemning even the most intolerant, war-like or authoritarian communities. If the moral standpoints of communities are totally incommensurable, then it is doubtful that they will reach any agreements about justice. But for those who do not hold these extreme positions it seems possible to retain an anti-transcendental perspective and yet advance an international theory of justice. One way in which this might be done is to argue that the international world itself is or could be a community – with its own relationships, traditions and standards.

This is what Walzer can be understood to be doing in *Just and Unjust Wars*. Having disposed of Thucydides' version of realism, which if true would take international relations beyond the reach of any moral reasoning, he sets out what he calls 'the legalistic paradigm' – the principles of law and order and assumptions about the entitlements of states which constitute the tradition of what he calls 'international society' (1980a: 161ff.). He then develops and revises this paradigm in the light of particular problems and conflicts which international society has had to face. So understood, Walzer's version of Just War Theory is not founded upon theological premises or appeals to natural law or on a contract made in the 'original position'. It appeals to ideals, principles and agreements which leaders and citizens of states have come to accept and value.

The problem with Walzer's approach, as I have argued, is its inherent conservatism. If international society is changing as drastically as Beitz and some critics of realism suggest, then the legalistic paradigm deserves to be challenged. But since we can respond in different ways to interdependence, what we really want is a ground for thinking that one response is better than others as far as the promotion of justice is concerned. Why should we value and want to maintain the traditional relations associated with the 'legalistic paradigm'? Walzer answers this question by appealing to the value of the 'common life', which individuals through their shared experiences and co-operation over a long period of time have developed within the territory of a state. 'Most states do stand guard over the community of their citizens, at least to some degree: that is why we assume the justice of their defensive wars' (1980a: 54). The international order, in other words, is a means for preserving communities which are of value. But this defence provokes an obvious question: why should the national community be valued so highly? Walzer not only has to counter the critics of the state – those who argue that state authority is basically repressive and destructive of individual liberty and true community – but also those who believe that justice would be best realised in a world society in which state sovereignty is valued less or not at all. Walzer's defence of the legalistic paradigm is thus inadequate, or at least incomplete.

As these remarks suggest, this book will be centrally concerned with two approaches to questions about justice and world order: what I call the cosmopolitan and communitarian points of view. Those described as cosmopolitan do not all operate with the same moral theories or arrive at the same principles of justice; but what they have in common is the idea that a social order must be justified in terms of how it affects the entitlements of individuals or their general welfare where these entitlements can be specified, or comparative benefits evaluated, independently of commitment to any particular social relations. A community or world order is good or bad, just or unjust, depending on whether in it human rights or individual autonomy are respected, or human happiness or the satisfaction of individual preferences is maximised. A cosmopolitan position, in other words, provides an external standpoint from which any community or social order can be judged, and its approach is 'individualist' in the sense that it insists that societies are to be evaluated in terms of what they do to or for individuals considered as such. Cosmopolitanism is clearly 'universalist' and 'totalising', but whether it necessarily rests on transcendental premises remains to be seen.

Communitarians insist that cosmopolitan criteria are an

unsatisfactory standpoint for moral evaluation. For if individuals are constituted wholly or in part by the social relations of their communities, if their goals, their ethical judgments and their sense of justice are inextricably bound up with community life, then why should they accept the criteria or evaluations of cosmopolitans? Where do these 'external' criteria get their authority? But communitarians not only bring into question the criteria and methods of cosmopolitans; they also claim that justice requires respect for communities and the values associated with community. What communities deserve respect, whether there is any satisfactory way of determining this, are questions that a theory of international justice obviously has to face.

Formulating a practical theory of international justice clearly requires that we go beyond abstract discussions of cosmopolitanism and communitarianism. For this reason I begin my examination of the issues raised by these two basic positions with a discussion of the theories about society, morality and international order of philosophers who belong to the modern political philosophy tradition: the tradition of Hobbes, Locke, Rousseau, Kant, Mill, Marx, Hegel, Fichte and their more recent successors. This tradition contains both cosmopolitan and communitarian perspectives, but in the context of theories which attempt to deal with the basic problems of modern political life.

The theories which belong to this tradition were from the beginning a response to historical developments – above all, to the problems created by the development of modern states, of political societies whose institutions of government are supposed to exercise sovereignty over a population of individuals who belong to different classes, races, religions, ethnic groups, and at the same time maintain the integrity and independence of the body politic in a world of sovereign states. For such societies to be viable, individuals have to be prepared not only to obey the laws of the state and when necessary subordinate their other interests, including other community interests, to the authority of its political and legal institutions. They also have to be loyal to their own particular state and prepared to defend it against other states. Central to the modern political philosophy tradition is the question of what justifies this requirement of obedience and loyalty. The very nature of the modern pluralist state makes it difficult to answer. First of all, it might be doubted whether there is any rational basis for political consensus in a society so diverse. But even if there are ideals, principles which everyone acknowledges ought to be realised in their political society, these are likely to be too general to serve as a justification for loyalty to any particular state. If the institutions of my society deserve support because they respect human rights (for example), then the question still remains why I should be any more obligated to my state than to any other equally just state; why I should value the continuation of my political society, as opposed to any equally just alternative political arrangement.[7]

The problem of justifying the state is clearly bound up with the problem of justifying a world order. If the state as a sovereign political body has no good reason for being, then the question arises why individuals should not advocate and try to establish a new kind of political order – perhaps a world state or a system of large regional states. Are the problems which stand in the way of establishing a new world order merely practical, or are there moral grounds for objecting to the disappearance of existing states? Is the 'common life' that people in a state are supposed to share something that justifies us in defending our state in the face of proposals for a new world system? If not, what kinds of community should the international world contain? The political theories advanced by philosophers in the modern tradition implicitly or explicitly take a position on international organisation and international justice, and in so doing provide answers to these questions. Their views thus deserve examination as a starting point for a theory of international justice and as a way of making concrete the opposition between cosmopolitans and communitarians.

There are other equally important ways in which the concerns of the thinkers in this tradition are central to an inquiry into the nature and possibility of international justice. As philosophers they are essentially concerned with questions of moral justification. As social theorists they advance ideas about the nature and development of modern societies. One way of approaching the problem of justice from a practical point of view is thus to try to determine how well their justifications and theories meet the problems already discussed and whether their perspectives can be made relevant to the issues of our times. Using the resources of this tradition, I will advance a conception of international justice and world order which is respectful of difference and the value of community, but at the same time takes as central the liberty and well being of individuals. Though I argue for a particular idea of international order, this book is more of an exploration of problems than the presentation of a theory. It is one contribution to a discourse which I hope will become more widespread.

Part I

From a cosmopolitan point of view

Chapter 1

Being realistic

The world would be just, as well as peaceful, if every agent in the international world were willing and able, now and in the future, to act in accordance with universally acceptable principles and procedures of justice. In an age when disputes and acts of aggression can lead to enormously destructive wars there are both prudential and moral reasons for wanting to achieve a just and peaceful world. Why, then, can't we do so?

There are, as we have seen, various answers to this question, but among the most powerful and persuasive are the ideas about international politics propounded by those who call themselves 'realists'. Realism is not merely one theory or doctrine, but a large number of related views, some more extreme in their implications than others. Thus those who refute one version have by no means defeated realism, and indeed philosophers who oppose what they call realism may be realists of another sort – as I have suggested is the case for Walzer.

There are two basic kinds of realism. The first is a set of explanatory theses intended to account for the international world as it is and to explain why idealistic hopes for a just and peaceful world are bound to be frustrated. The second is a collection of moral doctrines which tell us that leaders of states ought to concentrate on pursuing the interests of their states in world affairs, or, alternatively, that they ought to strive to achieve and maintain a balance of power – and that in doing these things they cannot afford to pay much, if any, attention to what is just.[1] The various theses and doctrines which can be labelled as 'realist' have different justifications and sometimes incompatible results. For example, realism as a moral doctrine is inconsistent with the idea that there is and can be no morality in international affairs. Those realists who maintain that leaders have an obligation to pursue the interests of their state are likely to reach different conclusions about what ought to be done from realists who believe that leaders ought to strive to maintain a balance of power. For the second objective sometimes requires that national interests be sacrificed.

What all of the versions of realism have in common is that they deny, explicitly or implicitly, the possibility of realising a just world society. The more extreme forms, as, for example, the realism espoused by Thucydides, deny that morality of any kind has an application or makes any sense in world affairs. The less extreme forms merely assert that, given the realities of the world, leaders cannot always afford to act justly. For they will be faced, more or less frequently, with what Walzer calls 'a supreme emergency'. Realism as a moral doctrine attempts to persuade us that for the sake of the national interest, or for the sake of peace, we cannot afford to worry too much, or at all, about requirements of justice.

The relation between the cosmopolitan point of view and realism is a complex one. On the one hand, they are at odds with each other: realism is what cosmopolitans have to defeat in order to provide sufficient scope for the operation of a cosmopolitan idea of justice in international affairs. On the other hand, realists often presuppose, and themselves subscribe to, a cosmopolitan moral outlook. Realists have often been concerned with questions about world order, and post-World War II realists in particular have often had as their aim to determine how we can achieve peace and security, to the extent that these are possible in an imperfect world. Behind their pronouncements on this matter is often the idea that it would be nice if justice in the form of a universal respect for human rights and individual freedom could prevail in the world, but unfortunately international realities make that impossible; or, in the case of the moral versions of realism, they imply that the morality appropriate to world affairs is some version of consequentialism – another form of cosmopolitan morality. The well-being of everyone in the world, they are saying, is more likely to be maximised if leaders concentrate on pursuing the national interest or maintaining a balance of power rather than on pursuing idealistic objectives. The very term 'realism' suggests a cosmopolitan reference point – it invites a contrast between universal moral principles and what it is possible to achieve in the real world.

There are, it is true, doctrines which might be regarded as forms of realism which reject cosmopolitanism, even as a reference point. Hegel, for example, holds that our ethical duties flow out of the relationships we have to others within our state and to the state itself. Outside of what is entailed by the 'ethical life of the state' there is nothing on which to base an appeal to justice – not even as an ideal which cannot be realised. Requirements of justice fail to apply to international affairs, not because of the necessities of world politics, but because the very idea of such cosmopolitan prescriptions is incoherent.[2] This more radical objection to cosmopolitanism will be examined in Chapter 6.

Why is it impossible for the international world to be a just world? The answers realists give to this question differ in detail, but virtually all, including those who think that the perversity of human nature has something to do with our predicament, believe that the answer mainly lies in the peculiar nature of international politics. There is a logic in international relations, they say, which leads inevitably to conflicts in which agents act as they must in order to secure their own survival and are justified in doing so. This situation exists because states are in what the political philosopher, Thomas Hobbes, called the 'state of nature'. Thus in order to determine whether (or to what extent) the realist view is true about our world, let us look critically at this Hobbesian logic which is supposed to govern world affairs, particularly at the assumptions that are being made about the nature of agents and their situation.

Hobbes, as is well known, insists that agents who are not governed and controlled by an effective political authority inevitably fall into a state of war of all against all. In the state of nature, he claims, there is no peace, and appeals to justice make no sense. Hobbes' primary concern is the problem of ensuring peace and order among individuals within a state, and thus the war of all against all is, predominantly a struggle among individuals, a civil war. But he clearly believes that the same reasoning applies to states. In fact he uses the international situation as an illustration of what we can expect in the state of nature:

> But though there had never been any time, wherein particular men were in a condition of war one against another; yet in all times, kings and persons of sovereign authority, because of independency, are in continual jealousies and in the state and posture of gladiators, having their weapons pointing and their eyes fixed on one another
> (1651: 61)[3]

I will look first at Hobbes' arguments for saying that individuals in a state of nature inevitably fall into a state of war, and then at how well they apply to states.

Crucial to Hobbes' argument that the state of nature is a state of war is his insistence on the natural equality of individuals: 'For as to strength of body, the weakest has strength enough to kill the strongest, either by secret machination, or by confederacy with others, that are in the same danger with himself' (1651: 60). The physical and intellectual differences that exist among individuals are not so great that anyone can make himself secure or ensure, in a reliable way, that another shall do his will.

However there is another, equally important, aspect to Hobbes' idea of equality: he insists that there are no natural relations of authority and subordination (except between parents and young children) (1651: 77). This means that there is no moral ground in the state of nature for one person to demand that others defer to him. Hobbes is rejecting those traditional ethical standpoints which use metaphysical premises or ideas about human nature to argue that some kinds of people have a natural or god-given right to rule, and he is more insistent on this point than most philosophers: even the relation between husband and wife is not, he insists, naturally a relation between a superior and a subordinate.[4]

Given that individuals frequently want and need the same thing, Hobbes argues, and all cannot satisfy their desires, given that there is no reason on earth or in heaven for one person to defer to the other, each will be prepared to do what he can to obtain what he desires, and will be justified in so doing. This means that the only way that the issue can be settled is through force or the threat of force: 'If two men desire the same thing, which nevertheless they cannot both enjoy, they become enemies; and in the way to their end endeavour to destroy or subdue one another' (1651: 61).

This conclusion, it seems, is reached too rapidly. If the nature of the object of desire permits, rational protagonists in the state of nature should be prepared to reach a compromise, since all will be rightly fearful about the outcome of a struggle. Hobbes is supposing, in addition, that compromise is often impossible, or that there are a sufficiently large number of individuals in the state of nature who, for one reason or another, are not prepared to reach an accommodation, or at least that agents generally believe that this is so. As a result even those individuals who are prepared to live according to the law of nature and simply want others to leave them in peace can never be certain that they will survive to enjoy the fruits of their labour so long as there are others who want what they have:

If one plant, sow, build or possess a convenient Seat, others may probably be expected to come prepared with forces united, to dispossess, and deprive him, not only of the fruit of his labour, but also of his life or liberty. And the invader is in the like danger of another.

(1651: 61)

For the sake of security these peace-loving individuals will be forced to destroy their enemies and potential enemies before they can be assured of living in peace. They must get their enemies before their enemies get them; and they are entitled to make war on them since this is the only way that they can protect their own lives. But since there is no end to potential enemies, the struggle for life and security also has no end, and what such a person most desires, the peaceful enjoyment of the fruits of his labours, can never be achieved. War, which is only supposed to be a means to an end, becomes the centre of existence, and the struggle for survival comes to dominate all human activity with the consequence that life in the state of nature is 'solitary, poor, nasty, brutish and short'.

This situation, like the much-discussed Prisoners' Dilemma, is created not because individuals are driven by irrational passions or don't know what is good for them or don't understand the position that they are in.[5] On the contrary. Hobbes' individuals are not only rational; for the most part they also want to live together in peace, and know that doing so would require that they treat each other justly – that is, obey what Hobbes calls the 'Laws of Nature' (1651: Ch. 15) which require that they keep their agreements, treat each other as equals and respect each other's rights. Their problem is that they can't manage to do this. Nor will they be able to solve the problem of war, Hobbes argues, by simply agreeing to do so, for no one can trust anyone else to keep the agreement: 'And covenants, without the sword are but words, and of no strength to secure a man at all' (1651: 85). The only solution to a brutal existence is thus to leave the state of nature through agreeing to be ruled by a sovereign who has sufficient power to enforce law and order, punish transgressors and thus ensure peace.

The question still remains why the peace-loving individuals who possess 'convenient Seats' cannot manage to achieve and maintain peaceful relations with each other by agreement, and at the same time deal with aggressors through some form of collective action. In his own account of the state of nature in the *Second Treatise on Civil Government* (1690), John Locke sees no reason why individuals should not be able to uphold justice against the encroachments of 'corrupt and vicious men', on their own behalf or on the behalf of others – well enough, at least, for just relations to be possible.[6]

In *Hobbesian Moral and Political Theory* Kavka argues on behalf of Hobbes that the introduction of a sufficiently large number of aggressors ('dominators') into the picture decides the issue in favour of war of all against all (1986: 105). For people who want to live in peace but are prepared to attack others for the sake of their own security (the 'moderates') will fear that other moderates in striking against dominators may attack them by mistake; and moderates may seek to conquer other moderates to use in future battles against dominators (and other moderates will know or fear this). Hence there will be a war of all against all even among peace-loving individuals. Kavka is right to suppose that this could happen. But the outcome is not so inevitable as he implies. Given the right circumstances, it may be unlikely that moderates will make a mistake: it may not be so difficult to tell foe from friend and to attack the former without attacking the latter. Given the right circumstances, moderates may judge co-operative defence to be easier and more in their interest than conquest of other moderates (and the others know that the others do). In any case, why should we suppose that there will be a large number of aggressors in the state of nature? Aggression is, after all, a risky business.

These considerations indicate that Hobbes' conclusion is not as well supported as his comments lead us to suppose. He is depending upon assumptions about agents and their situation which may not always hold. It is important to bear this in mind when considering how his arguments are supposed to apply to the international state of nature.

Hobbes' own position on international affairs is unclear, and apparently inconsistent. On the one hand, as we have seen, he uses international relations to illustrate what happens in a state of nature, and he insists that in the international world there is no such thing as justice. Since states are in a state of nature in relation to each other it is not wrong, he says, to injure a foreigner for the benefit of the commonwealth or to kill innocent people in a war (1651: 165). For all those who are outside the state are enemies, or potential enemies, and we are entitled by the original right of nature to exercise whatever power over them is necessary for our self-protection. Neither, presumably, is it wrong for one commonwealth to attack and try to invade another.

On the other hand, he also notes that the state of nature among states does not pose the same kind of problem as the state of nature among individuals. Culture, science can still thrive, he says, individuals can live in security, even while their state is carrying on perpetual hostilities with other states (1651: 63). Ending the state of nature among individuals is an urgent matter, but the state of nature among states is something Hobbes thinks we can live with. This big difference between the situation of states and the situation of individuals, along with other related differences, suggests, as critics of realism have often pointed out, that there may be more room for peace and justice in world affairs than Hobbes allows (Cohen 1984: 319–29).

First of all, as Hobbes admits, states are not so vulnerable and insecure as individuals. Their relative security is assured by two factors: being a collective body with control over territory, they are in a better position to provide for their own needs, and thus their reasons for coming into conflict with others are likely to be less pressing. Compromise ought to be in most cases a viable option. Furthermore, the state is less vulnerable to attack and more able to defend itself effectively. States do not sleep or turn their backs, and those who attack them have to fear retaliation. Moreover, states are not equals. Some states are considerably more powerful than others, and those which are weak have little choice but to be allies or subordinates of those which are strong. There are only a few very powerful states in the world, and they can without too much difficulty keep each other under surveillance and at bay.

What these differences between the state of nature among states and the state of nature among individuals suggest is that given the right conditions, confrontation between states can take the form of threats rather than actual fighting, and thus in a world where dominant powers can police the behaviour of smaller states, and at the same time can deter other big powers from attacking them or their allies, peace is possible and requirements of justice have some meaning even if they are often ignored. In fact the great powers, to the extent that their leaders are rational, will be inclined to treat each other fairly, for this contributes to perpetuating a system which it is in their interest to maintain. Furthermore, in a world where most confrontations take the form of threats rather than actual fighting, and states are not generally driven by desperation, there is no reason why leaders and citizens should not on most occasions be able to acknowledge and act in accordance with the Laws of Nature with respect to foreigners. Their security will by no means be jeopardised by acts of justice, and in fact treating foreigners and other states justly may increase security by giving others fewer causes for conflict.

Hobbes does sometimes insist that without a sovereign there is no such thing as justice, and he might be prepared to argue that this will continue to be so for the international world, whatever form the state of nature takes. But if so, he and other realists must rest their case on something other than the right of each agent to do whatever is necessary to preserve his own existence. For states, though in the state of nature, can often ensure their own security without destroying or fighting others.

What the right conditions are for achieving this result is a matter of debate. Is a world system with two dominant powers safer than a world system with three or more? Does the existence of nuclear weapons make the world more dangerous, or do nuclear weapons provide a reliable means of keeping the peace? What system of nuclear deterrence is most likely to do this? These questions, especially the latter two, have been discussed endlessly in the last forty years. But however optimistic the outcome of the discussion, it is clear that the result of this challenge to Hobbes' argument is not the defeat of realism, but realism in another form. Peace in this realist world will be possible, but only in the form of a balance of threat. A peace based upon trust, co-operation and good will – the kind of peace many people desire – remains outside the realm of possibility. Moreover, keeping the peace will never cease to be a precarious and uncertain business. The best we can hope for in this world is that the confrontation between great powers will become a formal, habitual affair – a very cold Cold War – and that war, or at least major war, will become a more remote possibility. But the contingencies which could affect such a peaceful modus vivendi are never likely to be completely controllable. The balance may be upset by a change in power relations, the rise of a new power, the invention of new technology, a change of government, an ambitious or irrational leader, internal political and economic factors of the sort discussed by E.P. Thompson. In the past, attempts to maintain a balance of power have always been upset sooner or later. There is no reason to think that in the nuclear age all the relevant factors are under control.

Furthermore, the pursuit of justice in this realist world will always have to be subordinated to the goal of security. It is this point which Walzer is probably making when he says that in an age of nuclear deterrence, supreme emergency has become a permanent condition. It is this point realists are making when they say that the common good – namely preserving the balance of power or the system of deterrence – has to become our over-riding moral goal in world politics. For the sake of their own security and in the name of this 'common good' powerful states have justified aggression and other violations of sovereignty, subordination of populations, support of unjust political systems. In the name of peace and security, and to prevent the spread of Soviet power, the US during the last forty years went to war in Korea and Vietnam, blockaded Cuba, invaded Grenada, and supported dictatorial regimes in Central and South America, etc. And for the sake of peace and its security the Soviet Union has dominated eastern Europe, invaded Poland and Czechoslovakia, invaded Afghanistan, etc. In many cases, no doubt, the consequentialist reasoning of leaders of states leaves much to be desired as far as moral justification is concerned, but in an insecure and dangerous world it is natural for leaders to define the common good and make judgments about consequences in a way that serves the interest of their state. Hobbesian logic suggests that we cannot expect them to do otherwise.

Moreover, a world in which powerful states dominate the weaker and force them to do their will is not, according to most people, a just world. States are not as a matter of fact equally powerful, but the idea that they should have equal rights of sovereignty in a world society is a common one. In other words, the moral ideal of equality plays a role in the affairs of states, and those who subscribe to it are not going to accept the subordination of their state to the needs of the bigger powers, if they have any chance of doing anything about it. They may be prepared to engage in war, acts of terrorism, and even threaten the uneasy peace between the great powers, for the sake of what they regard as justice. We have good reason, then, to consider whether the logic of Hobbes' argument can be challenged in a deeper way.

A common complaint made against Hobbes' arguments about the state of nature is that he assumes that morality is based on prudence (Beitz 1979: 50ff.). He presupposes, in other words, as does the Prisoners' Dilemma, that agents are not reliably motivated by the desire either to be altruistic or to do the morally right thing, especially if this puts them at risk, and thus no one can expect anyone else to be so motivated. If, on the other hand, agents were strongly motivated to obey the 'Laws of Nature' and were prepared to do so even at risk to themselves, then the situation would be changed. For if agents are generally motivated to act in accordance with moral requirements, if they get into the habit of being just, then each can generally rely on the others for just treatment. This will in turn reinforce their habit, for they will know that they can go on acting justly without the risk of being seriously harmed.

How effectively the state of nature rules out peaceful and just relationships depends upon whether and how individuals, or states, can establish the habit of being just. This habit will be impossible to establish if individuals are incurably selfish. Hobbes, it is usually assumed, takes it for granted that individuals in the state of nature are motivated solely by greed and glory, not by altruistic or moral ends – though recently this understanding of Hobbes has been questioned (McNeilly 1968: Chs 5, 6). Whatever Hobbes' view of human nature, there is no doubt that he recognises the existence in the state of nature of confederacies, alliances and other associations in which individuals are generally inclined to act according to mutually determined rules and to keep their agreements with each other. But these concessions are, for the purposes of his argument, largely irrelevant. The reason why the agents in his state of nature are assumed to be predominantly self-interested has to do with the problem of justifying the authority of the state, and thus giving people a reason for obeying a sovereign, when there is no common interest or objective or idea of the good to bind everyone in a commonwealth together; when traditional habits of obedience can no longer be relied upon; when, indeed, there exists no reason in nature why one group of people should obey another.[7]

Hobbes is dealing with the problem posed by modern pluralist political societies and their disparate and sometimes competing classes, faiths, races, cultures and interest groups. Since people who are so diverse cannot be expected to have a universal love or concern for each other – the kind of bond which inclines individuals to be altruistic or trusting – it does not seem unreasonable to try to base morality on prudence, to demonstrate that individuals and groups, whatever their particular interests and ideals, will be better off if they obey laws and a ruler. The idea of justice that Hobbes embodies in the 'Laws of Nature' is similarly designed for a society in which individuals have nothing in common apart from being individuals, and it appeals to their appreciation of what obligations all must accept in order to live in peace. It is, in other words, a non-transcendental conception: political, not metaphysical. Hobbes' idea of what makes justice possible and what is just depends on his conception of the kind of society for which he is legislating. He is attempting to formulate the moral obligations which, when underwritten by sovereign power, will be practical for such a society. This suggests that the best way of challenging Hobbes' account of what is required in order to achieve a peaceful and just society is to challenge his conception of the possibilities inherent in a pluralist society.

Rawls claims in 'The idea of an overlapping consensus' (1987: 20ff.)

that people in pluralist societies have managed to develop a moral commitment to acting justly that is different in kind from the compromises accepted by self-interested agents for the sake of peace. At the first stage of this development their agreements will be Hobbesian in nature. Wishing to avoid perpetual war, they establish a modus vivendi, the terms of which depend upon the relative strength of the parties. But as they become accustomed to co-operation and the benefits of peace, they will become more inclined to act out of a sense of moral commitment. A sign of this will be that their rules and agreements will remain unchanged even when shifts in the balance of power occur. Finally, Rawls says, they come to value the principles on which their co-operation depends and become bound to each other through this allegiance. Having developed a commitment to justice, they do not need the overwhelming power of a Hobbesian sovereign to keep them in order.

Rawls is presenting an account of what he thinks has actually occurred in some national societies over a period of centuries: religious and other ideological divisions which plunged people into a state of war were eventually bridged, first by a modus vivendi, and later by mutual commitment to principles and institutions of justice. In a society which has gone through the development described by Rawls, people are generally prepared to co-operate, do their fair share, obey laws, and are even prepared to make some sacrifices for the sake of helping the needy or disadvantaged. Hobbes, it seems, was overly pessimistic about the possibilities for peace and justice within a state, and wrong about what sort of peace and what kind of justice can be achieved.

Why shouldn't we suppose that the same development will occur in the international world? For this world, as Walzer suggests, is a society of sorts in which agents generally recognise a law and have developed customary ways of relating to each other. All recognise that if universal peace is to be possible, leaders and citizens must be prepared to abide by these laws and procedures. So it seems possible to imagine that under the right conditions – if trust becomes more widespread – obedience to the requirements of international law will become a universal habit and leaders and citizens will generally be able rely on each other to be law-abiding. A modus vivendi will gradually turn into a moral order. The world will become a safe environment for the exercise of justice, and being just will be a primary motivation for action in it.

How plausible is this idea of how the international world might become a just world? A realist would respond with two basic objections: the first is that it is simply improbable that the international world, or any state of nature, will ever be safe for the exercise of justice. For even if most agents become law-abiding, not all will, and this is enough to ensure that a state of nature will be in a state of war (whether this consists of actual fighting or of threats backed up by force). The second objection is that even if it were possible for a just and peaceful society, once achieved, to maintain itself, the logic operating in the state of nature makes its achievement impossible – short of the exercise of the kind of sovereign authority envisioned by Hobbes. For the problem in the state of nature is that people cannot trust each other, and therefore cannot afford to begin acting in a way that requires trust.

The first objection, as we have seen, is embodied in Hobbes' insistence that even agents who are peacefully inclined, who simply want to occupy their 'seats' and cultivate their gardens, will not be able to guarantee their own security. For there will always be some people – whether driven by need or greed – who will be prepared to disturb the peace. I have argued that Hobbes is overly pessimistic about the possibility of justice in the state of nature, but Hobbes' worry is, perhaps, best understood in relation to the problem which he was most concerned to solve: how law and order can prevail in a large, complex, pluralist society where agents cannot easily keep track of each other, where there are needy as well as greedy people, where it is not easy to tell friend from foe, where alliances are constantly shifting, where individuals are vulnerable and can easily be injured and harmed by intent or by the negligent or careless actions of others, where informal arrangements for collective security are difficult to make and maintain. Even if most people are prepared to be law-abiding, even if a Hobbesian sovereign is not necessary to keep the peace in national society, we would not like to get along without courts, police, jails, etc.[8]

It could be argued, however, that the situation in international society is more favourable to maintaining peace and justice through agreements among states which are prepared to be peaceful and just. For in world society agents are more likely to be able to keep track of each other, monitor each other's actions; they are less vulnerable to surprise attacks, etc., and not so likely to be harmed by mistake. Moreover, it seems more reasonable to suppose that they can protect themselves through collective security from encroachments by corrupt and vicious states. It is true that collective security has so far not proved itself to be a very effective means of keeping the peace or punishing unjust aggressors in the international world. States are understandably reluctant to undertake actions which are costly and can put them at risk, and when they do go to the aid of others, they are generally motivated by self-interest at least as much as justice. But if conditions change, if aggressors become fewer, if most states become accustomed to acting out of justice, then there is more chance that peaceful states acting together without much risk to themselves, and perhaps without war, will be able to counter injustice effectively and will be prepared to do so for the sake of justice. Whether this idea of a 'new international order' is practical (especially in a world where nuclear weapons exist) requires more consideration, but the realist logic of international relations cannot be used to rule out a priori the possibility of maintaining a just and peaceful world.

But even if the idea of such a society is coherent, it may nevertheless not be possible to realise it. The realist argues that the state of affairs in the state of nature makes it impossible for us to leave the state of war – there is simply no way that our world can gradually evolve into a peaceful and just world society. Hobbes himself obviously thought that only a qualitative change, the institution of sovereign authority, could bring about peace, security and justice. Agreements made in the state of nature are not adequate because they do not make people secure enough to trust each other to honour their commitments. The habit of being just must exist before agents can rely on it, but in the state of nature it cannot begin to exist.

In tackling this problem it is worthwhile considering first the question of why Hobbes thought that the institution of sovereignty would be sufficient to secure peace. If people are not going to be prepared to keep an agreement in the state of nature, then why should we suppose that they will be willing to keep their agreement to obey a sovereign? The coercive power which a sovereign can exercise will not guarantee law and order. We know very well that coercion by state authorities does not prevent people from fighting each other, if they are really determined to do so. We know that a government which depends upon fear of punishment to keep its subjects in order may not be able to prevent civil war.

What Hobbes is supposing, I believe, is that given that people are rational, given that the sovereign has considerable coercive power, and given that most individuals are inclined to respect the contract they have made and indeed regard this as their obligation, this will tip the balance in favour of law and order: a sufficient number of people will be prepared to abide by the agreement, and will be able and prepared to back up their sovereign in his efforts to enforce the law. Once the balance is tipped, law-abiding behaviour will become more and more prevalent, and those who are vicious and corrupt can easily be dealt with. Of course there is no guarantee that the balance will be tipped. Hobbes is not offering us a sure route out of the state of war, and this is perhaps why he emphasises so strongly that individuals have an obligation to keep a covenant if it has any chance of success and an obligation to obey any government they happen to have (Kavka 1986: Ch. 5).

What Hobbes' reasoning does not establish is that there is no other route out of the state of war into a peaceful and just society. In the international world it is possible that there exist ways of tipping the balance which do not depend upon the existence of world sovereignty. One may simply be this: a stable balance of power based upon nuclear deterrence develops among the significant powers of the world. Since all are concerned to avoid any action or threat which could lead to nuclear war, leaders and citizens prefer to settle disagreements and resolve problems by a process of conciliation and compromise according to mutually acceptable rules and processes, and in time they establish the habit of doing so. They value their co-operative achievements and come to regard the rules on which they depend as being obligatory. Threat becomes a less significant factor in international politics and eventually drops out of the picture. The realist world has become a law-abiding international society.

There are reasons, as already mentioned, for being doubtful about the stability of any balance of power, including one that depends on nuclear weapons, and thus about whether states will ever settle down into a peaceful modus vivendi and whether the rules which govern it can ever become the foundations of a truly moral order. There is also reason to doubt whether a status quo imposed by an agreement between the great powers would be accepted universally as just. Nevertheless, neither Hobbes nor modern realists can rule out the possibility that in the right environment justice could become a primary motive for acting in the world of states. In the next chapters I will explore in more detail what these circumstances might be and consider how probable they are.

Another route to a peaceful and just world may become possible if states and other international agents become convinced that they can benefit more from co-operative economic and political relations than they can from aggression or hostility. Motivated by self-interest, they will develop co-operative institutions and the habit of co-operation. In time they come to appreciate each other's needs and come to value the institutions and rules which make the mutual satisfaction of these needs possible. When Mill, Beitz and others suggest that 'realist' relations of suspicion and hostility are being replaced in the international world by relations of economic interdependence and co-operation, they are calling our attention to the possibility of this route out of Hobbes' state of war. They are claiming that assumptions about the world made by the realists are no longer true (if they ever were) – that states are no longer in a Prisoners' Dilemma type situation – and a new, more just and peaceful world order is becoming the primary interest of all international actors.

Why people should think that economic interdependence is capable of encouraging co-operation, fair play and peaceful relations among individuals or states is not difficult to understand. If we assume that all individuals (or other agents) have a source of wealth and security in their property, whether this is land, goods or simply their talents and abilities (that they are not, in other words, destitute and desperate), if we assume that they are self-interested enough to want to increase their well-being as much as possible, or at least that they cannot provide everything that they need by their own efforts, then it is likely (if not inevitable) that they will find it worthwhile to establish and maintain a system for exchanging some of the fruits of their labour for those belonging to others. Since all are better off because of the existence of this system than they would be without it, they are predisposed to do what they can to ensure its effective operation. In the course of doing so they will police and control each other's behaviour.

For example, if an economic agent A tries to further his/her own interests by cheating B in an economic transaction or by failing to keep a promise, he or she is likely to suffer worse in the long run. B will punish A by refusing to trade with him/her in the future, and B is likely to inform other economic agents about A's misdeed, and they may well refuse to trade with A as well. If A murders B or forcibly wrests away his/her property, then the other agents, fearing that the same could happen to them, are also likely to co-operate in boycotting trade with A, or perhaps may undertake more direct action. But murder and invasion are not so likely because they are risky, and A will generally reckon that he/she is better off carrying on peaceful trade with B, especially if B has skills that A is not likely to acquire. Thus since A and the others know that they will be punished for bad behaviour and that they generally benefit more from good behaviour, they will be inclined to exercise that promise-keeping, contract-honouring behaviour, that respect for rights of property, which Hobbes and others regard as central to justice. Once they get into the habit of being just, they will become more and more inclined to act for reasons of justice even on those occasions when this does not directly benefit them. The world will become peaceful and therefore safe for the exercise of justice.

In order to reach this result, we do not have to suppose that the agents are altruistic with respect to each other or that they have any other bonds or common interests. The existence of mutually beneficial exchanges simply alters the situation sufficiently for co-operative behaviour to be rewarded and uncooperative behaviour discouraged. And thus it is plausible to suppose that imported into the state of nature these relationships could convert a state of war into a state of relative peace, and that once this happens agents will be more inclined and more able to act justly. It is notable that one of the differences between Hobbes' state of war and Locke's more peaceful, natural law-abiding state of nature is that in Locke's state of nature trade exists. Commerce in his view belongs to the state of nature and so do all the developments associated with it, including the use of money which, as Locke explains, allows individuals to accumulate wealth without the disadvantage of spoil and decay.

Why people have supposed that economic interdependence between states, or between agents within different states, will encourage peaceful and, eventually, just relations in the world as a whole is not difficult to understand either. They point out that it is reasonable to believe that states are less likely to act aggressively or unjustly to other states if the well-being and prosperity of a significant part of their populations depend upon the maintenance of mutually beneficial commercial relations. Invasion or some other form of aggressive behaviour remains a possibility in this world, but it is not so likely to occur, for not only is carrying on warfare a dangerous and expensive business but, even if successful, a war may end up destroying the very resources which it was fought to obtain. Moreover, peaceful states will have additional means to deter aggressors: they can deny war-like regimes the economic goods which their population and military forces have come to depend upon.

However, we have already seen that there are, in reality, serious problems with the idea that economic interdependence will make the world more peaceful and just. For one thing, not all agents receive benefits from the world economy or willingly participate in it, and some agents are economically powerful enough to exploit others. So long as this is true even a peaceful modus vivendi may be impossible to achieve, let alone anything that can be called a just world. Whether economic interdependence really does provide a route to a peaceful and just world thus depends on how difficult it is to overcome these problems. It also depends upon how likely it is that economic relations will ever encourage relations of justice. Can the fabric of a just world order really be spun out of the cloth of economic self-interest? Those who believe that commerce and trade are conducive to peaceful and just relations have never supposed that economic interdependence by itself can bring about this result. They assume, as did Mill, that trade encourages and goes along with favourable social, political and psychological developments of other kinds; that it paves or smooths the way for relations based upon morality rather than mere self-interest. But how this is supposed to happen remains unclear.

My critical examination of the realist view of the world is thus inclusive. There is no logic of international relations which entails that states are bound to threaten or exploit each other. Hobbes' view cannot be used to establish that the state of nature among states is a state of war. On the other hand, it is not yet clear what relationships or developments would make the state of the world more peaceful and just: what circumstances are likely to encourage states to develop the habit of justice; whether and how world economic relations can create a just world order. I will consider one influential attempt to map the route to a perpetually peaceful world in the next chapter.

Chapter 2

Achieving perpetual peace: Kant's universal history

For Kant, as for Hobbes, the chief problem of human existence is the problem of war. But for Hobbes, seeking peace is the prudent thing to do – something necessary for the protection of life and other things that individuals value – and he thought that the problem would be solved well enough if people could manage to live at peace within states. The law of nature which enjoins us to seek peace does not require that we make peace universal. Kant, on the other hand, was convinced that as long as war or the threat of war exists, the security of citizens cannot be assured and civilised life is not truly possible. If things do not change, he says, how can we avoid the conclusion 'that discord natural to our race, may not prepare for us a hell of evils, however civilised we may now be, by annihilating civilisation and all cultural progress through barbarous devastation' (1784: 20)?

Kant's perception of the danger of war is therefore similar to the perception of many presently existing people: war in any form is a threat to our existence and we have good reason to want to prevent it. But the difference between Hobbes and Kant runs deeper. The destruction of civilised life which Kant feared is not simply a destruction of lives and property but a moral degradation. War is a blot on the record of the human race; a result of the failure of human beings to be what they can and should be. Kant (1784: 21) goes so far as to say that if 'civilised' human beings are incapable of solving the problem of war, then we must admit that Rousseau was not wrong in preferring the state of savages to existing civilisation.

Kant's condemnation of war is, above all, a moral condemnation. War and respect for the moral law are incompatible:

Now our moral-practical reason pronounces its irresistible veto: There ought not to be war, neither between me and thee in the state

of nature nor that between us as states. . . . For war is not the way
in which each one should seek his rights.

(1797: 128)

Even if we could live in security while our states carried on perpetual
war or threatened each other with war, this would not be an acceptable
state of affairs. And peace, he insists, if it is to be in accordance with
morality, must be different from an armed truce, from a carefully
constructed balance of power or from a system of co-operation based
upon economic self-interest. It must be founded on mutual respect and
obedience to moral law. In his essay 'Perpetual peace' and in other
political writings he attempts to show what such a peace requires and
how it might be brought into being and maintained.

The irreconcilability of morality and war does not rest for Kant on a
particular conception of justice or the good, or on a theory of human
rights, but on the demands of 'moral-practical reason' as such. These
demands presuppose that the moral law is made by individuals acting as
moral legislators, individuals who recognise themselves and others as
being free to determine their own future actions and capable of moral
reasoning. People differ in intelligence, experience and sensitivity, but
considered as moral legislators, Kant insists, all are equal and all
deserve respect. That individuals should respect each other and not use
each other as means is basic to Kant's moral standpoint, and thus
'moral-practical reason' contains a conception of how human beings or
human groups ought to relate to each other. The use of force or threats
to bring about an end is always unacceptable – not only because the
right does not always prevail in such struggles, but because forcing
others to do our will is not treating them with the respect that their
status as free moral legislators requires. Nor is it allowable to treat or
regard individuals simply as useful contributors to our particular ends.
Morality requires that we respect each other equally and live according
to universally acceptable rules which we as free and equal rational
legislators have established for ourselves.

One obvious difference between Kant and Hobbes is that Kant insists
that the requirements of morality exist even in the state of nature.
Moreover, he regards us as being essentially free and moral individuals,
thus suggesting that we have a freedom to choose and are motivated by
moral considerations in a way that Hobbes often seems to deny. But
these differences should not be exaggerated. Kant's view of the state of
nature, and how human beings would act in it, is not essentially
different from Hobbes'. 'The state of peace among men living side by

side', he says, 'is not the natural state; the natural state is one of war' (1795: 10). And in war agents can be expected to do what they must for the sake of survival. Kant's account of how individuals emerge from the state of nature into a civil society depends, like Hobbes', on a self-interested desire for security. These individuals need, and if they are rational will accept, a strong master to rule over them. For the requirements of moral-practical reason are not likely to be appreciated, let alone respected, by people in a state of nature.

Nowhere is lack of appreciation and respect for the requirements of morality more evident, Kant acknowledges, than in international relations.

> One cannot suppress a certain indignation when one sees men's actions on the great world stage and finds, besides the wisdom that appears here and there among individuals, everything in the large is woven together from folly, childish vanity, even from childish malice and destructiveness.
>
> (1784: 12)

Kant's perception of the perversity of human affairs raises the question of how he could have believed that the peace required by moral-practical reason is realisable (and whether he in fact did believe this).

The essential difference between Hobbes and Kant, as far as their understanding of social relations is concerned, is that for Hobbes the solution to the predicament of war is dictated by the nature of human beings and their motivations and needs as these are revealed in the state of nature. But Kant does not think that human motivations or desires are fixed and immovable. Though always imperfect, human beings are capable of improvement, capable of developing a greater appreciation of moral requirements and aptitude for moral behaviour. Therefore it is not, for Kant, possible to determine what form of political governance is necessary, what hopes for peace are practical, by imagining what human beings would be like in a state of nature. The state of nature is only the beginning of a story about the evolution of human relationships and consciousness, which can end, Kant thinks, with perpetual peace. In other words, Kant is trying to solve the problem discussed in the last chapter: how the world can find a way out of the realist predicament.

What perpetual peace means for Kant and what practical arrangements it requires are explained in his essay 'Perpetual peace' (1795). This is set out, in its initial section, as if it were a contract or treaty containing the articles which parties who desire to lay the foundations for a lasting peace with each other can be expected to agree to: no treaty should be made which contains the seeds of further conflict; the independence of states should be respected – sovereigns should not attempt to partition them, cede them or claim them by inheritance; standing armies should be abolished; national debts should not be contracted for the sake of building up armaments or extending external influence; no state should by force interfere with the political affairs of another; nothing should be done in war which will make a satisfactory peace difficult or impossible. Kant adds that the first, fifth and sixth requirements 'demand prompt execution'; action on the others can be delayed until conditions are more favourable – but this should not be an excuse for delaying too long.

In these 'preliminary articles' Kant is doing something similar to what Hobbes did when he set out the Laws of Nature. He is specifying how agents must act if they are to have any chance of maintaining a satisfactory peace. In this case, those who have to make the agreement are leaders on behalf of their states, not individuals, and the parties must pledge to respect the autonomy and integrity of states. In prescribing for the world of states Kant is thus treating states analogously to the way he treats individuals: the autonomy of each requires respect.

If peace is to become possible, if the agents of world society are to be able and willing to satisfy the requirements of the preliminary articles, they must be of a law-abiding nature and disposition, and thus the focus of Kant's concern is to determine what this nature is and how it can be encouraged. The only states which can be perpetually peaceful with respect to each other, the only ones able or likely to satisfy the requirements, Kant says, are republics. Thus it is necessary that 'The civil constitution of every state should be republican' (1795: 11). A republic for him is not necessarily a democracy – certainly not rule by a majority – nor is it necessarily a state without a monarch.[1] Kant makes a distinction between the form of a government, whether monarchy, aristocracy or democracy, and the mode of government, whether republican or despotic. The essential feature of a republic is that it is founded on a rule of law which is guaranteed by a constitution and the separation of legislative and executive powers. It is based upon the consent of the governed and represents their will, but at the same time it ensures that this will is bounded by constitutional requirements and can be rationally and impartially executed.

Kant's idea of a republic is supposed to resolve both moral and practical problems associated with the requirements he places on states. By ensuring that the authority of government is an expression of the will of the governed and is based upon their consent, he underwrites the existence of states as juridical persons, as deserving of respect. Moreover, by having a constitution, proper procedures, states are also rendered capable of rational, consistent action. They can act as responsible agents in world affairs. But what Kant emphasises above all is that republics are less inclined than despotic states to go to war:

> In a constitution which is not republican, and under which the subjects are not citizens, a declaration of war is the easiest thing in the world to decide upon, because war does not require of the ruler, who is proprietor and not a member of the state, the least sacrifice of the pleasures of his table, his chase, his country houses, his court functions and the like.
>
> (1795: 13)

If the consent of the citizens is required in order to declare a war, Kant argues, then war is much less likely. For citizens will be reluctant to call down upon themselves the sacrifices and calamities of a war.

If states are republics they should be inclined to satisfy the preliminary articles, but in order to leave the state of war and the state of nature behind them, a definitive action is needed, similar in some respects to the action by means of which Hobbes' individuals left the state of nature. 'Each of [the republics] may and should for the sake of its own security demand that the others enter with it into a constitution similar to the civil constitution, for under such a constitution each can be secure in his right' (1795: 16). But this league of nations, Kant insists, would not be a state; its members would retain their sovereignty and would be able to leave it voluntarily. The association of states will be a free one and the laws which govern it must be acknowledged and honoured voluntarily. Among the laws which all will accept will be those guaranteeing the entitlements of individuals as 'world citizens' – the entitlement not to be treated as enemies, not to be enslaved or exploited by foreign governments. Perpetual peace based upon moral respect for individuals and their national societies will finally be secured when all states become republics and join the league of peace and accept its laws.

Kant rejects the idea that the only and best way of ending the state of war is to institute a world government – a sovereignty capable of enforcing a law on member states. Such an authority, he often says, would be a tyranny. If states are forced to submit to the authority of outside forces, then this would be a violation of the will of citizens upon whom the legitimate sovereignty of their state rests. But even if world government were established by consent it would be, Kant supposes, inefficient and impractical: no authority could effectively rule a society which encompasses such a large area and so many cultures, or guarantee individual rights and security. Inevitably local bodies would rise up to fill the gap, and this would eventually undermine the exercise of sovereignty and dissolve the state (1797: 124).

Since Kant rejects a Hobbesian solution to the problem of war, it might well be doubted whether he can solve it at all. Why should we think that sovereign states, even republics, will be inclined to establish or maintain in perpetuity a voluntary league of peace? Waltz, in 'Kant, liberalism and war' (1962: 338), argues that the equilibrium achieved by the league of peace would be as precarious as a balance of power (which Kant elsewhere ridicules as an unstable basis for world order): 'Kant's structure fall[s] to the ground whenever one major state chooses to forsake the international federation and flout its universal law.' He concludes that Kant could not have believed that perpetual peace – a world society founded on mutual respect and just dealings – is a realisable goal. In 'Perpetual peace', Waltz claims, he is merely setting out what conditions would have to be satisfied if perpetual peace were to exist.

Kant's fear that civilisation is itself threatened by the existence of war, the seriousness with which he approaches the problem, suggests that he did not think that he was engaged in a merely academic exercise. On the other hand, his proposal doesn't seem to take sufficently into account what he elsewhere describes as the perversity of human nature. Republics have sometimes degenerated into despotic regimes, as did Germany in the 1920s; even in republican states ambitious leaders, ideologically motivated citizens, have sometimes been known to ignore international law. One way of dealing with this problem in the framework of Kant's proposal for perpetual peace is to insist that the federation have some powers and means to counter aggression or threats against it and punish members for breaking the law.[2] A world federation with such powers is not necessarily the same as a world government. Separate states could retain the right to make and enforce laws within their territories, but those who agree to federate would have to cede some of their sovereignty, above all the power of making war, for the sake of peace. But this concession, it could be argued, is no more objectionable than the insistence that individuals, when they leave the state of nature, must give up some of their freedom.

However, this way of developing Kant's proposal does not get to the heart of Waltz's objection. For he is arguing that Kant's world federation, in spite of what is claimed for it, is not different in kind from a balance of power, a modus vivendi. States will accept its authority only so long as it is in their interest to do so, or so long as they don't feel threatened by what others do. But as soon as these conditions are not satisfied, the federation will break up, and 'perpetual' peace will prove short-lived. Even a federation with some power to enforce the law will probably not be able to remedy the situation if leaders of states are determined to pursue their own interests or carry on hostilities with each other. The failure of the League of Nations, established after World War I to promote peace and provide for collective security, seems to demonstrate the difficulty of establishing a successful world federation.

Waltz's objection comes out of a realist view of the world. He assumes that agents act out of self-interest, or at least that they cannot trust each other not to do so. What he doesn't sufficiently appreciate is that Kant is attempting to change the parameters of world politics; he is trying to show how the realist world can be superseded. The league of peace can and will maintain itself, Kant thinks, because its members are basically law-abiding. They are in the habit of acting justly towards each other and towards individuals, whatever their own interests, and thus can be trusted by other agents to do so. The plausibility of Kant's proposal thus rests upon an idea of how human affairs and human consciousness can evolve from a situation in which war or threats of war are endemic, towards a state of affairs in which leaders and citizens work for peace effectively. Kant's belief that this can happen depends upon an idea of social and political progress, an idea implicit in his prescriptions for perpetual peace and developed more fully in 'Idea for a universal history from a cosmopolitan point of view' (1784).

Once again in this work Kant poses the problem which human nature presents for morality, the fact that human material doesn't seem a very promising basis for a moral and peaceful world order. We cannot expect perpetual peace to be established through the good intentions of individuals, since the intentions of individuals are not reliably good.

But human beings are part of the natural order, an order which operates according to natural laws, and historical developments are governed by these laws. Thus while human beings desire and struggle, fight and die, nature in the form of history produces consequences which no one aims for and goes through movements which only hindsight can appreciate. It is historical evolution, happening largely behind the backs of human individuals, which makes possible progress towards a peaceful world.

The way in which nature can make a moral life possible is already evident, Kant thinks, in the history of states. In coming together to form states individuals were motivated by nothing more than the desire for self-protection. By forming a political society they put themselves into a situation in which their desires and competitive vanity, so destructive in the state of nature, could be a source of mutual benefit, stimulating their ingenuity and use of talents. And at the same time political society and the enlightenment that went with it converted 'the coarse natural dispositions for moral discrimination into definite practical principles, and thereby changed a society of men driven together by their natural feelings into a moral whole' (1784: 15). In this way nature has taken unpromising material and used it to create something fine, though not without a lot of individual suffering along the way.

As the result of the struggle to avoid civil war on the one hand and tyranny on the other, states in the course of time become republics with all the benefits and increase of moral sensibility that this promotes. For if a government is founded on the consent of its people then, according to Kant, its laws can be understood by them as being products of their rational will. Living under such laws is thus a way of coming to appreciate the nature and requirements of practical reason – something that is true as much for the rulers as for the ruled. Moreover, the laws of a republic protect the freedom of individuals and ensure their equal treatment under law, thus promoting the respect for persons which is the foundation of the moral law. And further, the existence of law makes it possible for people protected by it to develop moral relations without the fear that they will make themselves vulnerable to the self-interest of others. Kant believed that living under the laws of a republic promotes morality and provides for both rulers and citizens a moral education – an education which can even have an effect on those who only obey the law because they fear punishment.[3] Gradually individuals and states are prepared for the task of achieving perpetual peace: they now appreciate the incompatibility between morality and war, they are civilised enough to regard war as unacceptable, and moreover they are in the habit of obeying a law.

So long as states are in conflict, the requirements of moral–practical reason cannot be fulfilled, but it is not difficult to identify tendencies which are leading in the direction of peace. War itself is pushing us in that direction: 'All wars are accordingly so many attempts (not in the intention of man, but in the intention of Nature) to establish new relations among states' (Kant 1784: 19). Stimulated by the threat that war poses to their existence and livelihood, leaders and citizens will be moved to make agreements and treaties. And once again a development brought about by self-interest will make moral progress possible: once relations between states become more peaceful, leaders will develop the habit of being law-abiding, and the foundation for perpetual peace will be laid.

Kant's universal history is teleological. Kant often speaks in his 'Idea for a universal history' as if Nature has a purpose and that it 'wills' or 'intends' a particular end for human beings, which it sets out to fulfil regardless of the motivations of individuals. Behind history is the hand of Providence pushing us along towards ends which we cannot yet appreciate. However, in spite of his deterministic language, Kant is not supposing that progress is inevitable, or that his 'philosophical history' must be true. Kant does not believe that he knows the purposes of Providence or that there is any way of finding them out. His philosophical history is a construction put on the facts of history – a construction based upon hope. But our hopes may be dashed, and in any case, different ideas about what progress means or how it is accomplished are possible.

What is especially notable about this history is that it embeds Kant's ethical standpoint in history and political life. Like Rawls' account of justice in 'The idea of an overlapping consensus' (1987), it shows how the will to be moral can arise in the course of the development of social life and how what the ethical will wills can be understood as a response to practical political problems. Kant's transcendentalism, the metaphysical views about self and will which post-modernists and others criticise, drops out of the picture. The transcendental standpoint appears in the universal history as Providence, but in this form it seems dispensable, for the idea of progress that it is supposed to underwrite is presented as a practical political goal which many people, whatever their metaphysical views, will share.

Kant uses his philosophical history to deal with two problems which inevitably arise as soon as we ask the questions: what ought we to do?

or what can we hope for? How well he deals with these problems will determine how plausible and desirable is his conception of a perpetually peaceful world. The first problem is the practical one of showing us a plausible route out of the state of war. The main difficulty which Kant faces in 'Universal history' and elsewhere is that our ability to satisfy the requirements of moral–practical reason, or even to appreciate them, is affected by the social and political state of affairs. If we are in a situation in which lawlessness is common, then we will not only in most cases be unable to behave justly, but we will also be disinclined to do so even when we can. Before the habit of acting justly can become established, the proper political and social foundations must be laid. However, if people don't appreciate moral requirements, and thus aren't inclined to honour them, or if they can't do so, then how can they be expected to bring about a circumstance in which law-abiding behaviour is the rule rather than the exception?

Kant assigns to nature the task of bringing about favourable circumstances for human development before human beings are generally prepared to will and strive for them. By invoking nature, he can be understood as making the point that what happens in human affairs is often contrary to, or at least different from, what individuals want to bring about, and that, looking back, we can sometimes discern a pattern or direction in events which human actors were at the time not aware of. Sometimes it is also reasonable to project such a pattern into the future – though of course we remain profoundly uncertain about what will actually happen. In appealing to nature Kant does not have to suppose that history has a necessary end or that the intentions of individuals are irrelevant to what happens. Kant's claim, properly understood, is that developments associated with the creation of modern, constitutional states will (if they continue on their present evolutionary course into the future) make it more probable than it might at first seem that citizens and leaders of states will eventually find it possible and desirable to make peace the object of their endeavours. Indeed Kant's discussion, especially in 'Perpetual peace', suggests that the time has come when willing peace and effectively striving for it have become more possible. Leaders can begin taking some definite and practical steps towards perpetual peace, even if it remains a distant prospect. Thus though Kant's universal history is based upon hope, it is at the same time supposed to serve a practical purpose: it is supposed to give us some ideas about what moral individuals can actually do to achieve its desirable end.

Nevertheless, the peaceful international society was not something that Kant expected to occur in the near future. He makes it clear that its creation is the work of generations, and that this work may not be completed for a very long time. The idea of an international social contract, like all social contract stories, treats a development that may take centuries as if it were something accomplished in a moment of agreement. The universal history cannot make definite predictions, nor can it guarantee the end result. The indefiniteness and uncertainty attached to Kant's attempt to make projections into the future raise some crucial questions. How can moral agents be sure that they are contributing anything positive to the achievement of the goal? What are moral agents justified in doing to achieve it?

In answering the last question Kant unconditionally rules out the use of war to achieve peace, or lawlessness to achieve the rule of law. We are not justified in carrying on war or violating the sovereignty of other states for the sake of laying the foundations for perpetual peace, nor are citizens justified in using revolutionary violence in order to make their state into a republic:

> No attempt should be made, however, to realise this idea precipitously through revolutionary methods, that is, by the violent overthrow of a previously existing imperfect and corrupt government, for in that case there would be an intervening moment when the entire juridical state of affairs would be annihilated. Instead, the idea should be attempted and carried out through gradual reform according to fixed principles. Only in this way is it possible to approach continually closer to the highest political good – perpetual peace.
>
> (1797: 129)

The means that we adopt in striving for perpetual peace must be moral means.[4] We are not justified for the sake of any end in departing from the framework of the moral law. However, this prohibition poses a problem: what if perpetual peace can never be achieved by peaceful, moral means?

It may be thought that this problem only exists because Kant and those who accept a Kantian approach to morality refuse to allow an action to be justified in terms of the good consequences it achieves. A consequentialist, it might be argued, will have no problem advocating that we do whatever is necessary in order to bring about the desirable end. But this is not so. Conscientious consequentialists, once they take into account the uncertainty of the outcome (which will come about, if at all, only in the distant future), once they acknowledge the amount of suffering which the use of force (whether revolution, war or intervention) is likely to cause in the short and long term, and add to their calculations the recognition that in political affairs what is achieved is often very different from what was desired, it is unlikely that they will be able to justify committing violent acts for the sake of bringing about perpetual peace. This does not mean that we have to agree with Kant that revolution or intervention is never justified. But given that revolutions and interventions are dangerous actions which harm large numbers of people and have uncertain consequences, justification is going to be difficult under any circumstance, and an uncertain indefinite goal like perpetual peace is not likely to be a good enough reason for embarking on such a morally problematic exercise.

However, Kant's prohibition means that perpetual peace may never happen: what moral individuals in the framework of the moral law can do to bring about this goal may always be ineffective. Worse, what they can do may be counter-productive. Given the uncertainty about the future and how our actions will affect it, it is reasonable to fear that the actions we perform, though within the framework of morality, will have bad or indifferent, rather than good, consequences.

The second problem, which Kant uses his philosophical history to solve, is this problem about the consequences of being moral. Human progress, he admits, does not take place without a lot of suffering:

> It remains strange that the earlier generations appear to carry through their toilsome labour only for the sake of the later, to prepare for them a foundation on which the later generations could erect the higher edifice which was Nature's goal, and yet that only the latest of the generations should have the good fortune to inhabit the building on which a long line of their ancestors had (unintentionally) laboured without being permitted to partake of the fortune they had prepared. However puzzling this may be, it is necessary if one assumes that a species of animals should have reason, and, as a class of rational beings, each of whom dies while the species is immortal, should develop their capacities to perfection.
>
> (1784: 14)

In the course of human history individuals suffer pain, failure, they are killed, they suffer and die, their efforts seem to lead them nowhere, and those who are most merciless and immoral are often the most successful. The universal history gives us hope, not only that in the long run even bad actions can produce some good, but that our good actions will also not be in vain. It is perhaps for this reason that Kant believes that some conception of human progress is embedded in the moral outlook. Even if people do not act in order to produce good consequences – something that the Kantian moral standpoint rules out – their confidence as moral beings would be undermined if they believed that their morally motivated actions tended to produce bad or useless results. Kant's universal history gives us a faith in what we are doing. But it also assures us that what must be done will get done. Nature does whatever dirty work is necessary to bring about species perfection, even at the cost of human suffering. And thus it accomplishes what individuals are not allowed to do.

However, nature in the case of history consists of human actions and their consequences, and human beings are free and subject to the moral law. This means that Kant's attitude towards some historical events is necessarily ambivalent: on the one hand, he believed that those who brought about the French Revolution were acting immorally – they caused enormous suffering, as well as overthrowing a legitimate government. On the other hand, he also believed that the French Revolution represented an enormous step forward as far as human progress is concerned. It created in those who witnessed it an appreciation of the importance of having a civil constitution, a recognition of the unity of humankind and the possibility of progress (Reiss 1977: 182). So long as we are merely spectators of an event, this ambivalence is possible. But in respect to future events whose outcome we can influence, we have to make a choice. We have a duty not only to obey the moral law, but a duty, presumably, to prevent immoral acts if we can do so. So even if we believed that a revolution or a violent act could contribute significantly to bringing about perpetual peace, we should not allow it to happen, if we can prevent it. We may have a duty to stand in the way of 'progress'.

This will not be a serious problem for Kant's account of progress towards perpetual peace if we can, through peaceful evolution, eventually achieve our end. Kant seems to assume that this is possible, at least in civilised times; that indeed the best way of promoting perpetual peace is through peaceful means. Even the accomplishments of the French Revolution could have been brought about by peaceful means, and leaders and citizens are now in a position to take the gradual steps required to achieve perpetual peace without using violence – in fact violence is likely to be counter-productive. But what if Kant is wrong about this? What if the evolutionary path is blocked and progress can only be made by revolution or war?

The accomplishment of both the practical and moral purposes which Kant's universal history are supposed to serve thus depends on its adequacy as an account of historical evolution. Considered from our perspective, almost 200 years after 'Perpetual peace' was published, how plausible is Kant's idea of how we can achieve peace? The mere fact that perpetual peace has not yet been achieved, and that attempts in our century to form 'leagues of peace' have failed to accomplish their purpose, does not by itself show that Kant's universal history is flawed, since he did not make any predictions about how long the process is supposed to take. Nevertheless, it is clear that there are weaknesses and uncertainties in his scheme.

One of the critical parts of Kant's evolutionary story is the creation of republics, the development of states as societies ruled by law rather than by a despot. But what counts as a republic? Is it likely that all states will become republics? From a modern perspective the problem with Kant's division between despotic and republican states is that it seems to make it too easy for something to count as a republic. Most modern states have some kind of constitution and separation of powers, however imperfectly this works in practice, but in many cases the governments of these states do not rule by consent of the governed and citizens have little chance to influence what their leaders do. Perhaps we should insist, in order to preserve the spirit of Kant's account of what justifies the entitlements of states, that to be a republic in a true sense, a state must be a liberal democracy. Its government must be truly representative of the people through elections in which there are choices of leaders and policies; it must reliably guarantee individual rights and uphold a constitution. However, in this case it is reasonable to doubt whether the world ever will consist of liberal democracies. Among the states of the world liberal democracies are in a minority, and they exist mostly in wealthier regions of the world.

Nevertheless, as Kantian optimists, we can hope that changes in eastern Europe, the USSR and South Africa in the early 1990s mean that the ideal of democracy and its effective practice are gradually becoming more widespread, even though there are bound to be disappointments and lapses back into despotism here and there (as in China). But is Kant right to suppose that the relations between republics, however these are defined, are likely to be peaceful? In his contemporary version of the Kantian thesis, 'Kant, liberal legacies and foreign affairs' (1983), Doyle points out that liberal democracies have, in fact, a good record of peaceful relations in respect to each other, though they have been willing enough to conduct wars and hostilities with states that are not liberal democracies and have sometimes done so with missionary zeal. He argues that Kant was therefore basically right about the disposition of such states, and that realists, who believe that ideology and political systems make little or no difference to the 'necessities' of international relations, are wrong. But the evidence is too meagre to support the optimistic view of Kant or Doyle. The fact that liberal democracies have not gone to war with each other may be because they have so far happened to have common enemies, similar economic interests, thriving economies and, as yet, no serious reason to engage in hostilities. In any case, it would be naive to suppose that being a liberal democracy is a permanent unchanging condition: under difficult economic and political circumstances liberal states have been known to become more despotic and less concerned with peace and individual rights. Critics of militarism or exterminism believe that this danger is universal and very real.

Developments in the last 200 years give us additional reasons to believe that Kant's account of world politics is over-simple. It does not take into account the rise of nationalism, its effect on states and international relations, and the new questions about the legitimacy of states that nationalist demands have raised. It does not allow for patriotic and other ideological enthusiasms which can encourage the citizens of states, even in liberal democracies, to hate a perceived enemy.[5] Neither morality nor prudence has proved to be a sufficient deterrent to such hostility. It has not foreseen technological developments which make the armed forces of states more threatening to their neighbours. When Kant advocated the abolition of standing armies he was attempting to reduce the climate of fear among states, but in our times this fear is created even more effectively by arsenals of nuclear and chemical weapons and the production and stockpiling of more and more deadly 'conventional' weapons. A contemporary Kantian prescription for peace would not only have to include disarmament, but also some means of ensuring that states cannot build up their deadly arsenals in secret. So far this has proved difficult to accomplish.

These difficulties concerning the means for achieving peace would somehow have to be taken into account by any late twentieth-century attempt to write a universal history which ends in perpetual peace. However, it is not merely Kant's means which are problematic, but also his ends. Some of the difficulties and developments briefly discussed in the Introduction can be used to bring into question the conception of world organisation which he takes to be the goal of history.

One of these problems is the division of the world between rich and poor. The existence of states which do not possess the means to provide for the basic needs of the population is for obvious reasons a hindrance to Kant's idea of progress towards perpetual peace. For one thing, commonsense suggests that such states are the least likely to become or remain republics in his sense of the word. People driven by desperate need are likely to demand desperate remedies, and their leaders will tend to be either demagogues or despots. Furthermore, a government based upon consent, a liberal democracy, seems to require that citizens have enough education, wealth and leisure to be able to concern themselves with public affairs. This is not going to be the case for most people in impoverished states. Moreover, an impoverished, unstable state may be driven to desperate actions in world affairs. It cannot be relied upon or expected to keep the articles of a league of peace, and will thus be a danger to any world order.

However, the problem posed by poverty is a deeper one. For Kant was not simply concerned with how the world can become peaceful, but also with how it can be just. Perpetual peace is peace in the framework of just laws and the recognition of individual entitlements. If, as many people believe, being forced to live in poverty is itself a violation of an individual's rights, then a world society which allows this to happen is not a just world. But if so, then Kant's idea of a peaceful society of sovereign states which respect each other's rights and do not actively harm individuals from other states is questionable as a goal – whether it is practical or not.

Interdependence, as we have seen, exacerbates this problem. Kant assumes that one of the factors pushing us towards peace is relations of trade: 'The spirit of commerce, which is incompatible with war, sooner or later gains the upper hand in every state' (1795: 32). But when he supposes that economic developments encourage peaceful relations, it is likely that he was thinking mostly about economic developments within states: the growth of manufacturing, the increasing influence of the commercial classes, the creation of a unified legal system. These are the sorts of development which curb the ambitions of rulers and encourage citizens to mind their own businesses and cultivate their own domestic economies. They can also help to ensure the stability of a state and the general prosperity of citizens. However, in an increasingly interdependent economy even wealthy states can no longer supply their own needs, and the ways in which states can drastically affect each other's interests, whether intentionally or unintentionally, have increased. Taking interdependence into account may require substantial revisions to Kant's story – not only to his account of how perpetual peace can be achieved, but also to the conception of what a peaceful and just international society should be like.

How should we revise it? One of the problems in answering this question is that it seems that there is no right way of anticipating the future, given that it will depend upon what we decide to do. Kant's references to Providence and nature tend to suggest that there is just one route into the future, but given that we are free to choose, the possibility of other philosophical 'histories' cannot be excluded. As far as the human future is concerned, 'nature' does not speak with one voice.

This becomes especially evident as soon as we start contemplating the future of our world. I earlier suggested that debates about interdependence raise in an obvious way the question of what kind of world order is possible and desirable. The world economy is becoming more interdependent in some respects, but on the other hand most states take some steps to protect their national economies, their sovereignty and the culture of their people. The question which these apparently contrary developments raise is not merely which tendency is going to win out in the long run, but which is likely to produce a more desirable and just future world. If we are going to engage in the Kantian exercise of writing a 'universal history' for our times, it is not enough to find a way of circumventing the problems which Kant didn't anticipate or of revising the conception of history's goal according to recent tendencies. We must also take into account the likelihood that there will be rival accounts of the future, which exist not simply because of different beliefs about what is possible, but because of different ideas about what end we should be aiming for. I will look at two of these rival accounts in Chapters 4 and 5 and consider how we should assess them.

However, there is another pressing issue which must first be considered. What is essential to Kant's account of progress to perpetual peace is not only the idea that a peaceful and just world is possible, but that it can be achieved through gradual, peaceful means. We have seen that there are good reasons, even from a consequentialist point of view, for Kant's prohibition on using violent, revolutionary, lawless means to bring about a peaceful world. Any modern attempt to write a 'history' in the spirit of Kant must therefore try to abide by this prohibition. The question raised by the Marxists is whether this is possible – whether there is a peaceful, evolutionary road to a just world. Since Marxist views about social organisation could so drastically affect our ideas about whether and how we can achieve peace and justice, and what a just world would be like, I will examine their views in the next chapter.

Chapter 3

Marxism and international relations

The Marxists have been among the most significant and persistent challengers of the idea that a peaceful and just world will result from an evolutionary development of economic or moral relations. At the same time Marxists themselves are advocates of a 'universalist' perspective and a universal history which also ends in world peace and a society in which everyone contributes according to ability and receives according to need. But in order to progress to this end, they say, the people of the world must go through a period of radical social change and whatever revolutions or wars are necessary to bring it about, and the cause of these struggles is precisely the social relations and developments which so many people have believed would encourage peace – relations of commerce and trade, the development of manufacturing and industry.

The most concentrated Marxist attempt to work out the relation between capitalism and international relations took place in the early part of the twentieth century when Bukharin, Lenin and others developed their theories about the relation of imperialism to war. The outbreak of war between the great powers of Europe and the hostilities which preceded it seemed to be a refutation of the Kantian view that civilised and moral people will avoid war and work progressively for a just world order, and of the Millian view that world commerce encourages peace. These Marxist theories were meant not only to explain what had gone wrong, but to demonstrate that war was endemic to a world capitalist system.

The early twentieth century Marxists were anxious to represent their position as an application of Marx's views to the problems of their time. However, they were in fact making a substantial revision to the Marxist theory of capitalist development, and contemporary Marxists who theorise about the relation of capitalism to oppression and injustice in the Third World are in turn revising Marxist theories to fit the facts of their times. So a discussion about what Marxists have contributed to understanding the connection between social relations and the possibility of a peaceful, just world has to take into account these changes of doctrine and the reasons for them.

Marx himself identified two kinds of antagonism built into the capitalist system: the struggle between capitalists and the opposition between capitalists and workers. The first is the competition between individual capitalists for markets, cheap labour, resources, investment opportunities. Marx commonly describes this competition as war and indeed paints a much grimmer picture of capitalist competition than did Mill. For what Marx understands by capitalism is a society in which the means of production are privately owned and where these private owners produce commodities, goods meant for sale in the marketplace. This means that their economic fate hinges on how well they can compete in this arena, and so each is continually and desperately searching for ways to lower costs of production, to create new products, find new markets. The system is inherently dynamic; it goes through cycles of boom and bust, and those who cannot weather these storms, innovate, expand or cut costs, will go under.

The fact remains that Marx did not think that this competition makes relations between capitalists into a Hobbesian state of war. What makes their relations more or less peaceful is not simply the existence of state authority as an agency to ensure the honouring of contracts or the mutual benefits which capitalists can get from trade. Conflicts of interests are transcended by a common class interest: by an interest in ensuring the continued subordination of the working class – of those who must live by selling their labour to capitalist employers. This common interest is expressed in the activities of the state which Marx described in the *Communist Manifesto* as 'nothing but a committee for managing the affairs of the entire bourgeoisie' (Marx and Engels 1848: 486). The state so conceived is by its very nature dedicated to protecting the inequalities and injustice built into the capitalist system, and Marx regarded talk about equal rights, liberty, consent of the governed as hypocrisy or 'bourgeois ideology'.

It is the relations between capitalists and the working class which Marx believed are potentially 'war-like' in a literal sense. For the survival of capitalists depends upon the exploitation of labour, and it is in their interests to ensure that workers work as intensively as possible and/or to keep wages low and hours of work long. What is in the interests of workers means the ruin of capitalists, and what is in the interest of capitalists means poverty and degradation for the workers. There is thus no common interest to bind classes together and no social contract that could possibly be satisfactory to both, and workers have no reason to regard themselves as having an obligation to obey the political authorities of the capitalist state. Thus as the working class becomes more numerous, more aware of its situation and more able to resist, as economic crises become more severe, concentrating ownership in fewer and fewer hands, class confrontation will become more open, more uncompromising, more like open warfare. The state will finally be unable to contain the conflicts created by class division, and revolution will destroy the capitalist state, along with the system of capitalist production. This is what Marx anticipates in the *Communist Manifesto* and elsewhere.[1]

What Marx says about the relations within a state among capitalists and between capitalists and workers he also applied to world society as a whole. Capitalism will inevitably expand over the boundaries of states. Though this expansion will cause disruption and suffering, Marx makes it clear that the march of capital through the world is progress: it makes the next stage of human development possible. Though capitalists need governments to protect their property, as capitalists they owe allegiance to no particular country, and as they move out into the international world, doing business wherever it is profitable, the cosmopolitan nature of their activities will become more evident. Marx suggests that there is nothing to prevent the international expansion of capital taking the same course as earlier developments within states, and no reason why international capitalists cannot peacefully manage international political affairs for the benefit of their class as a whole. Like Mill, Marx tended to think that rivalries between states were due to reactionary forces, that they were a hangover from a feudal period.[2]

As capitalists bring their relations of production to the world as a whole, they also swell the ranks of the working class. The potential for revolution develops in every country. Marx assumed that workers would organise themselves across national boundaries, and that when revolutions began to occur in the separate states they would spread rapidly through the world. Though the first aim of the revolutionaries in every country will be to destroy capitalist institutions and create a proletarian state capable of fighting against internal and external enemies, states as instruments of class rule will have no intrinsic reason for existing and will eventually disappear. In the new international society production will be managed on a world scale according to the needs and desires of all. However, Marx does not have much to say about how this international socialist society will be formed: how it will develop from a system of proletarian states; what would have to be done about backward or recalcitrant areas, etc. Nor does he have much to say about how an international socialist or communist society would be organised. But it is reasonable to count Marx's idea of a post-revolutionary society as a conception of a just society and one that belongs unambiguously to the modern political philosophy tradition – even though Marx himself generally eschewed or ridiculed talk of justice or equality. For he tells us that it will be a society in which each individual counts equally and thus is assumed to have an equal entitlement to the satisfaction of his/her needs, a society where each individual can freely develop his/her capacities.[3] In time, Marx sometimes suggests, human relations and consciousness will develop to the point where individuals will freely endeavour to satisfy each other's needs without the governance of either external authorities or an internal sense of duty. This development will be made possible not only through the co-operation and solidarity which socialism will encourage but also through the abundance produced by such a society. There will be no need to make appeals to justice – but this is because in such a society the needs and desires of every individual can be fulfilled and the equal worth of each will be recognised as a matter of course.

Though the story is different and though it ends in a different way, Marx's 'universal history' has much in common with Kant's. Like Kant he begins with the world as it is and considers how, given its propensities and possibilities, a truly civilised and peaceful society can be brought into being. It is a story of human progress, of the evolution of consciousness and the perfection of the species. Like Kant's, it supposes that most of this progress will take place without being willed or intended by human agents. But like Kant he also supposes that, at a certain stage, agents (in this case, the working class) will actively and consciously strive for the end which the story foretells. Thus Marx's history, like Kant's, functions both as a source of hope and as something that tells agents what they ought to do.

The differences are also significant. In Marx's history, nature has decreed class war and revolution, and there is no other way to a truly peaceful and just world. War in Marx's view is not something capitalists can avoid by being more sensible, less greedy or more knowledgeable about what they are doing. To survive as a capitalist, each must compete, and thus exploit, and the inevitable result of the activities of each is the war that brings about the destruction of all.

Capitalists can no more avoid this than they can avoid economic crises. There are for Marx, as for Hobbes, necessities governing human relations which are the result of agents doing what they must in order to secure their own existence. Thus Marx's history proceeds with an inevitability which Kant's lacks. Indeed Marx prided himself on uncovering the true moving forces of history, on identifying not merely the tendencies of social development but its 'necessities'. This does not mean that Marx supposed that he could account for everything that would happen in the future, but he did offer definite predictions and therefore his account can be put to the test more easily and definitely than Kant's.

This consideration helps us to appreciate the problem posed for Marxists by events in the early part of this century. These events ran counter to Marxist expectations in two respects. First of all, the enmity between capitalist states, which led to war on an unprecedented scale, did not accord with classical Marxist views about bourgeois co-operation. The international implications of capitalism required further examination. But more critically, Marxists did not anticipate, and found it difficult to account for, the factor which made such a large-scale conflict possible: the willingness of ordinary citizens, including working-class people, to support the interests of their states and fight and die for them.

The theories which Bukharin, Lenin and others developed about imperialism and war were an attempt to respond to these difficulties in the framework of Marxist theory. What they argued is that imperialism and war belong to a later stage of capitalist development when the tendency of the system to create monopolistic enterprises and fall into economic crises has reached a culmination. The new state of affairs, Bukharin argues in *Imperialism and World Economy* (1917), is the result of contradictory factors: the increasing integration of capital within the boundaries of states and the anarchic nature of its international expansion. The tendency of capital to become integrated reaches its ultimate conclusion: the conversion of all significant capital within state boundaries into a gigantic trust dominated by financial capital. In these new conditions the state becomes more than a mere committee of the bourgeoisie and more like the board of directors of an enormous holding company. But competition among these giant state trusts continues with a vengeance, for they now have all the powers of the state behind them. For one thing, they now have the ability to protect themselves by building a tariff wall around their territories.

Inevitably state trusts come up against the limitations of the system.

Consumption in the home market cannot keep up with production, and the possibility of making profit through export is thwarted by the tariff barriers of other state trusts. The rate of profit will fall.[4] Capitalist trusts will attempt to solve this problem by moving into parts of the world not yet exploited by capitalism and will use the military forces of their state to occupy and incorporate new territories – hence imperialism. In the early stages their armed forces are used mainly against peoples who try to resist incorporation. But when the whole world is divided up and turned into state trusts then the room for such expansion is at an end, and the only way a state trust can now obtain more territory to exploit is to try to take away the possessions of others. Once military power becomes a necessity for the expansion and protection of the capitalist state trust, the individual freedoms and parliamentary institutions of bourgeois society become increasingly subordinated to the interests of imperialists, and cosmopolitan ideals and the support of free trade, typical of the earlier days of capitalism, give way to national chauvinism and war.

Since state trusts, operating as monopolies, can afford to buy the support of workers, they will at first be able to seduce some of the working class into their imperial adventures. But this, both Bukharin and Lenin believe, is a temporary phenomenon: working-class patriotism will disappear as soon as workers become aware of the deadly implications of this capitalist logic. But in the meantime wars will become more ferocious and more extensive – until world socialist revolution puts an end to both capitalism and war. The Marxist theory of imperialism and war is thus an attempt to explain why the capitalist powers of Europe found themselves at war and why workers supported them. But even more than an explanation of the past, this theory is a projection into the future based upon what these Marxists saw to be the dynamics of capitalism in the modern period.

There is a superficial similarity between this view of international affairs and the realist one. They offer a similar description of the world: states have opposing interests which lead them into conflict, conflict which is exacerbated by the build-up of military forces. However, Marxism is a reductionist theory. It countenances no independent laws of politics, no generalisations about the behaviour of political agents in international affairs. This means, for one thing, that Marxists would deny that in a state of nature states are bound to come into conflict with each other. They would see no reason why socialist states could not exist together in peace. On the other hand, they hold out no hope that capitalist states can manage to coexist by achieving a balance of power. The dynamics underlying the capitalist system mean that any balance will be upset by the insatiable needs of capitalists. Bukharin does not believe that there is a political solution in the framework of international relations to the problem of war any more than Marx believes that there is a political solution within the framework of a state for class warfare.

It is this reductionism which has proved to be the chief problem for Marxist theory. Realism is inadequate because it does not sufficiently take into account economic and social changes in world affairs. Marxism is inadequate because it does not sufficiently account for non-economic forces and agents – particularly political ones. That there are difficulties with the Marxist account is revealed by developments in the world since Bukharin and Lenin's time: the fact that capitalist states have largely divested themselves of their colonies, that for the most part capitalist states have managed to live together in peace, that in spite of the increasingly international nature of capitalism, workers of the world have failed to unite in an international movement for socialism, that socialist states do not seem more able than capitalist states to live together in peace. But the tensions and contradictions which later Marxists have wrestled with are also evident within Bukharin's theoretical account of the tendencies of modern capitalism.

This account depends, on the one hand, on the idea that capitalists within a state can co-operate to form an integrated system which is no longer subject to the necessities of unbridled capitalist competition, and on the other hand, on the idea that international co-operation of capitalists or capitalist states is impossible. These two ideas do not sit together comfortably. If capitalists within states have become mono-polists, who can through political means assert control over their economic environment, then they can, for one thing, afford to make concessions to workers, to pay them higher wages, and this in turn will enable workers to pay the higher prices charged for commodities. Expansion of capital outward, the annexation of new territories, does not seem to be something which this new integrated form of capitalism absolutely requires. Bukharin assumes that if given a choice between making concessions to the working class and imperialist expansion, capitalists will choose the latter: 'One cannot imagine that the big bourgeoisie would begin to increase the share of the working class, in order thus to drag itself out of the mire by the hair' (1917: 79). But at least he concedes that they have a choice. Thus Bukharin's conception of capitalist development seems to support the idea, advocated at the time by Hobson (1902) and others, that there are alternatives to imperialism and alternatives to war.

More generally, Bukharin's idea of the 'corporate state' seems to anticipate a development which has run in a direction contrary to what Marxists of the nineteenth and early twentieth centuries anticipated. For Marx, the state is something which protects bourgeois property and represses attempts by workers to organise. It is not capable of controlling the anarchic tendencies of capitalism: of alleviating crises, dampening down class confrontation, running the economy. Thus even if capitalists want to curb the destructive, war-like tendencies of the system they cannot do so. But Bukharin anticipates a situation in which the state is more capable of doing these things, and thus his appeal to the necessities built into capitalist relations is no longer convincing.

Starting from the possibilities which Bukharin's idea of the state opens up, it seems that we can continue the story which Marx tells in the *Communist Manifesto* in a different way. We will assume that capitalists, being on the whole rational, will prefer, if they can, to overcome or counter those tendencies which seem to be leading to revolution or war. A radical disruption of the system is not in their interests. Thus as workers become more united and better organised (as Marx says they will) capitalists will generally be prepared to make concessions for the sake of peace. They should in most cases be able to do so: the protection their industries receive, their ability to negotiate industry-wide agreements with workers and inscribe them into law will ensure that none of the larger capitalists, at least, will be seriously disadvantaged by giving their workers better wages and conditions (O'Conner 1974). When workers earn more money they will also buy more goods, including luxury goods, and in the case of the industries producing them, increased sales will more than make up for the higher cost of production. Moreover, higher wage costs will stimulate the development of labour-saving technology, and in this way the tendency of the rate of profit to fall will be alleviated.

As workers become better off and better educated, they will increasingly demand a greater say in political affairs. In most countries they will gain their rights as citizens, and their unions and parties will increasingly be able to affect the political agenda and bring into existence reforms favourable to them: shorter hours of work, unemployment benefits, health and safety standards, recognition of the rights of unions, welfare measures. Most capitalists will concede ground unwillingly, and reforms will only come about as the result of strikes and political pressure. But on the whole they will be achieved peacefully within the framework of law. Workers, even those who regard themselves as socialists, will not be inclined to join revolutionary movements or engage in illegal activity. They will come to regard the state as their state and will feel committed to obeying its laws, participating in its political system and achieving their goals by democratic reforms. Capitalists will also accept this process, even when it means the diminution of their power. They will become accustomed to negotiation and co-operation with workers and their organisations. Though at first most of the concessions they make to workers will be a matter of prudence, over time they will become more and more inclined to be moved by appeals to justice; they will come to regard the welfare measures implemented by their state as desirable from a moral point of view, even when they complain about some of the details. Gradually the society will turn into something that can be properly described as a welfare state or even 'socialism' – though this will not mean the disappearance of capitalist ownership.

This story, an adaptation of Rawls', may not be an entirely accurate description of what is happening in capitalist countries or what could happen (Sweden is probably the country that it best fits), but at least it suggests that there is no reason why a capitalist society cannot gradually and peacefully become a more just and co-operative society. In the world as a whole transition through reform will be more difficult, for there is no government which can manage the economy or make and enforce laws. But peaceful progress towards a more just world order may nevertheless be possible. The story continues as follows.

We will assume once again that most capitalists will prefer to avoid, if they can, war, revolution and anything that disrupts their ability to do business. Since they have at their disposal enormous resources and can generally use their control over their economic environment to avoid the worst effects of competition, capitalist states (and in the modern world transnational companies) are not driven to exploit the Third World or to make war on each other. They can afford to make and keep trading agreements with each other and with the governments of the countries where they have their investments, and for the sake of orderly, profitable business relations they will be inclined to do so, making concessions where they must (Warren 1973). An imperialist or aggressive policy, they will usually find, is bad for business, since it encourages resistance, disruption and even revolution. It is also bad for business to keep people in poverty, for an impoverished population cannot afford to buy the goods which capitalists manufacture.

For their part, Third World countries need capital for development and they will be prepared to make deals in order to get it. Socialist countries too will want to engage in trade and will often be prepared to accept some capitalist investment. At first the arrangements with poorer countries will tend to favour overseas capitalists and trans-national companies, but as populations of these countries become wealthier and better educated, as their own industries grow, they will be able to win important concessions or make their own terms, as has happened to some extent in Taiwan, Singapore, South Korea, etc. In some cases, their possession of important resources will make this easier, as in the case of the petroleum-rich countries. As countries become wealthier, internal reforms will become more possible and likely. The poorer people of these countries will gradually win the rights and protection which people in wealthier countries now possess. As their influence on national affairs becomes greater, workers' parties and unions will be in the position, if they choose, to bring about reforms and changes to their political and economic conditions which can be described as 'socialist'. Thus, though progress will be slow, we can hope for, if not expect, a more or less peaceful evolution to a more just world order.

This story of progress can be regarded as a version of Kant's universal history which takes into account the problems Marxists find in capitalism. In some respects it is similar to Marx's own story. It assumes that the spread of capitalist industry throughout the world is progressive – that it lays the groundwork for a better life for all people – and that this development can occur without causing war among nations. Where it parts company with Marx is that it also insists that changes favouring workers and other less well-off people can occur more or less peacefully through political reform and concessions of capitalists, and thus that the world could become more just without revolution or war. However, this part of the story depends essentially on citizens of a country being able to better their conditions through political pressure and reform. One of its problems is that it does not take into account changes in the world economy which seem to be making it more difficult for most states to manage their own economies, and thus for governments to negotiate advantageous agreements or for citizens to bring about changes by means of political processes.

The fact is that the gradual improvement in the well-being of people everywhere in the world which this story of the future predicts doesn't seem to be happening. Critics of the international economic order point out that some Third World countries, particularly in Africa, have slipped backward in the last decade as far as their standard of living is concerned, and though there may be many reasons for this – war, bad government, etc. – they also suffer from a huge burden of debt, and as primary producers they are especially vulnerable to changes in the world market or recession. In other words, some countries are not in a very good position to make advantageous deals with transnational companies, capitalist governments or financial organisations. What this means is that companies and investors can, and sometimes do, exploit the vulnerability of desperate people: they take advantage of and aggressively maintain the conditions which keep workers in semi-slavery, ignore health and safety standards, pollute and destroy the environment, bribe local politicians, help to prop up repressive regimes, prevent the establishment of local industries, and contribute almost nothing to the development of the local economy.

Moreover, the power of some of these capitalist industries and the close relationship between capitalists and state authorities mean that local people are likely to have a difficult time reforming their government and fighting for better conditions. Even when reform movements manage to win a victory, their accomplishment can be undermined or destroyed by intervention, economic or military, from powerful states backing up capitalist interests. The US invasion of Grenada and the economic pressure and subversive tactics used against the Allende government in Chile are some examples of this kind of interference. This means, for one thing, that workers and other poor people in Third World countries will be able to gain little comfort from stories about how workers in wealthier countries have managed over time to win some concessions from capitalists. Their own fight seems much more difficult.

In any case, as modern critics of capitalism point out, conditions for many workers and other vulnerable people in capitalist countries are not so favourable as the story of progress suggests. People in wealthier countries do not generally starve to death, but many of them are homeless or impoverished, and depend upon charity for their basic needs. Their conditions of work can be dangerous or unhealthy, their pay inadequate, and their ability to improve their situation limited by threats of unemployment or laws which favour their employers. What most contemporary Marxists and other critics of capitalism are arguing is not that capitalism necessarily generates injustice and war, but that it is likely to do so. For it is a system which encourages greed and exploitation by rewarding those who are greedy – a system which makes it difficult for the most vulnerable people to change their situation and makes it unlikely that the wealthy will respond to demands or pleas for justice, even when they can.

Like Rawls' and Kant's account of the development of relations of justice, our story of progress is supposed to assure us that relations of war and exploitation can be converted into a modus vivendi from which all receive benefits, and that this modus vivendi will eventually turn into a just social order. But why these developments should happen remains unclear. Wherever in the world capitalists have the upper hand, they are likely to have less of an interest in making a compromise favourable to workers or local people or they may put their energy into finding political means for maintaining or increasing their power – as Marx supposed they would. A peaceful modus vivendi, more or less satisfactory to all parties, might never be found. Even if capitalists are willing to compromise for the sake of peace, they may never accept the idea that they are morally obligated to share their resources with the least well off. The problem is not just that a modus vivendi may fail to turn into a morally motivated relationship, but that capitalists may be inclined to subscribe to a conception of justice that serves their interests – as Marx also supposed they would. They may, for example, adopt the libertarian view that property rights are basic to individual freedom and all taxation is theft. This means that those who want to bring about a just world not only have to be concerned about how this can be done but have to be prepared to defend their idea about what international justice is. We have seen that even among cosmopolitans there is no general agreement about the 'goal' of history.

Realists do not succeed in establishing that there is a logic of international relations which precludes perpetual peace, and Marxists do not show that there is a logic of capitalism which makes peace and justice impossible. Nevertheless, Marxists, like the realists, pose problems concerning the development of a just world which have not yet been solved, as well as raising questions about the nature of international justice which need to be answered. Can we construct from the perspective of the late twentieth century a more satisfactory 'universal history from a cosmopolitan point of view' which ends in perpetual peace? In the next two chapters I will consider two attempts to do this and the idea of international justice intrinsic to each.

Chapter 4

Cosmopolitan justice in a federation of sovereign states

A theory of international justice must at one and the same time provide a conception of how world society could and should develop and the principles and procedures of justice which are supposed to be realised in it. What keeps this inquiry from being hopelessly circular is that we start out with views about what problems a theory of justice ought to solve and thus the objectives we want to achieve, and we have available facts and theories about the international world and about the needs, desires and loyalties of individuals in it. We can therefore engage in the exercise of making our moral theory fit the facts or ordering the world to fit the theory. That is, we can try to determine whether our moral ideas could prevail in the world as it is or as it could become, or formulate a view of justice which does fit the world as it is or could be. I will take it that what it means for a view of international justice to be acceptable includes the requirement that the just world be achieved peacefully and by just means. There are good reasons, as I have argued, for insisting on this condition, and no good reason for thinking that the logic of international relations or of international capitalism makes it impossible to satisfy.

I am not assuming that there is only one way of constructing such a 'history'. There are likely to be alternative means to the same moral end and there are different views within the cosmopolitan framework about what that end should be. I will begin by considering two common ideas about how international affairs could and should evolve and the two different conceptions of international justice which are associated with them. These two ideas about world development and organisation correspond to the two possible routes out of the state of war briefly discussed in Chapter 1. In this chapter I will try to determine whether a world federation, something like Kant's league of peace, could be the basis for a just world. In the next chapter I will consider whether a world state is a viable alternative, and what this entails as far as justice is concerned. These are not the only ideas about what a just international world would be like, and I will later consider others. But by looking more closely at the issues which these more familiar conceptions raise, we will obtain a better idea of what approach is most promising. We will also be in a better position to examine cosmopolitan assumptions about social organisation and world justice.

One obvious way of beginning the project of formulating a feasible conception of a desirable future world society is to take ideas about international justice which are already widely accepted by people in the international world and consider how they might be developed, modified, supplemented and made more adequate. We can then consider what kind of social and political environment would be most appropriate for this revised conception of international justice if it is to have any chance of prevailing, and whether it is reasonable to suppose that such an environment could exist. Like Walzer (1980a) I am relying on pre-existing ideals and standards in 'international society'. The task is to see whether these ideas can be developed and altered in a way that overcomes the problems that confront them.

What is attractive about the Just War approach to international justice is that it is firmly rooted in a political order which most people accept. States may no longer be the only agents of international affairs, as critics of realism point out, but they remain the most important agents, and it is therefore reasonable to suppose that a theory of international justice should take relations between states as central. Furthermore, the Just War approach underwrites the value that most individuals place on maintaining the sovereignty of their state. Even those who are at war with their own government, or who object to boundaries as they now exist, generally desire, and are often prepared to fight for, their national independence.

Even from a cosmopolitan point of view it is not difficult to understand why people generally value national sovereignty. States do or can protect and promote what individuals value – their lives, property, welfare – as well as the less tangible goods which Walzer includes in his notion of the 'common life'. Not all existing states adequately protect these things and none of them does it perfectly. But Marxists and other critics of the state give us no good reason for thinking that states, even under capitalism, cannot manage to serve the interests of all individuals or develop just institutions. This does not mean that a system of states is the only, or even the best, way of protecting the interests of individuals. But given that a system of states exists, that most people value the sovereignty of their state, and that it is generally reasonable that they should, then we have from a cosmopolitan point of view a justification for the existence of this system and perhaps for most existing states (though not necessarily for governments as they now are). So let us lay it down that the right of sovereignty is basic to international justice and that all states have an equal entitlement to it. Given this starting point, it is then necessary to consider what this right entails, whether the difficulties associated with the Just War approach can be overcome and what this would mean as far as international organisation is concerned.

From a cosmopolitan point of view the entitlement of states to exist and exercise sovereignty is a derivative and conditional right which depends upon how well states protect and promote the well-being, autonomy or rights of individuals. Given this understanding of what justifies the rights of states, there are two immediate problems with a conception of international justice that takes the equal right of sovereignty as basic. The first is that some states are much better than others at protecting individuals' interests. If the entitlements states possess depend on how well institutions of state treat individuals, then some states have no entitlement to exist and some, it seems, have a greater entitlement than others. Moreover, some states have a much greater population than others; in some states individuals are in much greater need than in others. How can it be just to assign equal entitlements to political societies which are so unequal?[1]

From a cosmopolitan point of view there are nevertheless good reasons for presuming that each state has as much of a right to sovereignty as any other state unless there are very good reasons in a particular case for denying this. First of all, we have to reckon with the value most individuals place on their national sovereignty. To interfere with their affairs in a way they do not want is to fail to respect their desires. Second, it is important to avoid imposing on the international world requirements of justice that are impossible or costly to fulfil. In a world of independent states the costs of refusing to recognise a state's sovereignty are likely to be prohibitive from a moral and prudential point of view. For if we deny that a state has a right to exist or claim that it has a lesser title, then presumably we are attributing to ourselves the right or duty to intervene (for who else but another state can ensure that justice prevails?). But the intervention of states into the affairs of others, whatever the intentions (and these are usually questionable), tends to cause harm, injustice and resentment, and sow the seeds for future conflicts. States are inept interveners.[2] There are thus good moral/prudential reasons for assuming that the integrity of a state should not be violated except for very good reasons – if, for example, the government is at war with its population and the people call for outside aid or if a minority group is being persecuted and asks for help (Walzer 1980a: Ch. 6). The fact remains that the inequality of states and the existence of unjust states are a problem for a cosmopolitan theory of international justice, and we will want to see whether we can retain a theory of justice based on states' rights and at the same time find a way of dealing with these difficulties.

What the entitlement of equal self-determination entails is that it is unjustified to violate the sovereignty of a state unless there are clear and pressing reasons for intervention. Armed aggression – the invasion of one state's territory by the armies of another – almost always counts as an unjust violation of sovereignty, and it is generally accepted in the international world that aggressors should not only be stopped but that they ought to make restitution or reparation for the harm that they have done to the state they have violated. In reality reparations are not always paid and there are serious disagreements about when they are due and how much they should be. But since the principle is accepted, even though the practice is uncertain, it is worthwhile to consider how this idea might be built into a more demanding conception of international justice.

One of the problems with the Just War approach, as we have seen, is that it does not deal adequately with other kinds of interference in the affairs of nations – interferences which can destroy or subvert the common life of citizens and interfere with their well-being just as effectively as armed aggression: economic embargoes, clandestine activities, support for rebel groups, etc. It is important to recognise that the same arguments that can be used to condemn armed invasions can also be used to condemn these activities. If, for example, a powerful state, through economic sabotage or political pressure, attempts to undermine the political system or economic stability of another state, then it seems reasonable to regard this as an unjust violation of sovereignty, something that interferes with individuals' interests and their political self-determination, and thus to require that the violation cease and that reparation be made for the harm done.

Moreover, by the same argument, it seems reasonable to require that states take responsibility for the unintended harm that they cause to individuals in other states or to their political life if this harm is the result of carelessness or negligence. If, for example, the industries in a particular state cause serious pollution problems in another state, and this is the result of a failure to exercise reasonable care or to institute proper standards, then it seems just to require not only that the harmful activities cease but that reparation be made for the harm done.

The idea of international justice which I am developing can be called the 'Just Interaction Theory'. According to this conception, the respect for the equal entitlement to self-determination forbids states and their citizens from disrupting, harming, destroying or negligently allowing to be harmed or destroyed, the rights and well-being of individuals of another state or their political institutions against their will (except in self-defence or to prevent gross acts of inhumanity). The Just Interaction approach clearly makes more demands on states than do most versions of Just War theory. But they are motivated by the same reasoning, the same regard for individuals, their interests and values. They take as basic the idea that cosmopolitans share – that it is unjust to cause harm to individuals or to violate their individual and political rights, whether deliberately or through negligence (except in self-defence or for some other equally strong reason). Moreover, they build upon a conception of justice which is fairly widely accepted in the international world, and thus there is good reason for regarding these demands as a reasonable extension of this conception – an extension which is motivated by an attempt to deal with problems faced by the Just War approach.

The theory seems to require further extensions. Another problem which the traditional Just War approach does not adequately deal with is the grievances of states or groups of people concerning the wrongs done to them by others in the past. It seems reasonable to suppose that if harm has been done in the past by states, deliberately or through negligence, to individuals of other states or their social and political institutions, then justice requires that some kind of compensation is due to them – especially if the effects of that injustice are still present. Therefore it seems that Just Interaction Theory must require citizens of states to take responsibility and make reparations for past violations or injuries done by their society to other individuals.

If, for example, our predecessors acquired by illegitimate means the territory we now inhabit – by invasion or some other act of force – then it seems reasonable to demand of us that we make some kind of reparation to the descendants of those who suffered from this violation, especially if they are still suffering from the results of this illegitimate act (J. Thompson 1990). This does not mean that we are required to give up the territory that our ancestors gained illegitimately – for this may cause injustice to individuals now living there. But we may be required to make compensation in the form of benefits, payments or the ceding of land rights, depending on the needs of the individuals whose ancestors' rights were violated. If our country has in the past pursued an imperialist policy and has increased its wealth by exercising domination over people in other parts of the world, we have a remaining responsibility to compensate for the harm done to these societies, especially if the effects of that harm are still present. What this responsibility entails will depend upon the nature of the harm and what the people in these societies now need.

The demand that we take responsibility for past wrongs raises the objections frequently voiced against the idea of collective responsibility: that individuals cannot be expected to pay for wrongs that they have not committed, and that no compensation is due to individuals who were not personally wronged. However, a conception of justice based upon entitlements of national sovereignty and the corresponding responsibilities of states seems to require an acceptance of some kind of collective responsibility. If we accept the first, then we should accept the second. The citizens of a state, to whom national sovereignty is a value, must ultimately take responsibility for what their state does (for no one else will do this), though this does not mean that all citizens have to be regarded as having an equal responsibility. This will include the responsibility for compensating for past wrongs. For debts, including moral debts, are, like assets, inherited. If we regard the territory and resources controlled by a state as being in some sense the collective possession of its citizens – which the idea of sovereignty seems to entail – then these joint possessors have to regard themselves as taking on the burdens as well as the assets of their predecessors. If these predecessors incurred an unpaid moral debt, then those who are their heirs are responsible for discharging it. And those to whom the heirs are indebted are, by similar reasoning, the successors of the people injured.

In summary, the Just Interaction Theory regards as unjust injuries done by states and other international agents to individuals and to the national societies to which they belong – whether these injuries are deliberate or the result of negligence. And it requires that they make reparations for harm done, including harm done in the past. I have claimed that the Just Interaction Theory has an intuitive plausibility – it builds upon accepted ideas about international justice – and that it is reasonable for a cosmopolitan to accept it. Whether this theory is in the end acceptable, however, depends upon two further considerations:

whether it does adequately overcome all of the problems associated with the Just War approach, and whether it is practical – whether leaders and citizens are likely to be able and inclined to accept and apply it.

One of the biggest problems for Just War theory, as we have seen, is the problem of inequality and poverty. The Just Interaction Theory, if it were put into practice, might, it is true, go some way towards dealing with some of the causes of poverty. It would be difficult to deny that imperialist policies carried out by wealthy states in the past, and sometimes continuing into the present – unfair trade policies, political interference, etc. – have caused or contributed to Third World poverty and the political suppression suffered by many people in poorer countries. So if wealthy countries were to stop this exploitation or interference and make reparation for harm done, including harm done by past generations, then most Third World countries and most people in them would undoubtedly benefit. There is, of course, the problem that compensation given to some Third World countries will not benefit those who are worst off; it may indeed be used by governments to buy armaments in order to suppress their population. In this case, wealthy countries may be justified in withholding payments until reforms satisfactory to the population are made – which in itself would be a strong incentive to reform. When such a course is justified and when it counts as unjustified interference in the political affairs of another sovereign state is, to be sure, not always easy to determine.

The Just Interaction Theory, unlike Beitz's theory, does not require a state to give aid to those it has not injured, however badly off the people of that state may be. Citizens of a state do not have a duty of justice to help people of another state who happen to lack sufficient resources within their territory to carry on a decent life (though they may be persuaded to do this for humanitarian reasons). Poor states that are not owed anything may thus be left to wallow in their own misery. The Just Interaction Theory is compatible with the existence of inequality, even severe inequality, within the international world. Those who, like Beitz, regard the very existence of such inequalities as a reason for regarding a state of world affairs as unjust will thus judge the theory to be deficient. Should we agree with them?

It seems that from a cosmopolitan point of view we must agree. For cosmopolitans are supposed to respect the rights or autonomy of all individuals, or they are supposed to be concerned with maximising the well-being or satisfaction of preferences of all. But to exercise rights or to be an autonomous individual, to have preferences satisfied, requires that all individuals have access to resources. A principle of distributive justice thus seems basic to any cosmopolitan ethic. Cosmopolitans, it is true, disagree among themselves about the content of this principle. Some would be content to ensure that the worst-off have enough of the basic resources to secure a decent life; others insist that the resources of the world ought to be distributed equally. But whatever the standpoint, a situation where some people starve while others have much more than they need for a good life seems intolerable from the point of view of justice.

Once again it might be argued that the international world is not a suitable environment for any principle of justice which requires interference in the affairs of sovereign states. To fulfil a requirement of distributive justice effectively there must be institutions for acquiring and distributing resources: for taxing groups and individuals and for ensuring that the goods acquired in this way benefit the least well-off individuals of the world. There must be international agencies with the power to collect taxes, direct resources to individuals and make sure that individuals and states do not evade their duty. But who has the authority to do this and on what grounds? So long as citizens value the sovereignty of their states they are likely to regard this kind of intervention into their affairs as an interference with their liberty or a form of imperialism. In other words, an idea of justice based on the sovereignty of states seems to rule out a principle of resource redistribution. In this world, it seems, inequality is simply the price that must be paid for valuing national sovereignty so highly.

However, this position is clearly not satisfactory. The continued existence of desperate poverty is unacceptable, first of all, from a prudential point of view. Poor and desperate people may not have the military means to challenge the international status quo, but we can expect that they will do what they can to relieve their distress, and this may result in an increase of terrorism or environmental destruction, or greater instability in world politics. Moreover, it is difficult to deny that poor and desperate people have some kind of moral entitlement to do what they can to preserve their own lives and what they most value. It is difficult to condemn people who are acting out of desperation – especially when others have more than they need. But if we find it difficult to condemn the violations of world law and order committed by desperate people, then we should also find questionable the principles of justice on which this law and order is supposed to be based – for these principles do not deliver us sufficiently from a state of nature in which people have a good reason for making war upon others.

An idea of world justice which tolerates extreme inequalities is also unsatisfactory from a moral point of view. For the rights of states are merely derivative from a cosmopolitan point of view and thus a world order in which large numbers of people suffer and starve is hard to defend. At the very least we have an obligation to consider whether there is a better alternative.

This suggests that the Just Interaction Theory, as it stands, is not demanding enough. On the other hand, in other respects it seems too demanding, and sceptics are likely to doubt whether states and other international agents will be inclined or able to respect it. For one thing, it might be doubted that citizens will ever be prepared to accept the idea that they are responsible for making reparation for harm that their state has done – especially if this entails considerable sacrifice of their own interests. But if states refuse to do what is just, then who is going to make them and at what cost? Moreover, there is no international body capable of laying down the law concerning whether and what reparations are owed. There is likely to be continual dispute about this matter – thereby laying the groundwork for future quarrels. More seriously, we can doubt whether states can be expected to refrain from harming or interfering with the sovereignty of others. For as realists point out, the security of a state, the economic well-being of individuals in it, can depend vitally on what happens outside its borders: on availability of resources, maintenance of supply lines, the existence of friendly neighbours; and for the sake of survival states will sometimes be forced or inclined to interfere in the affairs of another state – ensure that friendly governments remain in power, that vital resources continue to be supplied at a reasonable price, etc. We do not have to be realists in order to acknowledge that the governments of states in an interdependent world are sometimes going to be little inclined to honour the requirements of the Just Interaction Theory, and if they believe that they are only doing what they must in order to survive, then they also will be disinclined to pay reparations for harm done.

The interdependence of world economic and political affairs creates other difficulties for the application of the Just Interaction Theory. For in this interdependent world, the problem is not simply that leaders and citizens may, with some justification, refuse to accept the idea that they should never interfere with the sovereignty of others, but that the harm done to these others may not be anyone's responsibility. As contemporary Marxists rightly point out, the developments which cause misery to populations, destroy their culture and common political life, are often not willed by leaders or citizens of states and cannot easily be controlled by them. These are the effects of the operation of the international economy and the world monetary system or of technological change – effects which are caused by the actions of a large number of agents all over the world, including many that are not states – e.g. transnational companies, international financiers. It is not clear what responsibilities citizens of states can be expected to take for what these agents do or for the overall effects of the world economy. It is not clear that there are any agents who can be held responsible for this. I have argued that traditional Marxists are wrong to think that international capitalism inevitably leads to exploitation, misery, war, revolution. But it remains a plausible thesis that in a world in which the ability of states to control the course of economic and social development has been eroded by interdependence, a theory of international justice which focuses on states and their responsibilities is an unrealistic basis on which to try to establish a more just world.

It does not follow from these objections that we have to reject the Just Interaction Theory. I argued in my discussion of Beitz that one possible response to the problems created by interdependence is to try to undo or modify some of the developments which are taking world society in that direction. Since there are some reasons for regarding Just Interaction Theory as an appropriate basis for just international relations, then it seems that we also have reason for trying to bring about a world society in which states are able to act as responsible and just agents and are inclined to do so. Similarly, one response to the problem of poverty is to consider how the world as a system of states might develop in a way that makes it more likely that all individuals will have their basic needs satisfied. What would such a world be like? How likely is it that it will come into being? What moral problems stand in its way? The acceptability of the Just Interaction Theory, and similar conceptions of international justice, depends on the answers to these questions.

In order to be a suitable environment for the application of the Just Interaction Theory a system of states would have to satisfy the following basic conditions. All of these are either implied or made explicit in Kant's discussion of perpetual peace. The first condition is that all states be capable of acting as responsible agents in international affairs. This means that they must be able to make rational decisions, carry them out effectively and consistently, keep agreements and act in a predictable way over a reasonable period of time. To do so they need decision-making bodies and executors who are able and accustomed to act in a rational, law-abiding manner. When Kant insists that states should be governed by laws and constitutions, one thing he undoubtedly has in mind is what is required to ensure responsible agency. The problem with a despotic state is not just that the monarch may go to war without consulting his subjects, but that he may do so capriciously, according to the whim of the moment.

However, the problems raised by Marxists and by developments in the world economy indicate that if states are to act as responsible agents, able to make rational decisions about war and peace, able to keep agreements, it is also necessary that what they do should not be determined by economic necessities, the needs of a particular class or the demands of international companies and financiers. The political affairs of the world must be within the joint control of their decision-making bodies, and these bodies must have enough freedom of action to be able to avoid war and injustice if they want to. This presupposes, for one thing, that states be and remain the principal agents in the international world. This does not mean that there can be no international companies or international bodies active in international affairs, but their influence must not be so great that states cannot act with reasonable freedom and, in so doing, jointly determine the course of world politics. That this requirement should be fulfilled is also assumed by Kant and others who believe that international justice can be based upon a system of sovereign states.

If states are to be able to act freely, a third condition must also be satisfied: each state must have sufficient resources to ensure that the basic needs of all citizens can be satisfied and that citizens of a state can carry on their political life without endangering the lives and political institutions of the citizens of other states. Satisfaction of this condition makes it more likely that states in a system of states will be able and inclined to establish just relations, and less likely that the system will be disrupted by the desperate acts of desperate people. Moreover, satisfying this condition makes possible in the context of a system of states a solution to the problem of extreme poverty – a problem which most cosmopolitans rightly insist must be solved if the world is to be just.

The availability of resources does not guarantee the well-being of everyone or that all states will be able and inclined to be just. To have a world conducive to the practice of justice it is also necessary that states have just institutions. This requirement is central to Kant's conception of a just world order and also to Rawls'. To have just institutions, I will assume, it is not necessary that states all govern themselves according to particular principles of domestic justice or even that everyone within each state be in agreement about what justice is. The overlapping consensus may be about procedures rather than principles. To count as a state with just institutions, I will assume, there must be procedures and practices, which citizens in general regard as acceptable, for resolving disputes, for ensuring that the interests and views of individuals will be taken into account, and a means for ensuring that each can participate in determining through political representation the nature of these procedures and practices. In a state with just institutions individuals will be respected, their needs and values will be attended to, and their views will be properly represented in decision-making bodies. A world of such states is not only likely to be politically stable, but it should be, as Rawls claims, conducive to just relationships among them. For a just state, he says,

> is not moved by the desire for world power or national glory; nor does it wage war for purposes of economic gain or the acquisition of territory. These ends are contrary to the conception of justice that defines a society's legitimate interest, however prevalent they have been in the actual conduct of states.
>
> (1973: 379)

The four necessary conditions for application of Just Interaction Theory are closely related. A reasonably wealthy state is more likely to have just institutions, and a just state, so Kant and Rawls claim, is more likely to be a just international agent. If a state has the institutions and the independence required for being a responsible international agent, then it is more likely to be able to make the political and economic reforms required for it to be a just state. The joint satisfaction of these conditions cannot, it must be admitted, guarantee that the world will be peaceful and just, but it is supposed to make it more likely that leaders and citizens of a state will be able and inclined to avoid harming citizens of another state or their institutions, and more inclined to make reparation for harm done.

What changes in world society would have to occur in order to make it likely that these conditions be satisfied? What seems essential, first of all, is that states be more economically and politically independent than most now are. This does not mean that they should aim to be entirely self-sufficient (which is probably impossible) or that they have to give up economic relationships and political alliances which are mutually beneficial. But it is important that states have enough resources for governments to be able to make and carry out policies that promote the

well-being of citizens without being drastically hindered and constrained by outside influences, for citizens to be able to carry on a
satisfactory existence without begging or stealing from other states or
forcing them to do their will. It is important that the policies of states
should not be determined by economic or political 'necessities' – at
least to the point where the choice is between doing an injury to others
or putting at risk the state and the individuals in it.

The problem is that most states in the world are not in this position:
in some cases because they are saddled with a legacy of debt, and are
not able to make independent decisions about internal or external
policy; in others because they are in the grip of international economic
forces or developments beyond their control; or because they are
politically dependent on others. But even if all debts were discharged
and economic forces were curbed so that each state could become a
master of its own destiny, all the conditions would not be met. For
there are many states which are simply too poor, too lacking in
resources ever to be sufficiently independent. Moreover, in a world
in which industrial development, manufacture and trade are so important for well-being, even relatively wealthy countries are never
going to achieve the kind of independence that the theory seems
to require. Thus the question of how a system of states could become more just leads us to consider how the world might evolve, or
be made, into a system of states which is more likely to satisfy the
conditions required for the successful application of the Just Interaction
Theory.

The story might go as follows. For the sake of their own protection
and economic well-being, states within the various regions of the
world will become more and more integrated in their economic and
political affairs. At first the unity within regions will be mostly a
matter of economic convenience, but in time and in gradual stages
political union will follow. At first this union will be no more than a
loose federation of states in which each has its own system of defence
and foreign policy, but gradually the leaders and citizens of these states
will become accustomed to making joint decisions on these matters,
and in the end the federation will acquire all of the powers and
responsibilities of a state. At the same time citizens of the separate
states will become more and more aware of their interdependence and
more inclined to look to the government of the federation for aid,
protection and direction. They will come to regard this federation as
their state and will directly participate in its politics. Their national
state will become a province in this larger political body, though it may

retain some degree of decision-making power concerning internal matters.

The formation and history of the European Economic Community, especially in recent times, can be taken as an indication of how this development might occur. Western Europe is not yet one united state, but it is reasonable to suppose that it is moving in that direction – a process which is likely to be speeded up by the need to develop a common policy towards eastern Europe. Once one regional federation comes into being, then for the sake of their own economic development and protection, states in other regions will be forced into a similar development. The world will become a system of trading blocs, each protecting its own economy with tariffs and import restrictions, and behind these blocs political unity will gradually evolve. A system of 'super-states', each with more wealth and power than existing states, will come into being. Each of these regional states will have within its borders resources sufficient to carry on the activities vital to its economic and political life. This does not mean that world trade will disappear, but it will be carefully controlled and restricted by the policies of the states.

Though there will continue to be inequalities between regions, each regional state will be wealthy enough to ensure that the basic needs of its population can be satisfied. Having achieved a greater potential for wealth and security, the people of these states are more likely to be able and inclined to bring about the political and economic reforms which will make their regional state into a just state. At first there are likely to be severe inequalities within regions, but as the regional government comes to take on the powers and responsibilities of a state, as citizens become used to co-operating with each other, and conscious of belonging to an interdependent regional network, they will come to accept a more equal division of resources, and the whole population will enjoy the social services and benefits that are possible in a wealthy state.

This story is supposed to show how the world could develop into a system of states which are able to satisfy the conditions for applying the Just Interaction Theory. We could add to the story further develop-ments which would aid the administration of justice: the creation of a world council for discussing and adjudicating disputes and resolving common problems, a world court which determines what states owe each other for violations of justice, an independent arms control body which has the right to inspect and monitor developments in each state. Like Kant I am not supposing that these world bodies are anything more than voluntary organisations; they will have no power to force states to do their will. Nevertheless, also like Kant, I am supposing that in a world where the pre-conditions for justice are met, states will develop the habit of being just and will be inclined to abide by the rulings of courts, keep their agreements, and resolve their disputes peacefully.

Whether the Just Interaction Theory is an acceptable theory of international justice depends upon whether this story, or something like it, is plausible, and whether the end result is desirable from a moral point of view. We might doubt, first of all, whether a system of regional states is likely to be achieved in a peaceful way without injustice or use of force. In order to ensure a supply of vital resources or a larger scope for commercial activities newly formed trading blocs might forcibly incorporate new territories. The world could be recolonised. In the early stages of their development, these blocs might carry out trade wars against each other, vying for power and position. In other words, Bukharin's prediction for the future might turn out to be more correct than it first appeared. On the other hand, states which are not immediately incorporated into a trading bloc could have serious difficulties – and these are likely to include very poor states which have no resources and thus are not regarded as assets to any economic community.

Within newly formed regional states, there are also likely to be serious conflicts over power, position, ownership among the members. People who have fought for their national independence will be wary of subjecting themselves to the requirements of a federal state, whatever the advantages, and will fear that the cultural life that they value will be destroyed. Those states accustomed to exercising considerable power will be inclined to impose their will upon others in the federation. The rich and powerful will want to remain rich and powerful and will fight against any policy of redistribution which harms their interests. In the European Economic Community unity has not proceeded smoothly and has not progressed all that far. In regions where there are even greater cultural and political differences, economic inequalities and historical antipathies, the problem of adjustment may lead to war and subjugation.

Let us assume that leaders and citizens, with foresight, good will and luck, will be able to overcome the worst of these problems, and that the others will gradually be resolved over time. As in the case of Kant's history we do not have to suppose that the world of peaceful, just regional states will come into existence in one or even a few generations. Granted all this, would it be a desirable objective? Is a system of wealthy, more or less self-sufficient regional states really likely to be a just and peaceful world? Is it the kind of world people want to achieve?

Realists have given us no good reason for thinking that a world of states will inevitably fall into a war of all against all. Marxists have given us no good reason for thinking that states, even states with capitalist economies, cannot be just and behave justly in world affairs. Moreover, the imagined system of states is supposed to have overcome all of the problems which make realist and Marxist pessimism about justice among states plausible. Nevertheless, there is still room for considerable doubt about whether states in a world of regional states will be inclined to act in accordance with the Just Interaction Theory. Many of the most serious quarrels in world politics have taken place not over economic conflicts of interest but over ideological matters. There is no certainty that regional states, even if their internal relations can be described as just, would not fall into ideological rivalries, and if so, they would undoubtedly use their considerable economic resources to build up arms and threaten each other.[3] The world could remain a very dangerous place. Those who worry about the possibility of nuclear war (that is, every rational person) would probably like more assurance that this would not happen. For this reason we might hesitate to describe the world society I have imagined as being desirable.

There is another problem which is closely related to this worry. In the imagined world political requirements dominate policy making. States control their economies and regulate world trade in order to preserve their sovereignty and autonomy as agents. But this requires that some of the activities of citizens be carefully controlled by the authorities of their state: people will not be able to form whatever associations they please, buy whatever they please, or have the opportunities that have sometimes been associated with a freer world economic system. As in our world they will not be able to immigrate as they please, and it is even possible that they may not be able to emigrate freely. For some states may have to take steps to ensure that they do not lose skilled labour or the economic resources of citizens. This suggests that the controls which states exercise over world affairs are going to have costs as well as benefits – they will restrict the freedom of individuals, as well as in some cases reducing efficiency and increasing bureaucratic regulation. Even if these restrictions do not in themselves count as unjust, they will be regarded by many people as undesirable.

There may be other related effects which are also undesirable. Liberal advocates of free trade like Mill have clearly over-estimated the contribution to world peace and understanding made by international associations and contacts. But there may be something right about their position. They may at least be right to fear that a world of self-sufficient states based upon trading blocs would encourage attitudes detrimental to good international relations. For if citizens of states have no important contacts with those outside their borders, they may come to be indifferent about what happens to these others, or worse, they may become suspicious or chauvinistic and fall into quarrels about petty or imagined wrongs. It seems over-optimistic to suppose that these difficulties would cease to exist if all states were just states, or even if all states were liberal democratic states or socialist states or welfare capitalist states. The irony may be that having put themselves into a position where they can act justly in international society, the people of these independent regional states may end up losing their capacity for justice – losing any inclination to interact justly with outsiders or to rectify harm done.

What this objection amounts to is a doubt about whether Kant and Rawls are right to suppose that internally just states are likely to be just in their international relations. The habit of justice may not translate, simply because the relationships which in a state incline people to act justly towards each other do not exist in the international world. There is evidence to suggest that people living in states which are more or less just are not immune to chauvinistic attitudes towards foreigners and are capable of being unconcerned about how their state's policies harm foreigners. If Freudian views about group psychology or sociobiological theories about human nature have some validity, then we have further reason to fear that Kant and Rawls' conception of a peaceful, just world based on a voluntary association of sovereign states is flawed. The problem of how we get from a state of hostility to a peaceful modus vivendi to a just world is still not satisfactorily solved.

There are thus reasons for supposing that attempting to achieve a world system of independent states would be difficult, costly, and that in any case the results would not be desirable, as far as the promotion of justice is concerned. The objections are not decisive but they are serious enough to raise doubts about the viability of the Just Interaction Theory. For if this theory is not likely to be applied even when the best possible conditions for its application are realised, if in addition it leaves problems associated with the Just War approach unsolved, then we have reason to look for another conception of international justice, and along with it an alternative conception of what a just world society would be like.

Chapter 5

Cosmopolitan justice in a world state

Basic to the cosmopolitan position is the idea that in a just social order all individuals deserve equal respect, possess equal rights or have an equal entitlement to well-being. Therefore it is natural to suppose that the ideal world from a cosmopolitan point of view would consist of one society, one state, which embraces all individuals, binds them together in relations of co-operation and mutual aid, and underwrites through its laws and political processes their basic equality. In a world state, so it could be argued, all individuals will at last be able to develop the relations with each other which now only occur in the framework of national states, and this will make possible not only the solution of international problems: war, economic dislocation, poverty, environmental destruction. A world state will make practical a more robust conception of international justice. Rawlsian or egalitarian principles of distributive justice will be realisable in this universal society. For the world state will not only have powers and agencies capable of sharing out goods among individuals. It should also be able to promote or make possible the relationships among individuals which incline them to regard universal sharing as a requirement of justice.

Nevertheless, there are also good reasons from a cosmopolitan point of view for being doubtful about the desirability of a world state, and few political philosophers have actually advocated this idea.[1] Objections to the idea of a world government are not difficult to come by. Critics first wonder, like Kant, whether such a body could function at all, and then go on to worry that it might function in a way which would deprive individuals of their liberty and other things that they value. The managerial problems in such a political body would be enormous, the conflicts of interest which its government would have to deal with would be severe. Those who believe that a world state is simply impractical think that it is sufficient to point to the differences in culture, ideals, attitudes that exist among the people of the world. The mere existence of the mechanisms of government clearly cannot guarantee the absence of hostility, war and injustice. To have a viable state, Berns argues in 'The case against world government' (1959), you have to have universal, or at least widespread, agreement on the basic principles and goals of society. In the world as a whole it seems implausible to suppose that this amount of agreement can ever exist.

Whether a world government could manage to govern at all is thus a doubtful proposition. On the other hand, if it were effective, critics fear, it would be too intrusive. Jonathan Schell in *The Abolition* expresses a common view:

> We want relief from nuclear peril, but if we sign up for world government as the means of getting it, we find that global institution after global institution is inexorably delivered on our doorstep thereafter, each one equipped to meddle in some new area of our lives.
>
> (1984: 87)[2]

Critics fear that even if a world government were a liberal democracy it would be so big, so bureaucratic, that individuals would be rendered powerless, even more so than they are now in national societies. But the government of the world state may not be democratic. Struggles for power among conflicting groups are likely to be severe, rebellions frequent, and in the resulting atmosphere of crisis it is easy to imagine that well-off individuals would begin crying out for law and order, that constitutional rights could be suspended, emergency powers invoked. These are the conditions in which suppression comes to be regarded as necessary and dictatorial regimes come to power. If the world government were a dictatorship, then it could be more oppressive than tyranny on a national scale. For there would be no one to come to our aid, put pressure on our rulers, nowhere to seek asylum.

As far as most political thinkers are concerned, these familiar objections put the idea of a world state outside the realm of serious consideration. This, I think, is a mistake. For the objections treat the world state as if it were something suddenly imposed on a reluctant and resisting world population. They ignore the fact that national states, which now seem to most people to be a natural and desirable form of political organisation, are the result of centuries of evolutionary development during which people slowly became accustomed to new political forms and new social relationships. To those used to the political life of the clan, the tribe or the village, the idea of a modern pluralist state would have seemed as undesirable and improbable as a world state does to those who are now accustomed to living in national states. But surely we should not allow our present political perceptions to rule out the possibility that over time a united world political society might come into being.

Moreover, a successful world political society is not so unimaginable or implausible as its critics suggest. We live in pluralist societies among individuals who are of different races, ethnic backgrounds, religions, have different ideals and attitudes, etc. The national state is, so to speak, an international society in miniature, and thus the conceptual distance separating modern political societies from a world political society is not nearly so great as the distance which separated pre-modern from modern ideas about political organisation. This means, for one thing, that we shouldn't find it all that difficult to imagine what a world political society would be like and how it might develop. And it suggests, for another, that critics of a world state are wrong to suppose that diversity among individuals in world society rules out the possibility of a viable and just world state. If justice and good government are possible within a pluralistic national state, then why shouldn't they be possible in a world political society?

Furthermore, there are developments now occurring which seem to be leading in the direction of world political unity. These include not only the international economic developments which Beitz and others make so much of, but also the creation of integrated systems of communication and transport, the development of world agencies and regulatory bodies, the establishment of international non-governmental associations, companies and pressure groups, the increasing association of individuals and groups across borders, the need to solve environmental and other common problems. These developments can be resisted by those determined to preserve the sovereignty of states, but as we have seen, the outcome of this resistance is uncertain, its costs may be considerable, and interference with the movement of goods, people and money that such resistance entails is increasingly likely to be regarded as an unjustified interference with the activities and opportunities of individuals and groups. It is worthwhile therefore to try to imagine how the international world might evolve peacefully and without war and subjugation into a just world political society. At the same time we will try to obtain a clearer view of what justice might mean in this society, and whether the relationships and arrangements which are supposed to underpin it are possible, likely, and desirable from a moral point of view, or at least more desirable than the alternatives.

One way in which the story of the creation of a world state might go is as follows. The world economy continues to become more integrated, and even the socialist countries, the Soviet Union, China, Vietnam, etc., become bound up in a web of international relationships. Attempts by national states to restrict the movement and activities of individuals – what information they exchange, what associations they have, what they buy and sell – become more and more futile. Since a world economy requires international regulations and controls, more and more international associations are formed in order to monitor, advise, conciliate, lend money, adjudicate disputes. They are aided by an increasingly sophisticated system of international communication. At first these regulatory and adjudicating bodies will be limited in what they can do by their lack of power and by the nature of their membership. States can, and sometimes will, refuse to take the advice of these agencies or heed their decisions. Moreover, those who sit on these bodies are likely to be official or unofficial representatives of states and can be expected to pursue national interests. Either that, or they will be people associated with the transnational companies and financial organisations of the developed world. Thus on the whole these international regulatory bodies will tend to favour the interests of countries and companies from the developed world – they will, to adapt Marx's words, be committees to regulate the international affairs of the wealthy – often to the detriment of the poor of the world.

However, this situation will change, first of all because the resistance to the policies of these bodies and to developments in the world economy will become international. For example, workers in the developed world who want to protect themselves in this new international environment, to ensure that their living standard and rights as workers do not decline, will become more inclined to form links with workers in other countries, including the poorer countries, and more inclined to fight for higher wages for the least well-off in the international world. These regional and international labour organisations will become over time better organised and more powerful; they will sometimes engage in strikes, struggles and boycotts which are international in scope. The regulatory and judicial agencies, for the sake of peace and order, will have to take into account and learn to co-operate with these workers' organisations. They will also have to learn to respond to the regional and international pressure groups which will proliferate in this new environment – environmental groups, consumer groups, groups of indigenous people, etc. These groups will typically contain members from both the developed and the poorer regions of the world, for the problems with which they are concerned are worldwide. They do not only affect the poor.

The nature of the regulatory agencies and the attitudes of people who belong to them and deal with them will gradually change. They will become more responsive to the demands and points of view of pressure groups, unions and others who are capable of affecting economic and political developments. This will at first be a matter of prudence. If the economic and financial affairs of the world are to run smoothly, then it is necessary to make concessions to the people who can cause disruption. But as the members of these regulatory and judicial bodies, and the groups that deal with them, become more used to co-operating and come to appreciate the point of view of the others, they will develop the habit of treating each other in a respectful way and will try to make decisions which they perceive as fair to all parties. Their policies, in other words, will no longer be determined by the relative strength of the parties but will be morally motivated. Agents will now adhere to the processes and guidelines which they have established as a matter of principle, regardless of changes in the distribution of power.

The processes and guidelines these agents adopt will be designed to ensure that each group is able to pursue its own interests and protect what it regards as good within a framework of co-operation which encourages the settlement of conflicts in a mutually satisfactory way. Having achieved relationships which they acknowledge to be fair, the agents will develop an appreciation of these relationships and the rules and processes which underwrite them. They will come to regard these rules and procedures as principles of justice to which they owe allegiance. Once this occurs, they will be inclined to apply them more widely, even to their relations with agents who do not have sufficient power to affect the decision-making process. It will become axiomatic that the principles of justice are universal and apply equally everywhere.

As people who belong to these international bodies, or deal with them, develop a universal conception of justice, they will become less and less inclined to pursue the narrower interests of their particular states. Indeed states, including the wealthier ones, will have less and less ability to insist that the economic and political affairs of the world go in the way that they desire. Instead of controlling international bodies, they will become controlled by them, having little choice but to do what they are directed to do. For in an integrated world economy it will not be so difficult to 'punish' recalcitrant parties, and international agents will be less tolerant of unco-operative behaviour. Moreover, citizens of states, as they become involved in international associations and partnerships, and become dependent on them, will be less inclined to support 'selfish' nationalistic behaviour, more inclined to accept the conception of justice associated with good international relationships.

As international judicial and regulatory agencies become more powerful and their influence more widespread, people of the world will become increasingly dissatisfied with their organisational form. They will want to have some say in how these bodies are run, and will want a more formal and less ad hoc way of having their interests represented and ensuring that their rights are protected. Moreover, it will become clear by this time that international legal and regulatory bodies have become more than mere agencies of regulation and conciliation. They are in effect making law, deciding the course of world affairs. There will be universal agreement that a more regular constitutional way of making and enforcing international law is necessary.

What form this constitution will take, what legislative body it will bring into existence, how it will manage a separation of powers, is impossible to predict.[3] But one thing seems clear: people will no longer be satisfied with an arrangement in which individuals are represented by appointed officials of their state (as is the case with the United Nations). For one thing, individuals will no longer regard their interests as being adequately represented by state governments. Their requirements and interests will be bound up with the health of the international community and with the activities of other groups in it. They will have developed associations and sympathies with people in other countries. Moreover, it will be clear that an international organisation based upon states is no longer capable of governing a world in which many of the most influential agents are not states. It therefore seems likely that the embryonic world government will allow individuals themselves to elect representatives. Whatever form the government will take, there will be some kind of constitutional guarantee of the right of individuals to pursue their objectives and form associations of their choice within the framework of their co-operative relationships.

Once a world government is formed, however elementary may be its powers and responsibilities, we can expect in the short or long term considerable social changes in world society. When the constitution comes into force, the government will be expected to enforce its provisions, including its guarantees of individual rights. Agencies for that purpose will come into existence. At the same time pre-existing conceptions of the rights of national states will have to be revised. For one thing, it will no longer be regarded as acceptable or necessary for states to have armed forces and stockpiles of weapons. These will gradually be eliminated; and recalcitrant state governments will be forced by economic sanctions and pressures from their own citizens into complying. The people of the world will generally be in favour of this development, not only because it makes the world safer, but because they perceive weapons as now being unnecessary for their security. We can expect that other rights now held by sovereign states will also gradually disappear. For example, immigration restrictions will become increasingly irrelevant and inconvenient, and will probably be eliminated.

The ultimate authority for making laws and enforcing them will now be held by the world government, and it will tend to gain increasing powers in order to carry out this responsibility. States will continue to exist and to make laws for the people in their territory, but more and more they will become like provinces in a federation, like states, territories or provinces in the USA, Australia or Canada. Their powers will be limited by the ultimate authority of the world government. Though some people will grumble about loss of 'states' rights' (as they do in existing federations), on the whole they will regard this development as inevitable and desirable. It will provide them with new opportunities, the freedom to move and do business, associate as they please, the security of orderly economic and political arrangements. Moreover, as individuals become more aware of their dependence on others, accustomed to participating in the bodies and structures of the world state, they will come to regard themselves as first and foremost world citizens. They will develop an allegiance to the institutions and cosmopolitan principles which underwrite and make possible their relationships and guarantee their rights. As a result they will be prepared to insist that the rights of individuals and citizens be universally honoured, and predisposed to believe that this means that everyone should have the resources necessary to exercise these rights.

This does not mean that everyone in world society will be in agreement about what justice requires. As in national societies there will be debates between those who favour a more egalitarian idea and those who fear that state regulation leads to an unacceptable loss of individual and group liberty. Even those who accept the same idea of justice will disagree about what these principles mean and how they should be applied to particular cases. I have argued that for a state to count as just in cosmopolitan terms it is not necessary that everyone accept a particular conception of justice. What is necessary is that there be a recognition of the right of individuals and groups to pursue their own diverse ends and to have their interest and needs taken into account by political and judicial institutions in a way that they generally regard as fair. In my account of the coming into existence of a world state I have attempted to show how world society could create an environment in which such institutions and understandings might come into being on an international scale and be accepted by all.

There is another important aspect to this story: it makes possible and plausible the demand that resources and opportunities be distributed more equally among the individuals of the world. It shows how an international environment can be created in which the demands of a theory of distributive justice – whether egalitarian or Rawlsian – make sense and are widely, if not universally, accepted. In the world state institutions and agencies for redistributing goods among individuals will exist. The world government will undoubtedly have the power to tax, the power to direct the use of resources and the ability to enforce the laws and directives it makes. Even more important, the world society imagined is one in which individuals are more likely to accept the idea that they have responsibilities to all other individuals: they regard themselves as world citizens; they have developed a strong allegiance to the principles and procedures of their liberal, pluralist world society and they are thus inclined to take seriously the idea that everyone should not only have the right to pursue their own good (providing this does not harm others), but also that they have an entitlement to a share of the total social resources. Taking the story further, we can perhaps suppose that most people will come to regard it as a requirement of justice that the world government take responsibility for ensuring that all people in the world have at least the basic goods they need in order to lead a decent life.

This story is, to be sure, only one of many possible accounts of how a world political society might come into being. It may be more plausible to suppose that economic and political developments lead first to the creation of regional governments (as imagined in the last chapter), and that later, as these governments recognise the need to manage some of their affairs in common, world regulatory and eventually governmental bodies will arise. At first these may be run by representatives of the regional states, but as the affairs of people in the different states become more integrated (given that no restrictions prevent this from happening), there will be a demand by other agents, including individuals themselves, to have a more direct say in how the world is governed. The point of my story is not to try to predict how the future will go (such attempts invariably fail), but to try to show that it is not implausible to suppose that beginning from where we are now, a world state could gradually come into being in a more or less peaceful and just manner, and that in the course of this development, the political objectives, attitudes and social relations of individuals would change enough for them to regard the creation of this state as desirable and come to accept a conception of world justice which is similar to conceptions now only appropriate within national states. What we need to consider more carefully in order to assess this idea of international justice is whether the story really is plausible and whether the outcome is desirable – what practical and moral problems are likely to arise.

Critics are likely to be sceptical about whether my story adequately deals with common objections to the idea of world government. Is it really plausible to suppose that any body, however well supplied with information and modern methods of communication, could effectively govern six billion (and no doubt more) people? We can suppose that the world state is decentralised; that local bodies do most of the governing, but nevertheless the world government is intended to be able to regulate world economic affairs, and dispense justice to all. Whether it really could do this without causing an unacceptable amount of injustice through bureaucratic bungling, red tape or the corruption and irresponsibility of petty officials is questionable. One of the problems is that the system of checks and balances which is supposed to keep a government and its institutions from systematically perpetrating injustices may be impossible to set up and maintain if a political society becomes too large or complex. If the operations of a government and its institutions are conducted on a large scale over a huge area and affect people in many different ways, then it will be virtually impossible for citizens to exercise proper vigilance over the policies and activities of their elected officials and difficult for elected officials, to monitor the behaviour of bureaucrats and other appointed government servants. Perhaps in time people in the world state will find ways of surmounting the problems caused by the scope and complexity of world government. But from our perspective the viability, and therefore the desirability, of such a system must remain in doubt.

Moreover, it is not clear what relation individual citizens could have to such a large and extensive government. A basic idea of cosmopolitan political philosophy is that government is supposed to be a means for protecting individuals and their rights, allowing each to pursue his or her own good as far as this is compatible with the pursuits of others. Constitutional democracy has generally been advocated by cosmopolitans because they think it is the sort of government that best ensures that individuals through political processes will be able to protect their interests and ensure that their needs and desires count in the decision-making process. In a world government, it could be argued, the form will exist without the substance. For the vote of an individual, the participation of an individual, will mean virtually nothing, and his or her particular interests and views will be lost in an ocean of human needs and concerns. Individuals will thus have no sense that they are helping to determine their society's political objectives or that their interests count. The result is likely to be a widespread cynicism, an alienated, apathetic or hostile view of political processes. The point is not simply that such alienation places in doubt the future of a world government. It is also a symptom of a basic moral shortcoming: world government, whether democratic or not, is not what cosmopolitans can accept as a proper means for serving the interests of individuals.

This criticism may over-state the problem. Even in national states the votes and voices of individuals count for very little. People have an effect on political processes mostly by being members of pressure groups or political parties. If a national government is an adequate means for protecting individual entitlements and enabling them to participate in determining common objectives (which, it is true, some people doubt), then why could not a world government also be adequate in the same way? Individuals would join groups and parties and these would monitor and influence the behaviour of public officials. No individual or group is likely to understand or appreciate everything that happens in the political system, but this is probably not necessary for good government or for the effective representation of individual interests.

Whether this is so or not, the question of what relation individuals would have to a world state raises a further difficulty for any attempt to extend conceptions of national justice to the world as a whole. I argued that economic interdependence is not enough by itself to underwrite requirements of justice in the international world. People must not only have relations of mutual dependence, they must be aware of them, value them and value the institutions which make them possible. Furthermore, if international justice is going to be something more than a matter of tit for tat – keeping agreements and honouring promises – if it is going to include taking responsibility for the welfare of poor and vulnerable people who are never likely to be in a position to return favours, then world citizens are going to have to develop attitudes which encourage them to regard the well-being of everyone as their collective responsibility.

My account of the future therefore depends essentially on the development of social relations which encourage a change of political and social consciousness. In the story this occurs in two stages. Individuals and groups associated with regulatory agencies first progress from a situation in which their policies, agreements, activities are determined by what Rawls describes as a 'modus vivendi' to a situation in which agents are morally motivated. Those who at first are compelled by prudence to take into account the needs of others eventually come to act out of a desire to be just. This change in motivation, I have supposed, is brought about through co-operation on projects and enterprises which all parties value and want to continue. The second stage of the development requires that individuals broaden their conception of what their community is. They become world citizens; they come to value the institutions and principles which make their association possible and develop an allegiance to them and to the political system in which they operate. The story is a deliberate attempt to make use of Rawls' account in 'The idea of an overlapping consensus' (1987) of how people come to develop and adhere to principles of justice in the framework of a liberal pluralist society (which in turn owes much to Kant). The critical question is whether this account is intelligible and plausible, especially when it is applied to world society as a whole.

The weaknesses and uncertainties in Rawls' story show up clearly in this adaptation. There are good grounds for doubting whether even the first stage of the development is likely. There is probably no project on which everyone in the world would be willing to co-operate or a set of institutions which everyone will accept. There are, for example, people in the world who clearly do not value liberal pluralist institutions and would not willingly sacrifice their cultural values in order to support them, even for the sake of obtaining economic benefits or peace. There are people who believe that their values and interests are non-negotiable. There are people who value the sovereignty of their state more than they value whatever economic advantages or increases in individual freedom would come from a larger political association. Such people are likely to regard steps towards a world state as a form of western imperialism or as a threat to their values and will resist if they can. So co-operation in the international world, whether on economic or political matters, may always be, to some extent, forced co-operation – to the extent that it exists at all – and thus it will not give rise to the moral motivations which are supposed to underwrite a more demanding conception of international justice.

This objection might be met by supposing that the development of a world political society takes place over a long period of time. A lot can happen in politics in 100, 200 years, and it is possible that groups of people who are now strongly opposed to the very idea of a world state will gradually come to accept it. Once again we can look to the development of the national state as an example of a political organisation which over time has managed to bring together in co-operative relations people who before were indifferent or even hostile towards each other.

However, critics of the world state, even if they are willing to allow that universal co-operation could underwrite a morality of fair play among agents who are powerful enough to harm or benefit each other, will point out that such co-operation does not necessarily incline agents to think that justice requires a distribution of resources in favour of the needy and vulnerable. Theories of international justice, as we have seen, have typically required nothing more than mutual respect between states. Moreover, these critics might argue, the social prerequisites which make advocacy of a theory of distributive justice plausible in the context of national societies will never exist in the world as a whole. The second stage of the development of moral consciousness is unlikely or impossible.

In order to be the sort of people who regard our abilities and resources as 'common-wealth', as something that ought to be shared, argues Michael Sandel in *Liberalism and the Limits of Justice*, we have to have an attachment to our community which constitutes our identity as persons. Our ends as individuals must be, at least partially, defined in terms of common ends.

> And what marks such a community is not merely a spirit of benevolence, or the prevalence of communitarian values, or even certain 'shared final ends' alone, but a common vocabulary of discourse and a background of implicit practices and understandings within which the opacity of the participants is reduced if never finally dissolved.

> (1982: 166)

Sandel's objection to Rawls' account of justice in *A Theory of Justice* is that his difference principle presupposes the existence of this kind of community, but that this presupposition is incompatible with Rawls' attempt to justify his principles by appealing to what rational self-interested individuals would choose behind the veil of ignorance. For this method of justification presupposes that what individuals desire and value – what makes them the kind of individuals they are – can be determined independently of their particular social relations. Sandel's critique can be used to explain why philosophers and others typically prescribe different principles of justice for national and international society. People in a national society are assumed to have an identity with each other, a common bond, which people in international society lack.

If Sandel's criticism is correct, then it means that it is wrong to think that the acceptance of the requirements of distributive justice is a likely result of relationships of co-operation between basically self-interested individuals or groups. For if individuals and groups are primarily concerned with the pursuit of their own projects, then they are not likely to favour a policy which threatens their property, pursuits or idea of the good for the sake of a universal redistribution of resources. They will regard such a prescription as an unjust limitation on their liberty. To underwrite a Rawlsian or egalitarian conception of distributive justice they need, it seems, a collective identity, a common good, which binds them together and makes them willing to take responsibility for each other. But this means that Rawls' account in 'The idea of an overlapping consensus' of the social prerequisites of a just society is still incomplete. Individuals have to develop more than an allegiance to the principles which enable co-operation between independent self-interested individuals and groups. They need the kind of social bonds which incline them to accept a duty to promote the welfare of their community and everyone in it.

In the corresponding story about the creation of a world society, I have supposed that individuals and groups come to think of themselves as primarily world citizens, that self-interest and their loyalty to other communities is superseded (at least, partially) by an attachment to the all-inclusive world community, and as a result agents become willing to regard their resources and energies as belonging to one big world 'common-wealth'. But this development may be implausible or impossible. 'If we did not provide for one another, if we recognised no distinction between members and strangers, we would have no reason to form and maintain a political community', says Walzer in *Spheres of*

Justice, and he goes on to say that membership is a special relation which implies that we do not have it with everyone (1983: 64). Walzer is not necessarily denying the possibility of universal political institutions, but he is suggesting that a real community, as a group of people who are willing to care for each other's needs, is a limited community. The reason, perhaps, is that we need to have something in common besides political institutions in order to make our relationship special and worth preserving: a common culture, a heritage, shared ideals. The problem, then, is that it is implausible to suppose that everyone in the world could ever have anything like this in common. Or perhaps Walzer is suggesting that social bonds depend upon contrast or comparison to outsiders; a collective has to see itself as distinct from others before people can value membership in it. A 'we' requires a 'they'. If this is true, then the very conception of what he calls a 'common life' rules out the possibility that it be universally shared. Whatever Walzer means, he is clearly implying that justice in the international world can never amount to the same thing or impose the same requirements as justice within limited communities.

Speculations about what kind of communities people are capable of forming depend upon psychological premises which may turn out to be false. Walzer may be wrong about the limits of community. However, Sandel's critique of Rawls and Walzer's appeal to the value of the national 'common life' amount to more than an empirical objection to the idea of a world political society and more than a view about how individuals form their identity. They are implying that communities of some kinds are morally important, and that it is morally justifiable, even obligatory, to defend and preserve them. This means that ideas of world order which entail the destruction of these communities or threaten their integrity are objectionable, not only on the grounds that they go against the grain of human desires, but because they are a recipe for injustice.

What this communitarian objection to the idea of the world state amounts to can be better understood by contrasting it with the kind of criticisms that come from a cosmopolitan point of view. Cosmopolitans, as we have seen, will reject the proposal for a world state if it seems to them that there are more costs than benefits as far as the promotion of individual rights or the maximisation of individual welfare is concerned. They will reject the destruction or undermining of limited political communities if doing so is likely to lead to loss of liberty, a narrowing of opportunities, a general decrease in happiness or in the satisfaction of preferences. So like Kant they may prefer a system of states to a world political society on the grounds that the existence of independent political societies more reliably and effectively protects the rights and well-being of individuals. More generally, what system they advocate, whether it contains regional states or smaller national states, which states they think have a right to exist and which do not, will depend upon what arrangements they think are best for individuals. It is the entitlements of individuals as such which are the measure of all things political.

A communitarian, on the other hand, insists that the relation of individuals to their community is (or could be) of great moral value. First of all, because the relations of that community define who an individual is, his or her objectives and purposes, and therefore what counts as self-realisation. The destruction of such a community is therefore a destruction of what is essential to self-integrity, something an individual may well regard as worse than death. The relations between people in the community are, secondly, ethical relations, relations which determine in a central way moral motivations and conceptions of duty. To destroy a community is thus to destroy the life that individuals believe they are morally obligated to live. The destruction of a community is not simply a bad or unfortunate thing as far as the satisfaction of individual preferences is concerned. It constitutes a serious injustice, a grave violation of the moral order. Individuals are thus justified in defending their communities both from external attack and from attempts to create a new world order. Indeed, given the importance of community to their ethical lives and their resulting duties to other members, they are obligated to do so. They may be justified in believing that they are obligated to preserve their community even if it could be demonstrated that the world would be a better place in cosmopolitan terms – human rights would be more successfully promoted, individual well-being maximised, the autonomy of moral agents more respected – in the framework of a new world order.

There are good reasons for taking the communitarian point of view seriously. The first is simply that individuals often do have strong loyalties and attachments to communities which they regard as of great moral importance. The arguments against intervention in the last chapter presuppose what seems to be the case – that people are often prepared to defend the autonomy of their community with their lives if necessary and believe that this defence is justified and indeed obligatory. Communitarianism in one form or another is a force to be reckoned with. But there is another reason more relevant to an inquiry into the nature of justice for regarding communitarianism as important. What makes communitarian positions attractive is not only that they point out the importance of community to many human lives, but that they give a plausible reason for regarding the preservation of community as important. If it is indeed true, as communitarians say or imply, that in a community individuals can find a more satisfactory meaning and value for their lives than through a more detached, self-centred existence, if it is true that the well-being of individuals, including that of the poor and vulnerable, is most likely to be promoted in communities which encourage the development of a common identity and a sense of solidarity, then there are good reasons for forming communities and wanting them to survive. But the most important achievement of community, according to communitarians, is that it reconciles individual freedom with a social existence. Individuals who identify with their community, who regard its aims as their aims, can freely pursue their objectives and at the same time live the ethical life of their society. Morality is not in opposition to individual desires (as Kant sometimes supposes); it has become embedded in them.

The opposition between cosmopolitanism and communitarianism is not so total as it has sometimes been presented. Even Kant, the philosopher who most sharply opposes morality to inclination, shows in his philosophical history how the two can be reconciled, and Rawls in 'Overlapping consensus' presents a similar account of how being moral can become a primary motivation for individual action. On the other side, communitarians do not necessarily reject all appeals to individual entitlements; nor do they suppose that individuals have no interests and aims of their own. Nor do they generally suppose that communities have a right to exist whatever their nature. To claim that community is or ought to be centrally important to human life doesn't mean that it is the only thing of moral importance. Nevertheless, the communitarian position differs from cosmopolitanism in a way that is bound to have implications for a discussion of the nature of a just world order.

What exactly these implications are depends on what communities communitarians wish to defend, on what communities they think individuals ought to commit themselves to. Is it the state that we should take as our primary community, as Walzer's remarks suggest, or is it the nation (which is not necessarily the same thing, as nationalist theory and practice demonstrate)? Or should we be looking for a new kind of community – one which is more homogeneous and less 'alienating'? The answer we give will not only have ramifications for our political objectives but also for political and social relations in the world as a whole – and, inevitably, for a conception of world justice. How we assess the views of those who have a communitarian point of view will thus depend both on how well their particular conceptions of community fulfil the purposes that community is supposed to serve (and whether these purposes can or should be achieved), and on what kind of international relations they make possible and what problems they pose for world order. Running through the modern political philosophy tradition there is what can be called a communitarian stream. It includes Hegel's theory of the state, Rousseau's conception of a democratic society, theories of nationalism. The ideas about community in this literature imply or promote particular views of international relations, and in so doing provide a starting point for a critical examination of the communitarian approach to international justice.

Part II

From a communitarian point of view

Chapter 6

The state as a community

In his *Philosophy of Right* Hegel rejects Kant's idea of a history ending in perpetual peace. Bringing about perpetual peace is not for him a moral requirement. War, he insists, is not a failure of civilisation, but a positive contribution to social life:

> The ethical health of peoples is preserved in their indifference to the stabilisation of finite institutions; just as the blowing of the winds preserves the sea from the foulness which would be the result of a prolonged calm, so also corruption in nations would be the product of prolonged, let alone, 'perpetual peace'.
>
> (1821: Par. 324)

Moreover, war accompanies and enhances a moral consciousness which Hegel regards as the highest expression of the ethical spirit – a moral consciousness made possible by the existence of sovereign states.

Hegel's disagreement with Kant is not primarily about the moral costs and benefits of war. Hegel, like Hobbesian realists, insists that there is no moral law superior to the determination of states. The sovereign state has the entitlement to choose what law to obey and to choose whether to obey it: 'The relation between states is a relation between autonomous entities which make mutual stipulations but which at the same time are superior to these stipulations' (Hegel 1821: Addition to Par. 330). But examined more closely, the resemblance of Hegel's view to common versions of realism is superficial. Hegel is not denying that states are subject to a moral law because he thinks that they are in the grip of necessity. On the contrary. States are affected and sometimes destroyed by 'contingencies', but as autonomous agents they have a scope for choice and responsibility. Furthermore, he allows that the relations between states can be ethical: what states do, even in war, is the result of the respect that each has for the others – a respect that is not the result of fear but of states being the kind of agents they are and having a particular relation to each other. This respect is for Hegel the basis of all international relations. Its existence ensures that states will usually be prepared to abide by their mutual stipulations, but even when they go to war, their behaviour will be governed by restraint: 'war itself is characterised as something that ought to pass away' (1821: Par. 338). There is thus such a thing as international law in Hegel's scheme, but it does not arise from cosmopolitan moral requirements.

When Hegel says that states are superior to their stipulations, he means that there are no 'external' requirements to which states are subject – whether a sovereign or principles of justice. This is why Hegel's criticism of Kant does not amount to a consequentialist claim that war does more good for a society than harm. It stems from a radical rejection of the idea of universal moral law. Hegel is also in effect criticising every other cosmopolitan conception of international relations, for all of these depend upon the universal validity of certain ideals, standards, processes or principles by which the behaviour of states or individuals is supposed to be governed. Nor does Hegel allow that individuals can legitimately appeal against the authority of their state to some conception of human rights, justice, universal welfare. They have no basis from which to reject their state's sovereign authority or advocate a different kind of international order. For Hegel insists that the relationship between citizens and their state is not a contractual one – not one justified in terms of the protection of rights or promotion of individual well-being.

> The state does not exist for the citizens; on the contrary, one could say that the state is the end and they are its means. But the means–end relation is not fitting here. For the state is not the abstract confronting the citizens; they are parts of it, like the members of an organic body, where no member of it is end and none is means.
>
> (1840: 52)

Hegel's emphasis on the moral primacy of the community and his insistence that the objectives, interests, moral being of individuals – what they essentially are – are inextricably bound up with being members of a community makes it appropriate to label him as a communitarian. But he also has a definite idea about what is the highest form of human community, a conception that has, as we have seen, clear implications for international relations. These two aspects of his view seem difficult to reconcile: if the moral life of individuals is completely bound up with their participation in a community, then what can we possibly appeal to in order to argue that one kind of community is better than another?

To understand Hegel's position it is important to identify at what point exactly he parts company with cosmopolitanism and why. For in many respects his starting point is the same. It is, in fact, not inappropriate to regard him as belonging to the same tradition. He begins, like Hobbes, with a recognition that there is no intrinsic reason why one group of individuals should subordinate themselves to the wills of others, and that therefore each is free to decide for himself his personal and moral objectives. That all individuals are free and that freedom is a value for all individuals is a premise of his political philosophy.[1] Hegel is thus concerned with the same problems that have exercised generations of political philosophers: what form of political organisation is most appropriate for free individuals? What justifies the authority of the state and the demands that it makes on individuals (including the demand that they sometimes risk their lives for its sake)?

However, his treatment of this premise is significantly different from that of Hobbes, Kant and most others. The freedom which it claims all individuals possess is merely freedom in the abstract. It is not a meaningless abstraction because it can be used to rule out as morally unacceptable some forms of social organisation: e.g. slave societies. But from freedom as an abstract property of individuals, Hegel believes, nothing much more follows about what kind of social and political organisation we should prefer. From the same premise different and contrary conclusions are possible, as the history of modern political thought has demonstrated. To be meaningful, to have real content, 'freedom' must be interpreted in the context of concrete social relations. Hegel's account of historical evolution is thus not an account of how a conception of rights or a moral ideal is gradually realised in social institutions but an account of the evolution of the conception of what it means to be a free being. Human individuals, through their social relations, through conflict, errors, self-reflection, gradually develop a more satisfactory conception of what freedom is and thus of who they are as free individuals.

Hegel's treatment of freedom is the consequence of a more general criticism of what he calls 'morality' (by which he means, primarily, Kantian morality). Universal moral imperatives, he complains, are too abstract to give us a guide to ethical practice. The rules, which are supposed to be objective and universal, have to rely for their interpretation on the subjective vagaries of an individual's conscience – on intuitions – and given that individuals are equally free to determine their own moral objectives, there is no basis on which we can prefer one individual's intuitions to another. Hegel makes basically the same objection to the idea of a Kantian world federation founded upon a moral law. This moral law always requires interpretation; and not only is there the problem that different states might interpret it differently (and thus come into conflict), but that any interpretation, even if it happens to be universally accepted, is arbitrary.

Hegel's objection to 'morality' is often interpreted as a common criticism of Kant's categorical imperative: that Kant's injunction to 'Act as if what you do were to become the universal law for mankind' does not give us an adequate idea of what we should do. So interpreted, the effect of this criticism is limited. There may be difficulties within a Kantian framework in determining what duties we have, but on the other hand, in some cases the requirements of moral–practical reason are clear: we have, for example, a duty to seek peace. Moreover, a non-Kantian cosmopolitan will not be troubled by difficulties intrinsic to Kant's approach. Hegel's criticism of morality should be understood, not as an objection to some part of Kant's moral philosophy, but as a general critique of the cosmopolitan starting point. He is saying that cosmopolitan appeals to human rights or the requirements of autonomous agents or the general welfare of individuals are too abstract to be an adequate basis for a political philosophy. First of all, philosophers have never been able to agree on which ideal or principle is valid; and even those who manage to reach a consensus on principles can still fail to agree on how they should be applied. Furthermore, attempts to settle these disagreements by appeals to human nature, metaphysical principles, religious doctrine are equally unsuccessful, for these justifications are as dubious, vague or contentious as the principles they are supposed to justify. Therefore there is no higher court of appeal than the moral intuitions of individuals. But intuitions not only conflict; they depend upon accidents of individual psychology or environment, and are thus an unsatisfactory basis for morality.

However, this critique of 'morality' does not in itself distinguish Hegel's communitarian approach from some approaches which might be regarded as cosmopolitan. For as we have seen, some cosmopolitans, like Rawls, are prepared to concede that there is no metaphysical basis for ideas of justice, that a theory of justice, and perhaps other moral ideas, arise out of political life; in particular that ideas about individual entitlements and distributive justice are the result of developments in democratic, pluralist societies.[2] So the question remains: why is it that

Hegel ends up denying common cosmopolitan ideas about how political institutions and social relations should be justified? The answer, it seems, must be found in Hegel's own story of how human individuals find a 'rational life of self-conscious freedom'.

The evolution which Hegel's philosophy is concerned with is at a basic level the unfolding of a concept – in the case of political philosophy, the concept of freedom. What is contained in a concept belongs to it necessarily and inheres in it timelessly. Thus his account of human development is not a story about how things might happen. The historical and social are in reality a phenomenal manifestation of logical necessity. Hegel is a paradigm case of a transcendental philosopher, and reconciling freedom with necessity, logic with phenomenology, is a chronic difficulty in Hegel's philosophy – the heir to Kant's problem of reconciling the determinations of nature with the freedom of moral agents. In my account of Hegel's 'universal history' I will not attempt to discuss this issue, but will begin as he does in the *Philosophy of Right* with human agents who are free beings, but who must yet discover what it means to be free and what use should be made of their freedom. I will assume that his defence of political authority, his account of community and international relations, must stand or fall according to what he says about the historical and conceptual progress of these individuals.

The most primitive understanding of what freedom is takes the form of an immediate awareness by individuals that they have wants and can make choices. Expressing their freedom means overcoming the restrictions which prevent them from getting what they want. The state of nature, as conceived by philosophers like Hobbes, best represents, Hegel thinks, the relation of individuals who live according to this conception of freedom. Unlike Hobbes he does not believe that this state of affairs is incompatible with the exercise of justice. A conception of rights, above all property rights, arises out of the need of people in the state of nature to put limits on each other's activities for the sake of individual safety and freedom. And he believes that these prohibitions will develop as the result of the determination of a common will into legal and regulatory institutions and governmental powers.

What is unsatisfactory about the state of nature in Hegel's opinion is not that it degenerates into a state of war of all against all. What is wrong is that the form of freedom it promotes is limited and merely 'capricious'. The freedom independent individuals can enjoy is bounded and frustrated by the contrary desires and actions of others. Moreover, the objectives that people pursue are simply regarded as given. There seems no good reason why a person should have one set of wants rather than another, and thus there is no clear distinction between desire and drive, freedom and compulsion: if people are impelled by their wants, if they are acted on by them as if by an external force, then what seemed to be freedom turns out to be the opposite.

However, once rights are protected and institutions promoting justice come into existence, individuals no longer regard each other merely as a hindrance or a help in getting what they want. They come to respect each other's rights as individuals and recognise each other as objects of moral concern. When moral obligation becomes a motivation for action, individual caprice gives way to action according to universal rules, and the force of egoistic desire is vanquished by the will's obedience to the moral law. Human freedom has reached a higher stage of development.

So far Hegel's account of the evolution of human consciousness and society is very much like Kant's. Where he parts company, as we have seen, is in his view of morality. He does not think that the moral life, as cosmopolitans have understood it, represents the highest form of human development. For the rules which are supposed to be objective and rational turn out to rely on subjective interpretation. Moreover, morality, so long as it imposes duties on us, will be perceived as a restriction of our freedom rather than an enhancement of it; it is an inner legislator which opposes itself to our wants and inclinations. Hegel concludes that individuals can only find a concrete basis for moral obligation and overcome the opposition between duty and inclination in what he calls the 'ethical life': that is, in fulfilling the duties and performing the roles that they acquire as members of a particular community. Individuals who regard themselves as at one with their community do not regard their duty as an obligation imposed on them from without but as an expression of themselves. 'The subject is thus linked to the ethical order by a relation which is more like an identity than even the relation of faith or trust' (1821: Par. 147). Freedom can be truly realised in such an ethical life. The duties which Hegel believes individuals have to their community are thus the result of an understanding of what freedom in its real sense requires. Nevertheless, he is not supposing that every attachment is equally valuable. Freedom is realised in some communities in a higher form than in others.

The most basic form of ethical life is in the family. The relation members of a family have to each other, Hegel thinks, is a natural one and their duties to each other flow out of an almost instinctive feeling of mutual dependence and love. But the very naturalness of family relations, the fact that they are based on sentiment, makes them less than satisfactory as an expression of freedom. So long as individuals are immersed in family life, they are not developing themselves as self-reflecting agents capable of recognising their own freedom and defining and satisfying desires of their own. (Hegel would presumably say the same thing about traditional tribal societies and clans.) Furthermore, in a society which consists of a plurality of families, the ethical life of the family will no longer suffice. Practices and rules must exist to govern the behaviour of representatives of families towards each other. Hence the development of government and civil society.

Civil society, as we have seen, does not lack law and order; it has police, courts of justice. It is what Hegel sometimes calls an 'external state'. But inherent in civil society, as an association of self-interested, rational individuals, are the problems relating to individualistic expressions of freedom. The individual is driven by his wants and is at the same time vulnerable to the contingencies of fortune. 'Civil society affords a spectacle of extravagance and want as well as of the physical and ethical degeneration common to them both' (1821: Par. 185). What Hegel is complaining about is not simply the hardship created for some individuals by a system in which everyone pursues their own interests. He regards the kind of existence which divides individuals from each other and drives them to pursue conflicting aims as being basically limited and unfree.

Individuals can overcome these problems to some extent, Hegel thinks, by becoming members of 'corporations' – organisations united along the lines of crafts or occupations. As he conceives them, corporations will not only provide protection for their members, but will also give otherwise isolated individuals a community life. They are a kind of family. But the activities of the corporations are confined to the pursuit of sectional interest. Divisions and clashes of interest are endemic to civil society, and so long as they are not superseded by a higher form of social organisation, the ethical degradation will not be overcome.

The state for Hegel is not a government but an organism which incorporates the family, civil society and the corporations, as well as having at its head special institutions of state which bind these parts together. Considered by themselves, the family and civil society are an inadequate environment for achieving freedom. But within the state they not only work together harmoniously, but they prepare the individual for being a citizen of the state. Even the divisiveness of civil society plays a role in this process: being part of this society and having the civil rights associated with it makes individuals aware of their own capabilities and needs, and this means that when they find the true end of their existence in their relationship to the state, they will have achieved 'a life of self-conscious freedom'. Their attachment to this community will be rational and not sentimental.

The state comes into being as a unified organism and finds its highest manifestation in its constitution and in institutions capable of defining and pursuing 'universal' interests – i.e. the interests of the state as a whole. The will of the state is concentrated in the individual will of the monarch. He is advised by civil servants whose purpose is to serve the universal interest. Monarch, civil servants and a body representing civil society – the Estates – form together the legislature which determines how the constitution of the state, its laws and objectives, are developed. But the purpose of the Estates is not to debate issues but to integrate the organisations of civil society into the state and thus bring about an identity between individual interests and the interests of the state – to bring into existence what Hegel calls 'the moment of subjective formal freedom' (1821: Par. 301).

Hegel's state is in Kant's sense a republican state. But Hegel's idea of a constitutional state reflects his concern for ensuring unity of purpose and the emergence of the universal interest. He is opposed to any political institutions which tend to encourage or reflect divisions in society, and clearly prefers for that reason constitutional monarchy to constitutional democracy. He regards as detrimental a situation in which the conflicts and capricious opinions of civil society manifest themselves in the higher institutions of state. Moreover a state which does not achieve unity around universal interests cannot be a state in which individuals realise their freedom. Decisions which are made as the result of conflict, compromise or the will of the majority are likely to be regarded by individuals as external impositions, and thus even in the best of democracies people will regard their institutions and laws as something that puts limits on their freedom.

The form taken by relationships between states is both conditioned by the nature of the state as an agent and in turn makes the existence of the state as an agent possible. What is characteristic about the behaviour of states in international affairs, according to Hegel, is that they act rationally and with restraint. This means that they must, at least, be capable of acting as agents, and indeed Hegel treats states as if they were a kind of individual. Hegel's requirement that divisions and differences of civil society be overcome within the institutions of state ensures, for one thing, that the state is capable of acting as an agent, as a kind of super-individual. As an organism, it has an intelligence provided by the civil service, a will concentrated in the monarch, and a body of citizens organised to perform various functions in obedience to this will.

However, Hegel's view of international relations, as we have seen, depends upon states being ethical as well rational – respecting each other's sovereignty. One of the bases for this respect is contained in Hegel's account of the state as the community in which freedom is most satisfactorily realised. A respect for the equal freedom of individuals means respecting the political communities in which individuals are able to live a good ethical life. However, this justification of the state does not explain why we should respect the states that now happen to exist. Why shouldn't we look forward to the establishment of a world state in which all individuals can live a common ethical life? Why are war and international conflict so important in Hegel's world? These questions are answered, I think, by reference to the process by means of which states realise themselves as 'individuals'.

There is a similarity between Hegel's insistence that states must respect each other as equals and his view in the *Phenomenology of Mind* (1807) that individuals achieve an adequate self-conception by recognising each other as equals. The differences between the dialectic of individual self-consciousness and what Hegel says about the relations of states are, however, equally important and worth exploring. In the *Phenomenology of Mind*, individuals, engaged in a struggle to realise and express their existence as free beings, at first try to overcome the limitations which other individuals impose on them through an attempt to destroy each other. By risking death they obtain a higher conception of self – one that is not tied to the satisfaction of immediate desires. But a confrontation of this sort turns out to be an unsatisfactory means of self-realisation – certainly for the individual who is killed, but also for the victor who loses his chance to be recognised by another. Enslaving the other rather than killing him may seem for a time like a satisfactory solution but the slave can only give to his master a debased form of recognition. In the end, as we have seen, Hegel believes that individuals can become free in the most complete way by being integrated as equals into a social whole where their relations to each other are no longer external ones.

The reason why the dialectic of consciousness does not have as its ultimate objective a world state or federation rather than a system of externally related autonomous states, and perpetual peace rather than limited war, is because what makes the ethical life possible, in Hegel's opinion, is precisely this external relation between states. 'Individuality', he says, 'is awareness of one's existence as a unit in sharp distinction from others' (1821: Par. 322). Human individuals become aware of their distinctiveness by there being others resistant to their will. The existence of the state as an agent depends upon citizens taking as their primary objective the maintenance of the state and at the same time recognising that they have this objective in common. But for them to have this objective, Hegel is arguing, there must be other sovereign states to which they can oppose themselves, and if the contrast and opposition between states is to remain sufficiently lively, then war has to be a permanent possibility. It plays the same role in the spiritual life of the state as does fear of death in the dialectic of consciousness. It takes the mind of individuals away from mundane matters, heightens their identification with their state and unites them behind their leaders.

The main problem that Hegel sees with proposals for a world state or a world federation, however formed or ordered, is that these bodies could not provide a satisfactory ethical life. Without anything to contrast itself with or oppose itself to, there would be nothing to ensure that the consciousness of citizens in such an organisation would be properly united and elevated. This would not only increase the danger of internal division and civil war. It would also dispossess us of the self-conscious unity which makes possible a truly ethical life. Given that this is so, it is rational for people to want to maintain a system of states, rational for states to respect each other's existence and to conduct war with each other – but always with restraint.

The ethical life of the state and the associated view about international relations depend upon the state being a particular kind of community. First of all, loyalty to the state must take precedence over all other loyalties; there must be no contrary demands on the loyalties of individuals. In doing what the state requires, individuals must also regard themselves as doing what they as rational individuals really want to do. The existence of divided loyalties is not only a danger to the state but also an indication that individual freedom and political existence have not been perfectly reconciled. Hegel therefore takes pains to ensure that family, civil society, the corporations are thoroughly integrated into the state and cannot come into opposition to it. Second, as far as their duties to the state are concerned there is supposed to be complete ethical unity among individuals. People are supposed to have the same understanding of what their ethical life requires, and rationally acquiesce in the constitutional arrangements and decisions which determine what the state as an agent does. For if there were disagreements about the requirements of the ethical life, or dissent from decisions of leaders – disputes which could only be resolved, if at all, by compromise – then the same objections which Hegel makes to the requirements of morality could be made against his idea of the ethical. Thus the state, as Hegel presents it, is a community with which citizens identify absolutely and which has itself an identity created by the moral unity of its citizens.

The attraction of this idea of community is not difficult to understand. Charles Taylor points out that Hegel's insistence that freedom in a real sense requires identification with a community is a response to a modern problem: how to reconcile social order with the aspiration for radical autonomy, with freedom from forces without and impediments within (1975: 410ff.). It answers to a dissatisfaction which many people have with what they regard as divisive and over-individualistic tendencies in modern western societies, and it provides support for the widespread communitarian idea that we truly find ourselves, discover a meaning and purpose for our existence, overcome alienation from our social institutions and from each other, by identifying with a community and regarding the common good as our good. Marx, as we have seen, regarded the formation of this kind of community as the goal of social existence, and anarchists and other utopians have advanced similar ideas. At the same time Hegel's political philosophy attempts to provide an answer to a question which all communitarians must answer if they want their position to be regarded as either rational or ethical: what binds people together in a community and justifies them in believing that they have a special relation, and thus an over-riding moral obligation, to each other and to their social whole?

Because Hegel wants to give a satisfactory answer to this question he cannot allow identity to be a matter of natural relationship or sentimental attachment. Not every community provides a basis for satisfactory ethical relations. Patriotism must, first of all, result from a rational attachment – one that an individual accepts as the result of coming to understand himself, his needs and how they can best be satisfied. Second, to be ethically satisfactory, our attachment to the state must rest on the assurance that the ethical life of the state in a world of states is the best way of realising the freedom of all individuals. If Hegel has indeed managed to reconcile freedom with social order and show that the state provides the highest form of ethical life, then he has also provided a basis for opposing cosmopolitan conceptions of justice and world order. I will argue, however, that Hegel does not succeed in showing that an attachment to a state is rationally or ethically required.

Hegel's state is by necessity a complex organism. The possibility of discovering the highest form of freedom and knowing we have found it depends on individuals having experience of and being shaped by different kinds of community, becoming aware of their drawbacks and limitations, and in the process arriving at a clearer idea of the problems which a satisfactory community must be able to resolve. This process is accomplished within the state itself where individuals live in a family, belong to civil society and a corporation, and become aware of the requirements and meaning of the ethical life of the state. However, the very complexity of the state, the division of labour it requires, makes it reasonable to doubt whether ethical unanimity can possibly arise out of these relations.

In his 1843 criticism of Hegel's theory of the state Marx makes the point that no person, group or organisation can be depended upon to represent or pursue the universal interest of the state. The civil servants whom Hegel depends upon to recognise these interests and dedicate themselves to pursuing them will in reality be pursuing the interests of their bureau or their own career ambitions, conducting state affairs according to the habits and ways of thinking instilled in them by their particular position in the political division of labour (Marx 1843: 23ff.).[3] Marx's point here is not simply that the activities and perceptions of civil servants are likely to be affected by their class background (though he clearly believed this to be true). He is also pointing out that professions, bureaucracies, tend to generate and pursue interests and objectives of their own. Indeed, nobody, from the monarch on down, is going to be simply an agent or servant of the state. He will have other allegiances, attachments, relationships, interests which will affect what he does and how he does it.

This means, for one thing, that other individuals cannot depend upon any class or group in the state, however situated, to look after the interests of all. What is torn asunder in civil society cannot be patched together by means of institutions of state. But if all individuals are partisans, and no one reliably represents the universal interest, then individuals will be rightly critical of what their political leaders do and rightly concerned to ensure that their own interests are properly considered. Disagreement, dissension, clashes of interest will be as much a part of political life as they are a part of civil society, and to suppress this disagreement, to prevent individuals from expressing their interests and representing them politically, would be a clear violation of freedom. Hegel is not a proponent of anything that can be called totalitarianism, but given his unreal expectations about political unity, it is not surprising that he has often been taken for one.

This criticism of Hegel can be taken further. The problem with Hegel's idea of how universal interests are defined and pursued is not merely that monarchs and civil servants may be more interested in increasing the power of their family or bureau or pursuing their own ambitions than serving the common good (for this is not always true). The deeper problem is that what they understand to be the universal interest and how they pursue it is inevitably going to be affected by their particular situation or profession. Civil servants will view the affairs of state in a way affected by their training and situation, whether they realise they are doing this or not, and so will the monarch and all others connected with determining national policy. But this means that the definition of the 'universal interest' is as much subject to capriciousness, to the subjective perspective of individuals and groups, as the cosmopolitan principles which Hegel criticises, and individuals are entitled to regard political arrangements which allow one group's opinions to prevail as unfree. Hegel has not after all been able to reconcile freedom with social order or show how individuals can have a non-alienated relation to society or each other.

Hegel might reply to this criticism by insisting that subjectivity, as far as the interpretation of the universal interest is concerned, is not a problem. Individuals have an obligation to obey the will of their sovereign, however that will was formed. If they are rational, doing this duty will be in accordance with their own wills, and the threat of war will always be there to remind them that this is so. The important thing is not what the sovereign decides, but the relationships, both in the state and in the international world, which make it rational for citizens to acquiesce in whatever he decides. It is this acquiescence which brings about ethical unity and not agreement on any principles, policies or objectives.

However, it is difficult to regard acquiescence in the will of a ruler as being rational. It would not, for example, be rational to obey a despot (nor does Hegel advocate this). Individuals must at least be prepared to make a judgment about whether their leaders' actions are constitutional, and this in itself means that they have to exercise their own understanding of what this means. More generally, where different opinions are possible, as they are on any matter of political policy, it seems necessary that a rational person exercise his or her own judgment concerning the rationality of the decisions of leaders and whether or not they properly represent the interests of all. But since people can and do disagree with their leaders concerning objectives and policies and have no reason to believe that their leaders are always right, they are entitled to demand that their view be expressed and represented politically.

This criticism, if correct, brings into question Hegel's ideas about political organisation. It also throws into doubt his idea of how freedom is reconciled with political order. There may be no alternative to government by compromise, a political arrangement which forces citizens to acquiesce in decisions they don't always agree with. More drastically, it brings into question Hegel's way of justifying the state. For the question is not merely who decides what our duties are, but whether there is anything that can be required of us in the name of the state. If people have other interests and commitments which sometimes conflict with what the state requires of them, if Hegel is wrong to suppose that all these interests can be reconciled, then why should they, always or ever, regard loyalty to their state as their primary commitment? There is no reason, it seems, for regarding the ethical life of the state as a true realisation of our freedom if it fails to do what Hegel says that it should do. On the other hand, if the state is justified as a means for keeping peace or promoting co-operation among individuals and groups with conflicting interests, then we have abandoned Hegel's communitarian standpoint. The state is now clearly being treated as a means which needs to be justified in terms of what individuals and groups need and want. Moreover, it seems that we have no reason for defending the state against cosmopolitan proposals for a world order which promotes co-operation and peace. That some people are patriots is unquestionably true. The problem is that Hegel has not succeeded in showing that this commitment is reasonable, let alone that it is ethically required.

Hegel's conception of international relations is equally problematic. From our perspective, the difficulty with Hegel's celebration of war is especially clear. In a world where war has become so dangerous, the threat to populations and their institutions posed even by limited war is unacceptable, and there is, in addition, the worry that a limited war may not remain limited. If we had to choose between world government of some sort and a world in which war is common it would, arguably, be better for the sake of our lives and social stability to choose world government even if this means the disappearance of communities which individuals rightly value. But there are other, more basic, problems for Hegel's idea of international order.

As soon as Hegel's conception of the ethical life of the state is questioned, his idea of international order becomes questionable. Once we raise doubts about whether the decisions of political institutions are rational or consistent, it becomes correspondingly less plausible to regard the state as a super-individual, or as a rational agent of any sort. If decisions in a pluralist state are determined by a particular constellation of pressures from interest groups – if they are a resultant of forces – then it becomes less likely that a state will act in a rational way. Even to say that it is 'the state' which does the acting may not, strictly speaking, be correct. The failure of a state to be a proper agent will not, it is true, be such a serious handicap for a rational world politics if leaders and citizens are generally agreed on certain principles of international relations – if, for example, they are prepared to respect the sovereignty exercised by others. However, looked at more closely the ethical obligation of mutual respect which, according to Hegel, states are supposed to accept has uncertain implications.

Hegel did not think that states were obligated to respect the sovereignty of all other states. He argued, in fact, that politically developed states have no obligation to respect the independence of politically backward states. Colonialism is not ruled out. Nor is it clear that Hegelian considerations can be used to defend a system of states just as it is. So long as individuals have a state to be loyal to, does it really matter what state it is? There seems no reason why Hegel should be opposed to stronger states swallowing up weaker states, or to the establishment of a system of regional states. But if so, an individual cannot justify loyalty to his state just because it is his state. There are other considerations – e.g. the creation of a stable world system of independent states – which can be a reason for alterations to the system. But if there are such reasons, then the mere existence of a state is not a justification for it. Once again the state is reduced to being a means to other ends.

Furthermore, once Hegel's justification of patriotism comes into doubt, so does the idea that individuals have a duty to be loyal to their state and only to their state. If they have commitments to individuals or groups outside the borders of their state it is not clear that their loyalty to the state should always or ever come first. A further justification for the duty of patriotism is needed.

Hegel's theory of the state therefore fails to establish that there is a form of community life which we can defend in the face of cosmopolitan proposals for a new world order. There are, however, two obvious directions we might explore in a search for such a community. Both were explicitly rejected by Hegel – but for inadequate reasons. The first is to return to the idea that a democratic community, a community in which all individuals participate in decision-making, is the community in which freedom can truly be reconciled with social order, and is thus the kind of community which deserves to be the focus of an individual's ethical life. Hegel rejected democracy on the grounds that decisions of the people are bound to be capricious and changeable – and therefore not the basis of a rational domestic or international order. This was the lesson he drew from the French Revolution and its aftermath. But if there is such a thing as a universal interest, and if there is no person or class of people who can be relied upon to identify it, then it seems that it must be the people as a whole who define it or discover it, if anyone does. Democracy was Marx's solution to the problems that he identified in Hegel's theory of the state. However, we still have to determine whether Hegel's criticisms of democracy can be answered: whether there are conditions under which the people of a community can express something that can be called a 'universal interest'. I will discuss the democratic alternative in the next chapter.

The other possibility that we need to explore in the search for the ethical community is the idea that it is the nation, rather than the state, which deserves to be the primary focus of our loyalty. Hegel was an opponent of nationalism. It is true that sometimes he talks of 'a people' in terms that seem nationalistic. The principle of a people, he says in his *Reason in History*, is a particular national spirit:

> This principle defines the common features of its religion, its political constitution, its morality, its system of law, its mores, even its science, art and technical skill. These special particularities must be understood in the light of the universal particularity, the special principle of a people.
>
> (1840: 79)

But all the time he insists that it is the state which defines a people. The unity of a people is a derivate unity, and it cannot be used as a basis for either challenging a state or justifying it.[4]

One of Hegel's reasons for dismissing nationalist ideas and movements is that he believed that nationalist attachments were sentimental rather than rational – too much like the unreflective, non-rational attachments of people within a family. Another is that nationalists, like cosmopolitans, make the state into a mere means for accomplishing other ends – in this case, a means for protecting and furthering the life of the nation. But the first objection is not clearly true and the second begs the question. From our perspective nationalism has to be taken seriously, first of all because it happens to be one of the most influential and prevalent communitarian ideals in the world, and any account of what is possible in world politics has to reckon with nationalist ambitions and sentiments. Second, it is worth considering whether appeals to the nation are able to solve some of the problems associated with the state as a political community: whether the existence of nationalist ideas explains what binds people together within the borders of some states and makes them willing to take responsibility for each other's needs, and why in other less fortunate states there is no sense of community and sometimes no peace. In the context of an inquiry into international justice and its social basis it is above all important to determine whether nationalist ideas have any validity from a moral point of view: whether it is true that people ought to identify with their nation and defend it, and if so, what this means as far as international relations are concerned. I will discuss these issues in Chapters 8 and 9.

Chapter 7

Democratic communities

Democracy, Marx insists again and again in his 1843 critique of Hegel, is the essence of the state (Marx 1843: 64ff.). The state is the people; it is their creation, and Hegel as usual confuses subject and object when he makes the state into the supreme earthly being and ordinary individuals into its dependants and servants. The way in which this essence is best realised, he thinks, is through true democracy where people make decisions about their collective life without intermediaries and special institutions of state. The 'withering away of the state', as Marx later describes it, is the disappearance of institutions which stand between the people and the expression of popular will – an overthrow of political authority which will become possible once class divisions are overcome. In the 1843 *Critique* Marx says nothing about international relations, though they play such an important role in Hegel's theory of the state, and thus he invites the criticism that political institutions are indispensable in a world where states are likely to come into conflict with each other. In his later works he envisioned, as we have seen, the eventual formation of an international society without states. But how everyone in the world can become one people, whether this result is desirable from a democratic point of view, how the collective will of everyone in the world can be determined and carried out without the existence of a vast army of bureaucrats, is something he never discusses. As far as political theory is concerned, Marx never gets much beyond his early identification of the democratic essence of politics.

The development of a democratic theory of community owes more to the work of Jean-Jacques Rousseau, and many communitarian advocates of the democratic community trace their heritage back to his ideas about the social contract and the bond that it creates. Nevertheless, Rousseau's theory is highly contentious and its application uncertain. It is worthwhile to look briefly at some of the problems it raises before examining whether and how contemporary advocates of democratic communities deal with these problems.

The problem that Rousseau addresses is to find a form of political association which not only serves as a means of protecting the lives and goods of individuals, but 'in which each, while uniting himself with all, may still obey himself alone, and remain free as before' (1761: 23). What he aims to solve, in other words, is not simply the problem of war or the problem of ensuring that justice can be administered in a reliable way. The kind of political community he is looking for is one that can reconcile individual autonomy with social order. It is this concern which separates him from Hobbes, Locke and other contract theorists and makes it reasonable to regard him as a communitarian, as sharing the same concerns as Hegel.

Nevertheless, his account of the making of a social contract seems much the same as that of Hobbes or Locke. Individuals recognise that their interests are best served by leaving the state of nature and entering into a compact, and are prepared to give up their natural liberty for this purpose. What they contract to do in Rousseau's version of the story is to put themselves under the direction of the 'general will'. This means that they themselves become the sovereign; they do not subject themselves to the person of a ruler. However, Hobbes too allows that political sovereignty can be exercised collectively by the whole body of individuals who make the social contract – though he thinks that the problem of conflict within the state makes this a less desirable arrangement. Rousseau's starting point raises the question of how exactly his view of the social contract differs from that of Hobbes, Locke and other contractarians. More basically, how can a social contract which involves compromising liberty for the sake of peace, protection and order possibly be the means whereby individuals are united in a way that leaves them 'free as before'?

At first glance Rousseau seems to solve this problem by means of a verbal trick. Once an individual becomes the sovereign, gives himself absolutely to the sovereign, as Rousseau puts it (1761: 24), then whatever this body determines cannot be contrary to his will. But the obvious reply is that the individual is not the sovereign; he is only one of many, and it is all too possible that these many will do something detrimental to his interests and contrary to his desires. This will not be a problem, to be sure, if what the general will decides is in accordance with the will of each individual. Rousseau's description of the body politic sometimes suggests that this will be so – at least so long as individuals are rational. The sovereign's role, he insists, is only to determine the general rules of political life, rules which are not likely to change very much from generation to generation and which are obvious to all. It is up to the executive, though ultimately responsible to the sovereign, to apply the laws and determine specific policies. Rousseau does not believe that the sovereign will have to exercise its will very often; and on those occasions every rational citizen will have little doubt about what the general will should be. Long debates, rhetoric, argument will be unnecessary and counter-productive. Indeed, the community that Rousseau sometimes has in mind is made up of largely independent, isolated households who only have a need for a limited state (as in the independent rural cantons of eighteenth-century Switzerland). We can easily imagine that the heads of such families, being similarly situated and having similar requirements, will be able to reach consensus on the basic rules of their association. But this idea of political community encounters an obvious objection: what relevance has Rousseau's political philosophy to a social life in which the possibility of radical disagreement, persecution of minorities and civil war cannot be discounted?

To interpret Rousseau as a social contract theorist, who simply ignores the problems which Hobbes was trying to deal with, is to miss what has made Rousseau an inspiration to communitarian thinkers. For what he wants to determine is how people united by contract into a political body can be or become more than a collection of individuals who happen to have some interests in common. Each member of the political corporation, Rousseau says, is an 'indivisible' part of the whole (1761: 24), and thus in his view the exercise of sovereignty must involve more than a means of protecting or furthering individual interests. People have not made a social contract in Rousseau's sense until each individual freely undertakes as a citizen to pursue the good of the political body as a whole – i.e. the interests of all. The state is not for Rousseau an arena in which people use political means to pursue their individual interests. By being citizens, people come to have a new, uniquely political interest; they take as their objective the good of the whole community, and thus the well-being of all.

This idea is embodied in Rousseau's notion of the general will and its distinction from the will of all. The general will is the expression of the people as sovereign, and Rousseau insists that it is infallible. What the general will decides is by definition just, but this does not mean that citizens unfailingly express the general will. The general will is expressed only if citizens are properly concerned to bring about the good of all, and an indication of its existence is that it treats all equally. The will of all, on the other hand, arises out of the personal and separate interests of individuals, and even if in the pursuit of their own goals all happen to reach an agreement on a policy, they are not expressing the general will.

Rousseau stresses that political association is not simply a means of protection for individuals. From it arise 'rights' in the true sense of the word, including property rights, and justice and morality: 'The passage from the state of nature to the civil state produces a very remarkable change in man, by substituting justice for instinct in his conduct, and giving his actions the morality they formerly lacked' (1761: 27). In becoming citizens, individuals themselves are transformed and their objectives and interests change. They identify themselves with their political corporation, and thus the general will, by being an expression of the citizens acting as the sovereign, is also the will of each individual citizen. In obeying the general will the individual is doing what he himself wills, even if what he is required to do is to sacrifice himself for his political community. For being free in a real sense is obeying the general will. A person who refuses to obey, Rousseau says, 'shall be compelled to do so by the whole body. This means nothing less than that he will be forced to be free' (1761: 27). On the basis of passages like this Rousseau is sometimes accused of advancing a form of totalitarianism – a tyranny exercised in this case by the majority. But his objective is much the same as Hegel's: he is trying to establish that in political life of a particular sort an individual can best realise his own freedom. Being forced to be free is merely being required to be rational.

Rousseau's social contract is thus different from most arrangements that are described as contractual. Individuals come together out of self-interest and agree to form a political society, and if at some stage they choose to break their association, then the society no longer exists. This is what makes it apt to describe their association, as 'contractual'. Their commitment is chosen; a political society is not a natural association like the relation between parents and children. But on the other hand, if they are to succeed in forming a political community they have to become citizens and acquire the interests and sense of themselves that this entails. The self-interest which leads them to desire to make a contract cannot guarantee this result. A qualitative change in their motivations is required. Rousseau sometimes suggests that to found a state what is needed is a law-giver, a leader who through force of personality and persuasion manages to change human nature – to subject people to law so that they can eventually become the subjects who make law (1761: 46). Though Rousseau makes use of the social contract tradition, there is a way in which relationships in his political community are 'non-contractual' in Hegel's sense.

Where he differs from Hegel, as well as from Hobbes and Locke, is in his conception of the nature of the corporation and how it forms its will. If the general will as expressed directly by citizens is infallible, then nothing can be substituted for it – not a monarch or even a house of representatives. Rousseau's reconciliation of freedom with political order depends essentially upon an undistorted, direct expression of the people's will – a will in which each individual citizen recognises his own will. One person can express the general will, but for this to count as an expression, citizens must at least be in a position to confirm that this is so. The confirmation must be direct – one in which all citizens participate. Voting for or against politicians who purport to represent the people is not an adequate confirmation: 'The people of England regards itself as free; but it is grossly mistaken; it is free only during the election of members of parliament. As soon as they are elected, slavery overtakes it, and it is nothing' (1761: 95).

Nor can the people contract to be ruled by a monarch, for this means that the political will is alienated from them and is no longer theirs. They have become slaves rather than citizens. Nor can a monarch or a bureaucracy, however situated, be regarded as the expresser of the general will. For unless their judgments can be confirmed by the voice and vote of the people we have no reason to think that they do express the general will rather than simply a will of their own. Marx's insistence that democracy is the essence of the state seems also to express Rousseau's position.

Nevertheless, we still have to determine whether Hegel's criticisms of democracy can be met by Rousseau's conception of the general will. The ruling of the people at any time, it might be argued, is simply the resultant of individual opinions. Individuals, even if they are trying to be public-spirited and not self-interested, are going to be influenced by their particular circumstances and other capricious factors. More likely than not citizens will end up in disagreement, and then who is to say what faction represents the general will? But even if they don't, there is always something arbitrary about their determinations. In other words, Hegel's criticism can be taken as a doubt about whether citizens do or can express the universal interest – or more radically, a doubt about whether there is such a thing, especially since Hegel's attempt to locate it also fails.

Two questions are raised by this criticism. The first, and most easily dealt with, is why we should suppose that what the people collectively decide to be in their universal interest really is in their interest. This is much the same, it seems, as asking why we should regard what an individual decides is in his/her interest as being in his/her interest. There are all sorts of ways in which groups and individuals can be irrational (perhaps more than Rousseau imagined). But if we have no reason to think that an individual or a group is being unduly influenced by forces which make rationality difficult or impossible, then surely we have no reason not to regard the decision of that agent as a legitimate expression of will – for who else is entitled to decide what this is? The second question, which arises because in the political case the agent is a collective and not an individual, is how a person who disagrees with what the majority determine – someone who has a different idea of what the law ought to be – can possibly regard acquiescing in the decision as a realisation of his/her own freedom. The answer that Rousseau gives is simply that if that individual has no reason to believe that the majority decision is irrational or discriminatory, then as a citizen committed to political decision-making, he will regard the decision as being in accordance with his will even though he voted against it. If the assembly votes differently from me, Rousseau says, this just shows that I was mistaken about what the general will is (1761: 107).

The persuasiveness of this answer depends upon whether individuals have any reason for believing that the people in their community are capable of making decisions for the good of all. The general will can fail to exist because the group is not really a community or because the individuals in it are not capable of being rational or able to express a rational will. To be rational, Rousseau believes, citizens must be independent enough not to be influenced unduly by others. Rationality thus imposes certain requirements on a political society. Every citizen should have property and there should not be a large gap between rich and poor, Rousseau insists in the *Discourse on Political Economy*. The government must somehow ensure that individuals are not rendered poor and dependent:

> It is, therefore, one of the government's most important tasks to prevent extreme inequality of wealth, not by taking treasures away from those who possess them, but by removing the means of accumulating them from everyone; nor by building poorhouses, but by protecting citizens from becoming poor.
>
> (1755: 222)

In addition, there should be no political factions because these distort the decision-making process by encouraging alliances among citizens. But if there are political parties, then there should be as many as possible so that no one group can dominate decision-making (1761: 35). What Rousseau is trying to ensure by means of these recommendations is that everyone is in a position to exercise an independent and rational judgment, and thus that all can participate in the body politic as free and equal citizens.

A group can fail to count as a real community not only if its members remain predominantly self-interested but if their ideas about what is in the interest of all are irreconcilable. Not every collection of people can express a general will – no matter how democratic may be their procedures. If the group is to be a real community, then they must, above all, be able to agree on who is a member of their collective and who is not, and there must be some common basis for their politics. To be a fit subject for legislation, Rousseau says, a people must 'already be bound by some unity of origin, interest, or convention' (1761: 53). A community of sorts must exist before the state can, and its laws, Rousseau says, will take into account the peculiarities of local concerns and traditions.

Rousseau's insistence that the general will exists only if people collectively make decisions or can confirm or veto the decisions made by leaders puts further conditions on the political community. States should not be so large that citizens are unable to assemble and collectively pass judgment. Rousseau takes as his model political societies the city states of Geneva, Sparta and ancient Rome. Small states, he claims, also promote the love of country and the concern of citizens for each other which he regards as the basis for healthy political life and just relationships. The idea is that if citizens have some kind of acquaintance with each other, they will be more apt to understand each other's needs and more inclined to sympathise with them. This means that they will be able to legislate for the good of all and will be ready to do so. The preconditions that Rousseau imposes on the political community thus form the foundation for an ethical life which is realised in political relations. The commitment of individuals to each other and to their community will be confirmed and strengthened by their direct participation in the body politic as equal citizens. Since they find in their political life their own self-expression, they will value their state above all other associations and will rightly want to defend it from external attack and anything else that threatens its integrity.

Rousseau seems to be able to do what Hegel failed to do: to provide a justification for patriotism. For he gives citizens a rational, ethical reason for their love of their state and for believing that they have duties to it. They have freely committed themselves to the authority of the general will and have done so rationally, for their citizenship enables them to be free and at the same time promotes the equal freedom of others. They are rightly loyal to their own state and have duties to it because it preserves their particular political relationships and thus what all of them define as their good. The very fact that citizens actively participate with each other in defining the collective will gives them a reason to identify with it and thus a reason for accepting political obligation. Furthermore, they have a special responsibility for the welfare of other citizens of their state because equal freedom and general well-being are prerequisites of the existence of a free, rational and prosperous body politic.

The obvious problem with Rousseau's political theory is that there are not many political societies which fit his specifications. Rousseau was well aware that political units were becoming bigger, that the day of the city state was drawing to a close. Moreover, in a world of large states, small states are at a natural disadvantage. Rousseau suggests that this disadvantage might be overcome by a federation for the purpose of mutual aid and defence, but he doesn't say much more about what responsibilities that federation would have and how much independence member states would have to give up for it to function effectively (1761: 96).[1] But Rousseau's attempt to defend the small state now seems largely irrelevant. Given that his ideal is everywhere ignored, why should we take seriously what he says about the general will and the nature of political society? Hegel's criticism of democracy may simply amount to the point that the people who belong to the civil society of a modern state will not, left to themselves, be able to express a general will. Class differences, the fact that they are largely strangers to each other, will not only make them little inclined to consider the good of the whole society, but even if they do so, they are not likely to reach the same opinions about it. Nor is this problem likely to be solved by overcoming class differences through socialist revolution, as Marx believed. Large modern states are pluralist societies: they not only contain people of different classes, but also people of different religions, ethnic backgrounds, races, etc. In modern bodies politic, there will be little or nothing of universal interest, and individuals will thus inevitably regard political decisions, however made, as placing a limit on their freedom. Moreover, in large political societies there is no way that citizens can participate directly in decision-making. Either people will have to govern themselves through representatives, with all the shortcomings that this entails, or the body politic will have to find a non-democratic way of revealing the general will – the solution that Hegel attempts. Whether the search for the general will succeeds or fails – and my discussion of Hegel suggests that it is likely to fail – it seems clear that Rousseau's ideas about politics are irrelevant to our present situation.

One response to this criticism comes from the anarchist or the utopian socialist.[2] Why assume, says this opponent of the state, that we are now living in the best of all possible political worlds, or that there is no alternative to a mass, pluralist political society? There are, as a matter of fact, good reasons for wanting an alternative. All states are bad in some respects: their governments oppress minorities, allow abuses of power, corruption and suppression. Their institutions are often inefficient, unresponsive and sometimes downright destructive. In the modern state, these critics say, individuals are indeed unfree, for no one can regard a political decision as an expression of his/her will. Leaders are chosen through a party system in accordance with the wishes of the more powerful people and groups in the society, and all ordinary citizens are allowed is an occasional chance to express their approval or disapproval of the government in power. They are given the choice, as Rousseau says, of whom they will be enslaved by, and even at election time the options they are given are limited. Political alienation is thus an inevitable phenomenon even in liberal democratic societies, and it is not surprising that in countries where voting is not compulsory, many people do not bother to participate even in this minimal way. Given the nature of their political society, they rightly regard their state as, at best, a necessary evil, something to put up with for the sake of peace and order or because there is no alternative. If they are unlucky enough to live under a corrupt and vicious government, then politics is for them an unmitigated evil. But whether governments are good or bad, anarchists conclude, the modern state is not a real political community. So if Rousseau's general will does not anywhere exist, this is not a reason for rejecting his political philosophy, but rather a reason for rejecting the modern state and searching for an alternative.

How seriously should we take this condemnation of the modern state? I have argued that there is no reason to think that the institutions of a state cannot represent the interests of all, no reason to think that bad institutions cannot be made better. There is also no reason why institutions cannot be made more democratic. Political parties, work-places, local communities, etc. could be reformed in a way that would give individuals a more direct and substantial role in decision-making.[3] The anarchist criticism also ignores a development which Rawls (1987) takes to be especially important: the possibility within liberal democratic states of achieving relationships of justice between individuals and communities – the creation of what he calls an 'overlapping consensus'. If citizens are motivated to uphold this consensus and regard it as an expression of their will, then it seems a mistake to regard the law which underwrites it as an imposition on their freedom. So if the liberal democratic state can allow for some individual and community self-determination, and at the same time bind everyone together through principles of justice which are universally accepted, then why not regard such a political society as the best way of achieving Rousseau's objectives under modern conditions? What more is needed or desired?

However, I argued in Chapter 5 that Rawls never adequately explains why people in a large pluralist society should value co-operation enough to be prepared to sacrifice individual or group autonomy for the sake of maintaining it. Still less does he explain why people in such a society should take responsibility for satisfying each other's needs, including the needs of those who are unable to contribute much to co-operative activities. What Rawls' account of the develop-ment of a pluralist liberal society fails to provide, in other words, is any reason why this collection of individuals and groups should come to regard themselves as a community, any reason why individuals should be loyal to the state they happen to belong to or regard themselves as obligated to defend its integrity, or any reason to regard their relation to other individuals in it as something that generates special duties. Whether and how a large, pluralist society can become such a community remains unclear. We know as a matter of fact that people in these societies do not agree on principles of justice (they do not, for example, all agree with Rawls); they can even fail to agree on basic political principles. Given that this is so, it may be true, as some political theorists claim, that the stability of the modern state depends upon political passivity, on citizens allowing themselves to be ruled by an elite.[4] But even if the majority of the people in a state happen to be in agreement over basic principles, this is not enough to make them into a real political community. Why should they regard what they happen to have in common as important to their lives or as a primary source of moral duty?

We have reason, therefore, for considering whether there is an alternative to the modern state. Those anarchist and utopian socialist theorists who have taken up this challenge are, like Rousseau, concerned with the problem of reconciling community with individual freedom.[5] Ideally, they say, individuals develop their self-identity – their objectives and who they think they are – through their identification with their community, an identification made possible both by a shared way of life and by direct participation in decision-making. 'Participatory democrats understand', says Isaac Balbus, '. . . that collective decision making necessarily entails a struggle for human recognition in which the identity of the self is formed in and through its interactions with its political others' (1982: 361).

These advocates of community are not necessarily supposing that the reconciliation of individuals and society will ever be perfect. Individuals will continue to have objectives and interests of their own which sometimes come into conflict with community goals. In his defence of anarchy, Michael Taylor stresses that the small participatory societies which have actually existed have never been completely harmonious associations. There have always been clashes in them between individuals and groups and always problems with 'free riders' – with individuals who try to take advantage of community goods without making a contribution in return. Nevertheless, he claims that only in a community where each individual participates equally in decision-making will there be a true ethical life. 'Only in a participatory political order of this kind do individuals owe political obligations and they owe them not to a state but to each other' (1982: 10). The obligation Taylor seems to have in mind is not simply the obligation to obey the law for the sake of peace, an idea of duty which can be motivated by self-interest, but an obligation to maintain the particular association which individuals have together created and to carry out the decisions which they have jointly made.

Though Taylor, like many other theorists of the democratic community, takes Rousseau as his precursor, there are some significant differences between Rousseau's ideas of political society and those of contemporary advocates of participatory democracy. Contemporary advocates of participatory communities are more likely to regard political participation as a form of personal development; they assume that individual needs will be expressed in the process of political deliberation and will be reconciled with the needs of all through sympathetic understanding, discourse, compromise, bargaining, etc. Rousseau on the other hand wants to keep individual interests and preferences out of politics. He insists that in their role as sovereign citizens should restrict their deliberations to what is general and avoid bringing the personal into politics, and he opposes political decision-making which encourages debate and discussion on the grounds that rhetoric clouds individual judgment. Contemporary advocates of participatory communities generally assume that people will have close relations to each other. They will not necessarily love each other, but they will have a lot to do with each other; their relationships will be 'many-sided', as Taylor puts it. The community as it is sometimes envisioned by Rousseau consists of independent landowners who come together only rarely for strictly political purposes. Nevertheless, these differences are probably not as significant as they appear. The important thing is that people be committed to maintaining their community and that they know each other's needs and interests well enough, are able to associate with each other freely enough, to be capable of expressing a general will and be universally prepared to accept it as their will.

If this is to be possible, advocates of participatory democracy argue, then the community must be fairly small. It must also be, as Rousseau also insists, reasonably self-sufficient. If its members are to determine freely the future of their community, they cannot be dictated to by outside forces. Furthermore, if everyone is to participate equally, individuals must be more or less equal in their circumstances; no one should be the servant or the dependant of another. Their relations must be, Taylor says, reciprocal (1982: 28). On the other hand, we would expect people in such a community to care for each other sufficiently to regard it as a community responsibility to help those who because of bad fortune or incapacity are unable to care for themselves or contribute fully to the work of the community – the young, the old, the handicapped, the impoverished. The ethic of the community involves some sharing of wealth – whether this is accomplished by holding resources in common or by levies on private property or, as Rousseau suggests, by arranging things so that everyone possesses more or less equal wealth.

That small, self-governing, participatory communities are possible, Taylor argues, is proved by the fact that human beings for most of the history of the species have lived in them. On the other hand, critics of this idea of political community commonly argue that given our present situation a return to this form of society is impractical. The problem is not merely how a highly centralised industrial society can divide into independent communities, but how this can happen in a world where states must be able to defend themselves against other states. As Rousseau notes, small political bodies are at a disadvantage in a world of large powers. This means that leaders of presently existing states will regard themselves as justified in suppressing independence movements which seem to interfere with their state's ability to defend itself, and people will be loath to establish communities which will make their lives and livelihood more insecure.

Nevertheless it is possible, at least, to imagine how the world could become a system of independent small political communities. Let us suppose that people all over the world become more and more dissatisfied with the inefficiencies, inequities and lack of responsiveness of big government, and more inclined to think that environmental and other serious problems are best solved by a return to a less industrial way of life in smaller-scale communities. Local communities everywhere begin demanding more and more power to decide their affairs, and governments, not being able to cope with developments, have little choice but to give in. There will, it is true, be people who have an interest in maintaining the state as it is – those who obtain advantages from what has been called its 'military industrial complex' – but we can assume that the popular movement for decentralisation is so strong and persuasive that in one way or another it can overcome this opposition. Eventually institutions of the national state wither away, or are retained in a minimal form to co-ordinate the joint affairs of the independent communities.[6]

For such a change to be feasible we have to imagine that all the conditions are right. The change has to take place everywhere in the world at about the same rate – otherwise communities may be left vulnerable and virtually defenceless. We have to suppose that the conversion of a centralised industrial economy into ways of life suitable for small-scale, more or less self-sufficient communities can take place without serious hardship or disruption. This in itself is a dubious proposition. If communities are to be reasonably self-sufficient then they must, presumably, have land and resources enough to provide for their own needs, but this requires not only a movement of population from the city to the country, but also very likely a movement of populations between different parts of the world. For in some countries there are simply not enough resources to go round. Given the population of the world as it is, it may be impossible to settle everyone in an independent and reasonably prosperous community, however much people are moved around. But even if it were possible to do this, the question remains how territory and resources are going to be divided up and by whose authority. The irony may be that the only force capable of accomplishing this in a more or less peaceful way may be a very powerful world government whose decisions are generally respected by everyone. But if a world government has this kind of legitimacy and authority, then demands for independence are not likely to be made, or if made, not likely to be successful.

Could relations in a world of small communities be peaceful and just? Rousseau and others have argued that the small political community should be inclined towards peace. It has no interest in acquiring the territory of others or making itself larger and more prosperous. Being mostly self-sufficient, it would not have to interfere in the affairs of others. A world of small communities could therefore be peaceful, and Rousseau makes the suggestion that a world federation pledged to peace among members might be able to guarantee perpetual peace (1762: 430).

On the other hand, in the history of the human species, small independent communities have not always been peacefully inclined. Warfare between villages, tribes and clans has been a common occurrence, and there is no reason to suppose that a future world of small states would be much different in their relations with each other. 'We have no grounds', Michael Taylor says,

> for believing that growing up and living in a community necessarily engenders a tolerant, pacific and co-operative disposition towards outsiders. It is true that many primitive anarchic communities lived at peace with their neighbours . . . but many did not, and the world is a great deal more crowded now.
>
> (1982: 167)

One of the preconditions for peace, he suggests, is that communities be in a material sense more or less equal, so that no one of them is in need or has a reason to be envious of the wealth of others. But who is going to arrange this? If a federation has the power to distribute resources among communities, then it is no longer a federation of independent political societies. If it does not have this power, then it seems that gaps in wealth are bound to occur given that the resources of the world are not naturally distributed in an equitable way.[7]

If small states are inclined to fight each other over resources or for any other reason, then they also might be tempted to form alliances, to reconstitute the institutions and industries which decentralisation has dismantled. The knowledge of how to form and use large political societies, like the knowledge of how to build nuclear and chemical weapons, is not something that will disappear from the world. We can never be in the same situation as people of the Stone Age unless a catastrophe destroys all possibility of civilised life. The world federation must therefore prevent the reconstitution of large political units, but if it has the power to do this, it is, once again, not merely a federation.

The movement to a decentralised world, the maintenance of a peaceful, just relationship between societies, is likely to require, I have argued, the kind of central authority which anarchists and utopian socialists are supposed to eschew. If this is so, then the very possibility and viability of a world of small independent political societies is in serious doubt. Nevertheless, the small independent political community might still be regarded as an ideal form, which unfortunately we are presently incapable of realising – as Taylor's position suggests. But is it so ideal?

Iris Marion Young argues in 'The ideal of community and the politics of difference' (1986) that advocates of community wrongly suppose that we are or can be 'present' to ourselves and each other. The ideal of community denies difference, and by excluding those whom we do not identify or feel comfortable with, it encourages chauvinism. She is saying, I take it, that the problem which Rousseau and others are attempting to solve by means of a particular kind of political community – the reconciliation of individual freedom with social order – is not solvable, and attempts to solve it often have pernicious consequences.

As they stand, these criticisms do not do justice to the point of view of advocates of small communities. From Rousseau through the anarchist and utopian tradition, one of the main concerns has been to ensure that individuals remain free, able to make their own judgments and able to realise themselves as distinct persons. None of the utopians expects or desires a total identification of individual wills with the will of their communities. Individuals will always have interests and concerns of their own, and Rousseau, especially, tries to ensure that they will have plenty of room to live an independent life and develop the ability to make independent decisions. Nor does an advocate of community have to suppose that people will always be in agreement on political issues, let alone on everything else. What makes them into a community is that for each maintaining the good of all is a primary objective. They have to have enough in common for their political decisions to be regarded as expressing a general will, but this commonality is compatible with some dissent and disagreement. Nor does an advocate of community have to suppose that everyone in it likes and feels comfortable with everyone else. Community is supposed to go along with a toleration of differences and personal relations which falls far short of love.

Nevertheless, small self-sufficient communities – villages, small towns and cities, rural communities – have often been intolerant of those who are different, as well as suspicious of outsiders. They often do tend to encourage conformity – not so much by forcing people to do what they don't want to do, but by ensuring that they have no opportunity to do anything else. People in small communities have often been narrow-minded, bigoted, patriarchal, hierarchical, defensive, censorious and suspicious of outsiders. This is not only a problem for people who live in them – and sometimes a problem for those who have to deal with them. It also raises doubts about whether they can express a general will, for the general will is supposed to be a rational will and not a reflection of the prejudices of the majority of people in a community.

Perhaps things don't have to be this way. Rousseau tries to ensure that individuals will retain their independence and their ability to make independent judgments through having property and interests of their own and through an education which encourages rationality. Perhaps, as some utopians recommend, individuals should be encouraged to have connections with individuals outside their community, to travel around, try out different forms of life. But there are some obvious problems with these suggestions. If the opposition between individual and community is to be overcome, then individuals have to regard the good of their community as their good. Their independence as individuals cannot be allowed to compromise their bonds to the community or make it impossible for these bonds to form. Nor can they be allowed to develop any loyalties or ties with outsiders which could compromise the coherence of their community or its ability to make and carry out its own decisions. An advocate of small political communities must, like Hegel, require that the primary loyalty of individuals be to their political community. Thus there will always be, it seems, a tension between encouraging individuals to be independent and critical, and retaining community bonds.

The tension between loyalty and individuality raises the question of whether individuals in the small, independent political community can in any real sense be free. Hegel insists that true freedom is not experienced by the autonomous individual. But nor is it experienced by the person who is so deeply embedded in community relations that he/she becomes incapable of choice or has no other options. For members of an enclosed, exclusive community are not able to develop a sense of themselves as independent persons; they have no real opportunity to do anything but what tradition and role prescribe. Hegel relies on civil society to give the (male) individual a chance to develop himself as an independent agent with a mind and objectives of his own. In other words, Hegel is insisting that only by experiencing a complex and varied social life – only by living in a pluralist society where there are oppositions, divisions, the possibility of different associations and ways of life, where the necessity of choice exists – can individuals truly be free. From this point of view the small, independent, homogeneous community does not seem a favourable site for developing free individuals. If this is so, then the reconciliation between individual autonomy and social order is no real reconciliation. Social order is bound to triumph. This perception is perhaps what lies behind Young's criticisms and behind the dissatisfactions that people often express concerning life in small communities.

A similar point can be made about the other important social ideal which is supposed to be upheld in the independent community. It is basic to Rousseau's idea of political society that citizens have an equal political right and that the determinations of the general will reflect this equality. Social resources are to be distributed in such a way as to ensure that political equality is not compromised by social inequalities. Modern advocates of small communities have also generally insisted that there must be social and political equality in the political society. Everyone participates and everyone's voice and vote count equally.

However, small independent communities, at least those based on agriculture rather than on hunting and gathering, have not generally been societies in which individuals are treated equally. These societies were typically patriarchal, refusing women any direct role in political decision-making, and they have often had a rigid class system which ensured that slaves, servants and other dependants had no political existence. In the societies which Rousseau took as models only a small minority of adult people were actually citizens. Political and social equality has not in fact been a feature of these societies except (at best) among those who own property.

Furthermore, there is reason for supposing that this is not a historical accident, reason to think that equality is not likely to be regarded as an ideal in small independent political communities – let alone something that is achieved in practice. For equality as a political or social ideal has historically arisen in pluralist societies, where people of different religions, races, backgrounds, neighbourhoods have had to establish some mutually acceptable basis for co-operation and political association. The idea that being an individual is more important, as far as political and social rights are concerned, than being of a particular sex or race or class is the product of a social development in which people have learned to tolerate and even appreciate differences. But in a small homogeneous, independent community dedicated to preserving a traditional way of life, the roles individuals play are likely to be regarded as what determines their political and social status and their duties in the ethical life of the community. What 'rights' people have are likely to be fixed by their sex, class, occupation, lineage; and justice will mean giving everyone their due, according to traditional ideas about what this means. Utopian thinkers suppose that we will take our ideal of equality into the new society and realise it more fully. But for how many generations will such an ideal endure in a situation which is not going to be conducive to its perpetuation?

A communitarian might reply that I am illegitimately applying cosmopolitan criteria of judgment to condemn the ethical life of the small independent community – illegitimately because it is basic to communitarianism that individual rights, however these are defined, should not always take precedence over the values of a community. However, none of the communitarians I am criticising rejects the principle of equality; all of them wish to preserve the autonomy of the individual, and indeed they must want to do so if the attempt to reconcile freedom and social order is to mean anything at all. My criticism is simply that advocates of the small political community do not convincingly demonstrate that they can achieve this aim. It does not imply that the values of a community are not important or that they should always be sacrificed for the sake of individual entitlements or individual objectives. Unlike Young, I do not think that the project of reconciling autonomy with social order is misconceived.

However, if my criticism is correct, then it seems that we have good reason to doubt whether in practice any communitarian position will prove acceptable. Either the communities which are the basis for international organisation will be pluralist communities, like states, or they will be the smaller, more homogeneous communities of the kind advocated by Rousseau and others. But in the former, if my criticism of Hegel is correct, a common identity and the kind of community life which communitarians advocate are going to be difficult, if not impossible, to achieve and maintain. On top of that, states do not seem to provide a stable or satisfactory basis for a just world. The small independent community 'reconciles' freedom with social life at the cost of freedom, and it too seems to be an unsatisfactory basis for world organisation.

There is, however, an alternative which has not yet been explored. This is the idea explicitly rejected by Hegel: that it is the nation and not the state that is the individual's true community and the proper basis for international order. It is promising because the nation, as it is usually conceived, is by nature pluralist: it contains a large number of people of different classes, different religions, different neighbourhoods, and, according to some conceptions of the nation, even people of different races and ethnic backgrounds. On the other hand, the nation is supposed to provide that sense of identity with others, that ethical life of social responsibility, which Hegel tried in vain to realise in the state. Moreover, nationalists argue that the nation is the only proper basis for political order and international organisation: a state which stands in the way of the self-realisation of a nation, or an international world which does not recognise and respect the integrity of nations, is unjust. In the following chapters I will consider what these claims mean and whether they can be justified.

Chapter 8

The nation as a community

Nationalists typically claim that the nation is the community which above all gives meaning and value to our lives and defines who we are as individuals, giving us a duty to be loyal to our nation and responsible for the well-being of others who belong to it. For the sake of their nation nationalists make political demands which can have profound effects not only on the politics of states but also on the international world. Nationalism is a force to be reckoned with in any account of what world developments are possible or likely. But it is also something to which a political philosopher must pay attention. For nationalists are claiming that their loyalty and their demands are justified from a moral and rational point of view, and thus they are providing a particular answer to the questions: what is the best way of reconciling individual freedom with social order? what is a just international world?

However, nationalism, though studied as a social phenomenon by political scientists, has rarely been treated as a philosophical topic. There are no philosophers of the nation comparable in stature and influence to Hegel, Kant, Marx or Mill. But this is probably not the primary reason why this subject has been neglected. There are, first of all, political philosophers who believe that there is nothing more to be said about the nation than what can be said about the state. And there are philosophers who regard nationalism as basically an irrational doctrine, a suitable case for condemnation, but not something otherwise worthy of serious consideration. Both positions, I believe, are mistaken.

States and nations are not, apparently, the same thing. A state is a political society individuated by its boundaries. A nation is defined by its culture, way of life, language, history, by the conviction of its members that they form a distinct people. The people of a nation may not all live within the boundaries of one state and one state can contain more than one nation. Since nationalist loyalties sometimes come into conflict with the demands of the state, there is good reason to consider what exactly nations are as social communities and what reasons people have for their commitment to them. Nationalism is a distinct communitarian position and deserves to be treated as such. It tells us where our primary loyalties ought to lie and what follows concerning our ethical duties. It tells us when people are obligated to respect political authority and when they are justified in resisting or rebelling. Like other communitarian positions it is a source of resistance to cosmopolitan conceptions of world order: it says that justifications for a political order which appeal to individual rights or individual well-being are not sufficient. Nations, too, have a right of self-determination.

The idea that nationalism is a form of irrationality also needs to be challenged. The way in which philosophers often talk about nationalism is illustrated by Isaiah Berlin's consideration of it in 'Nationalism: past neglect and present power'. Berlin begins by defining 'nationalism' as 'the elevation of the interest of the unity and self-determination of the nation to the status of the supreme value before which all other considerations must, if need be, yield at all times' (1979: 342). This implies, he goes on to say, that the commitment to the nation is not something open to rational assessment; and it can be used to justify any action which seems to serve national interests, however harmful to individuals or to international relations.

This characterisation of nationalism begs the question. It defines nationalism as national chauvinism, and thus ignores a large body of nationalist literature which argues that nationalism is compatible with, and even conducive to, human freedom and well-being and a respect for other nations. It is in fact more accurate to regard nationalist thinkers as addressing the same problem as did Rousseau, Hegel and many others: how to reconcile individual freedom and equality with social order both within and between communities. Such a reconciliation does not require us to deny that individuals have ethically important interests and needs of their own. Still less does it entail a non-critical support of any community.

The reason why Berlin is motivated to understand nationalism in the way that he does is that nationalism has as a matter of fact sometimes been associated with authoritarian political relations, racism, aggression, intolerance. But this historical observation does not tell us what nationalism really is: whether nationalist movements, in spite of attempts to rationalise them, are inherently chauvinistic and aggressive, or whether they are basically peaceful and tolerant but sometimes perverted by fascist and racist ideas or the imperial ambitions of rulers (as Benedict Anderson suggests in *Imagined Communities* (1983: Ch. 6)). What we need to determine, before it becomes reasonable to condemn nationalism, is whether there are conceptual or moral inadequacies in the philosophical ideas of nationalists which might help to account for the sometimes unfortunate history of nationalist movements.

Those philosophers and others who put forward a defence of the nation have generally framed their ideas about ethical duty and national life in opposition not only to what they regard as political suppression of the life of their people, but to the 'degradation' which Hegel associates with civil society. Johann Fichte in *Addresses to the German Nation* (1807) develops a conception of what it is to be German in opposition to the self-seeking and intellectual frivolousness which he associated with the French influence, but which he feared was insinuating itself into German life. From his point of view the political domination of German states by the French is a bad thing, not so much because of any direct harm done to individuals, but because of the spiritual harm it is doing to the German nation. Giuseppe Mazzini in the *Duties of Man* (1860) opposes not only the political domination of Italy by foreign powers, but also ways of thinking which he regards as 'materialistic', a description which includes both liberal individualism and socialism. He finds in the nation the possibility of an ethic of community that transcends individual concerns and class interests and emphasises matters of the spirit.

The ethic of community requires that individuals take responsibility for each other's welfare. The rich, Mazzini says, must provide for the poor; employers and employees must deal with each other justly and honestly; men must respect and protect women. In the organic unity of the nation, says Fichte, 'no member regards the fate of another as the fate of a stranger' (1807: 3). This unity is made possible by a love of the nation itself and a willingness to make sacrifices to ensure its continued existence and well-being. Love of nation is thus supposed to overcome the anonymity of mass societies, class and other social divisions in what Anderson describes as a 'deep, horizontal comradeship' (1983: 16). The feelings it evokes have often been compared to religious sentiments. The nation, says Régis Debray, is one of the organisations 'through which life itself is rendered untouchable or sacred' (1977: 26). It is through the nation, Fichte insists, that an individual comes into contact with the eternal and the divine in a true sense; and it is only through this contact that life has any value:

> Hence the noble-minded man will be active and effective, and will sacrifice himself for his people. Life merely as such, the mere continuance of changing existence, has in any case never had any value for him; he has wished for it only as the source of what is permanent. But this permanence is promised to him only by the continuous and independent existence of his nation.
>
> (1807: 116)

The ethic of community which these advocates of the nation have in mind is similar in many respects to Hegel's conception of the ethical life of the state and Rousseau's conception of political community. Individuals are supposed to love and be loyal to their nation, and in doing so they become a new kind of person, one who identifies the good of the nation with the good of himself or herself. This loyalty is supposed to complement, contain, and at the same time surpass all other loyalties – family loyalties, friendships, class associations – and people of the nation are supposed to have a special relation with each other and duties to each other that they do not have to outsiders. At the same time a nationalist is supposed to respect the entitlement of these outsiders to live the ethical life of their own nation, for in doing so everyone can most fully realise and express himself/herself as a free individual. Nationalism is not necessarily incompatible with the existence of interests and moral concerns which unite all human beings, but for the most part individuals are supposed to contribute to the progress of humanity by identifying with their nation and working for its self-realisation:

> In labouring according to true principles for our Country we are labouring for Humanity; our Country is the fulcrum of the lever which we have to wield for the common good. If we give up this fulcrum we run the risk of becoming useless to our Country and to Humanity.
>
> (Mazzini 1860: 55)

The ethic of community advocated by nationalists has as a consequence that the state and its institutions exist as a mere means. Loyalty to the state is always provisional. If the institutions of state subvert or interfere with the life of the nation, if the rulers are foreigners, then the state does not deserve the loyalty of the people. On the other hand, if the state protects and enhances the life of the nation, then it deserves to be supported and defended. In this way nationalists explain why, and under what conditions, people ought to be patriots and what states and governments have a right to exist.

The state will best protect and enhance the nation, so it is often argued by nationalists, if it is a nation-state – if it contains all and only the people of the nation.[1] A nation is therefore entitled to a state of its own, especially if its self-realisation as a nation is being threatened by present political arrangements; and if it doesn't have a state of its own, it has a legitimate cause for complaint, perhaps even a legitimate reason for rebellion. What nationalists have in common with Hegel – an emphasis on the importance of community and the ethical life of the community – is thus overshadowed by a different conception of politics. In Hegel's state the will of the people is supposed to be subordinate to the will of the rulers, for it is the latter who best represent the universal interest. The idea that it is the nation, not the state, which is of primary ethical importance seems to require that the people themselves determine the course of their political life. For in the people reside the history, traditions, customs, speech which define the nation. Nationalism for both Fichte and Mazzini involves an appeal to the people over the heads of their rulers (who, they believed, had proved unreliable or hopelessly corrupt), and it insists that the people, being the true source of the nation's identity, should also be the definers of its purpose. Historically nationalism has often been associated with movements for democracy and political reform.

This means that there is a lot in common between nationalist thinkers and those who have taken their inspiration from Rousseau, especially since Rousseau also emphasises the importance for political community of people having pre-existing social bonds. On the other hand, for nationalists these social bonds – the customs, traditions and language of people – are of overwhelming significance. They, not political relationships, make a people what it is and dictate what its ethical life must be, and what counts as a true expression of its will. The role of political institutions in creating and maintaining social bonds and influencing the nature of an ethical life is thus often de-emphasised by philosophers of the nation. There are, indeed, anti-political tendencies in nationalist thinking. The institutions of state, according to Fichte, tend to hinder the development of the nation. And the problem, he makes it clear, goes beyond the failing of particular rulers. A nation is a living thing constantly developing and changing; a state is merely a means of keeping order and peace, and the static nature of its laws and structures stand in the way of the evolution of the nation:

> In the maintenance of the traditional constitution, the laws and civil prosperity there is absolutely no real true life and no original decision. Conditions and circumstances, and legislators perhaps long since dead, have created these things; succeeding ages go on faithfully in the paths marked out, and so in fact they have no public life of their own; they merely repeat a life that once existed.
>
> (Fichte 1807: 120)

The state is static and dead, rigid and formalistic; it is the nation which is alive. Taken to its logical conclusion, the idea that states hinder the development of nations suggests that it would be better if states did not exist at all, a view which was held by Herder (1791), one of Fichte's contemporaries. As in the case of Marx, his ideal is that people should determine their destiny without relying on an 'external' political apparatus. But in fact most nationalists have regarded a strong state as a necessary means not only for ensuring national survival but for making possible national self-realisation. Fichte and Mazzini were well aware that their own people could be so easily dominated by outsiders because they were not politically united. Furthermore, both insisted that the state play a role in educating people about the importance of their national heritage, for it is education, above all, which is supposed to counter materialist ideas and create the new person whom the ethical life of the nation requires.

Nationalists often blame governments for hindering the development and expression of their nation. They also commonly blame politics for international conflict and war. Rulers make agreements and alliances with each other according to their interests and convenience. The power plays they engage in, Fichte and Mazzini both insist, particularly their attempts to achieve a balance of power, are a threat to the integrity of nations and a threat to peace. If people could determine their own destiny, if they were free to have and develop their own nations, the suggestion is, perpetual peace would become possible. The idea is Kantian, but the conditions have changed. In place of Kant's requirement that states be republics, nationalists put the requirement that they be nation-states. That nations be able to determine themselves becomes a primary precondition of a just and peaceful world. 'There is no more certain injustice', says Hoffmann, than alien rule imposed against the will of a people: 'Self-determination is a precondition for peaceful co-existence. And if one ever wants to go beyond the nation

state, recognising the right of people to their own nation is the first
step' (1981: 34).

Why should we suppose that a world of nation-states will live in
peace and that each will treat the others justly? The answer nationalists
typically give to this question is much the same answer that Rousseau
gives to the question of why political communities should be able to
coexist peacefully. The identity of a nation comes from within, not, as
in Hegel's case, through a contrast with and in struggles with others. A
nation is basically inward-looking, and therefore individuals will find
meaning and value for themselves by concentrating on the collective
realisation of qualities intrinsic to the nation and the ethical life that
this involves. It is not in their interests to conquer others, rule over
them and try to assimilate them. Moreover, the respect that they have
for all other individuals will be expressed in world society as a respect
for their entitlement to their national independence. Equality of
individuals translates into an equal right of self-determination of the
nations to which individuals belong.

This conception of how peace is achieved in a system of nation-states
presupposes that nations do not have interests or objectives that conflict
in any serious way. This seems to require, as I have argued before, that
states be much more self-sufficient economically and politically than
most now are. Fichte, because of his fears that the pure German culture
might be polluted by foreign cultural influences, took this idea to an
extreme conclusion and argued that the German nation would best
thrive within a 'closed commercial state': a state which aims for
economic self-sufficiency, closing its borders to trade and even to the
movement of people. Most nationalists do not require total self-
sufficiency; they assume that nations can trade with each other and
learn from each other. But a nationalist will want to ensure that
relations between nations are such that peaceful national self-realisation is possible. National life should not be perverted either by the
political or economic dominance of outsiders or by the temptation to
imitate the culture of others.

There is clearly going to be a problem in fulfilling the preconditions
for a world of peacefully coexisting nation-states. For in putting
forward the nation-state as a political ideal, nationalists are opposing
not only proposals for a world state, but also for a system of regional
states. But it is only regional states, I have argued, that are likely to be
able to achieve the kind of economic and political independence which
nationalists seem to require – so long, at least, as we continue to live
within a highly industrialised, commercial society. Thus taking the idea

of self-sufficient nation-states seriously requires that some of the technological and industrial developments of the last two centuries be undone. If this seems unlikely or undesirable, then nationalist ideas about world organisation are thrown into doubt. Even if deindustrialisation were possible, there are too many national societies which wouldn't be able to be self-sufficient no matter what they did. The ideal of self-sufficiency could turn out to be a recipe not only for terrible poverty, but for environmental destruction.

Satisfying the nationalist preconditions for a peaceful and just world also seems to entail radical changes to international society. There are in the world many groups of people who regard themselves as a nation, but do not yet have a nation-state. In some cases the people who regard themselves as belonging to the same nation are scattered over the world or live in large numbers in the territory of a state dominated by people of another nation. There are continual disputes about what territory belongs to what nation. Considerable changes would have to take place in the international world if all nationalist ambitions were to be realised, changes which include movements of populations as well as borders, and it seems unlikely that any political arrangement would satisfy everyone. Whether a world of nation-states could come into existence and maintain itself without war, threats of war, subjugation and oppression is therefore a doubtful proposition.

The idea of a world made up of peacefully coexisting nation-states faces a more fundamental problem: if this world is ever to be settled, stable and peaceful, then there must be, at least in theory, an end to nationalist challenges to the international status quo. There must be a state of the world that people can finally agree is just. This requires that there must be a general agreement about what a nation is and who belongs to it. But the question, 'What is a nation?' is notoriously difficult to answer.

The way in which nationalists talk about nations invites comparison with the way in which liberal philosophers talk about individuals. Each nation like each individual has a unique character and its good is achieved through realising and developing this character. A nation, like an individual, is subject to change and development, but to be true to itself it must remain true to its essential nature. Its will, what it decides and does, must be in conformity with this nature. Just as individuals can be wrong about their character and false to their true selves by being conformists or too fond of sensual pleasures or material well-being, so the people of a nation can be ignorant about their heritage and deflected from their true good by being over-influenced by the culture of others or corrupted by the desire for riches or pleasure. A people, like an individual, sometimes needs to be enlightened about where its true good lies. One of the ironies of nationalist thought is that it emphasises the need to appeal to the people, but at the same time often despairs of popular judgment and insists that the people first need to be educated. But who will educate the educators? The problem of defining the nation can be directly related to the use of the analogy between individuals and nations: to regard a nation as a kind of individual is a source of difficulties, and so is the liberal notion of individuality itself.

Individual human beings are relatively easy to individuate. Philosophical questions about personal identity aside, there is usually no difficulty in distinguishing one person from another, hence we know at least whom we are talking about when we inquire into a person's nature. One of the problems with the analogy between nation and individual is that it is not so easy to individuate nations. French and Gutman emphasise in 'The principle of national self-determination' (1974) that uncertainties about who belongs to the nation translate into a problem of determining when a political decision is a proper assertion of the national will. Commonly used criteria of nationhood leave us uncertain. If we attempt to decide who the people of a nation are by reference to a common history or culture we are begging the question. How can we call a history or culture 'common' unless we already know whose history it is? As a matter of fact, within any population there can be considerable disagreement not only about how history should be interpreted or what the culture contains, but whose history and culture are being referred to. Even language, the favourite criterion for distinguishing between nations, isn't a decisive means of individuation. For people who share the same language can deny that they belong to the same nation.

The problem is not solved by investigating how nations differentiate themselves from each other in practice. The idea of the nation, say historians, is a modern conception made possible by Enlightenment ideas and the reaction to them, by the existence of modern systems of education, communication and transport. It was promoted by the distribution of literature and other writings in vernacular languages; its rise in western society was accompanied by the decline of religion; it has been encouraged and spread by the industrial revolution, capitalism and colonialism and the reaction to them. The ideal of the nation has marched hand in hand with the development of the modern state, and rulers have sometimes deliberately fostered nationalist sentiments in order to promote unity and underwrite their authority. People who have lived within the boundaries of a state for generations, who are bound together by the institutions of that state and share a political culture, will generally regard themselves, and be regarded, as belonging to the same nations – but who can say what slumbering national identities lurk beneath the surface of this 'common life'? The very popularity of the nationalist ideal may encourage populations to see themselves as a distinct nation whenever the opportunity arises – to translate their grievances into insults to their nation. For having a nation is part of what being modern means.[2]

These considerations suggest that there is no single or uniform cause of nationalism and no single form that it takes. Despairing of a universal criterion of nationhood, some scholars have concluded that people have to determine for themselves what their nation is and what it stands for: 'All I can find to say is that a nation exists when a significant number of people in a community consider themselves to form a nation, or behave as if they have formed one' (Seton-Watson 1977: 5). But this formula will be problematic if a population disagrees about who belongs to their nation and who does not. Moreover, by insisting that people define nations as they choose is to give up the idea that the nation can be a normative or explanatory concept. To have a philosophy of the nation, as Fichte and Mazzini understood it, is to be able to make a distinction between what a nation is and what people think it is. For otherwise we cannot determine whether people are being false or true to their nation or to what nation they should be true.

However, Seton-Watson's 'definition' might be used to argue that as far as international relations are concerned what is important is simply that people believe that they belong to a nation and regard this as being important. Why they believe that is their business. But given that they do, it is important that we respect their desire for national self-determination. One of the problems with this position is that respect won't take us very far if nationalists make contrary demands on populations, states, territories or resources. If the people of the world cannot be divided exclusively and uncontroversially into nations, then we have reason to question nationalist recipes for a perpetually peaceful world. French and Gutman's doubts about whether national self-determination is a viable political demand deserve to be taken seriously. Moreover, to say that anything goes as far as the definition of a nation is concerned is to take tolerance too far. Nationalism as a force in international politics has to be respected. But what kind of respect we give it depends on whether we have reason to think that nationalist loyalties are rational and ethically justifiable. If it turns out that nationalism is irrational and pernicious, as many liberal and Marxist thinkers believe, then our only hope is to find some treatment for it, some way of curbing or dealing with outbreaks of nationalist sentiment. A respect for the loyalties of other people should not be used as a reason for ignoring the difficulties of defining and defending the nation, or a reason for refraining from criticism.

French and Gutman object to the demand of national self-determination, but they do not deny that the concept of the nation is meaningful. Problems with criteria aside, identifying nations and who belongs to them isn't generally a difficult thing to do. There is usually no doubt about who is German, Lithuanian, Hungarian, French, etc., though there may be differences of opinion about the identity of some groups of people (the people of Britanny, Russians who have lived in Lithuania for a long time, etc.), and over time the idea of who counts as a German, a Lithuanian, etc. may change. The nation, it might be said, is simply a concept with fuzzy edges – perfectly useful for most purposes, but sometimes capable of creating legal and political difficulties. Nevertheless, if the analogy between individuals and nations is going to be useful in any context, then there must be some central characteristics essential to a nation. Furthermore, these characteristics must have ethical significance. Being a member of a nation must be something more than a way of classifying a person. There are thus two questions which nationalist philosophers must be able to answer satisfactorily: the empirical question: how do we determine what characteristics are essential to a nation? and the ethical question: why should individuals suppose that they have an ethical obligation to preserve and realise this essential nature?

The first question raises another difficulty for the analogy between individuals and states. Liberal discussions of individual self-realisation assume that individuals have a definite self to realise. There must be something that individuals really are, as opposed to those characteristics which they may adopt as the result of unjustified interference in their lives or social pressures to conform. We do not have to suppose that these defining characteristics are innate, but self-realisation makes no sense unless individuals can make rational judgments – on the basis of experience, self-reflection, psychoanalysis, the insights of friends, etc. – about who they really are and what they want and need. Philosophers who question the idea that individuals have such an 'essence' are also questioning the personal objectives and ethical ideas which go with it.

To attribute an essence to a nation is even more problematic, for a nation consists of a large number of individuals who come from different classes, backgrounds, communities, etc., and are likely to have different and sometimes conflicting ideas about what the essential properties of their nation are. The ideals, the interpretation of a nation's history or traditions accepted by one group can be disputed by another. What is commonly regarded as the national identity may simply reflect the ideals or traditions of a dominant group, class or sex. The problem is not merely how such distortions can be avoided or corrected, but how we can decide what definition is really correct.

The disputes, the agonising that goes on in many countries over the question of national identity, what is and what is not willed in accordance with it, suggest that this question is not easy to answer. The problem, it might be argued, lies not in the methods used but in the assumptions about essence and individuality which give rise to these attempts at national self-reflection. Perhaps it would be better to regard the nation as a family resemblance concept: there are overlapping common threads which unite people in a nation, but nothing that all have in common. But if this is true then the idea that the nation has a general will becomes doubtful, and the idea that the nation should realise itself in a particular way is also thrown into question. Alternatively, it might be argued that nations can only define themselves in contrast to and opposition with other nations. But if this is true, then one of the basic assumptions Fichte and Mazzini make about national self-realisation is wrong: nations do not realise themselves by turning inward but through their relation with others. This method of individuation will cause problems for the international world if war plays the same role in the spiritual development of the nation as Hegel thought it did in the life of a state. In fact the events which most people identify as important to the formation of their nation are wars, revolutions or struggles against colonial powers. But if war is essential to the life of a nation, then critics of nationalism have some reason for their fears.

A defender of the nation would thus have to find a way of countering these alternative conceptions of national identity, or at least a way of showing that nations do have some essential properties to realise and that relations between nations do not have to be war-like. But even if this is possible, and even if people can agree on the essential characteristics of the nation, the ethical relevance of this identity remains unclear. Why should individuals believe that it is their ethical duty to preserve and develop the characteristics of the nation? Why should this duty outweigh duties to the other communities to which they might belong?

These questions are answered, it might be argued, by an appreciation of the relation of individuals to their nation. If the good of a person and the good of their nation are identical, then interference with national life is a violation of individual integrity and individuals who reject their nation are denying the most essential part of themselves. Those who are true to themselves must also be true to their nation. But even if this answer is accepted, it remains unclear what makes the life of a nation so central to individual identity. Fichte thinks that the importance to individuals of national identity arises from language. The very way that we think about the world, he argues, is determined by our native language. Out of the language of a people flows a culture, a point of view, a way of life: 'Men are formed by language far more than language is formed by men' (1807: 48). What concepts, particularly what ethical concepts, people find intelligible or alien, how they understand them, will depend upon the structure and history of their native language. And the way that people think about things will make certain kinds of behaviour and social relations natural. From language comes a community, an ethical life, the character of individuals. People can of course learn other languages, but it is a person's native language, the language he learns as child, Fichte insists, which shapes his way of thinking, his identity, and gives him a community. The implication seems to be that those who try to adopt foreign ways of thinking are forgetting who they are. By being untrue to their linguistic heritage they are being false to themselves.

The empirical and ethical claims made by this argument have to be untangled. There may be something correct about the idea that our native language shapes our thought, including our ethical thought, though Fichte probably exaggerates its influence. Fichte undoubtedly also over-emphasises the cultural uniformity of people who speak the same native language. But his emphasis on the centrality of language in the formation of peoples is not so important as the ethical presupposition that seems to be embedded in his argument: that being true to oneself means being true to one's culture. If this is Fichte's position, then it raises the question of how we distinguish between an undesirable imposition on a culture and an acceptable development of it; when people are being true to themselves and when they are not. If, for example, a scientific theory challenges a people's religious beliefs, and thus some of their ethical behaviour, does this count as an undesirable disruption of their cultural life or simply a development of it? Are individuals who accept the theory and criticise their religion being false to themselves and their culture? Who is in the position to make such judgments? It seems that it must be up to individuals, who are, after all, the interpreters of their culture, to decide what being true means. To prevent them from making this decision counts not only as a violation of individual freedom, but the violation of their entitlement to develop their cultural life in their own way. So if people find that foreign ideas and ways of doing things are valuable to them, then it seems that there is no basis for an objection.

However, what Fichte really feared was not that his people might adopt a few new ideas, but that the Germans would simply abandon their traditional culture in the face of French imperialism or as the result of the competition of individuals for greater material well-being. So understood, he is presenting a common idea of how individuals should live their lives, what counts as a good life and what does not. It is not good for people to change their way of life according to fashion or in order to fit the expectations of others (and it is certainly not good for others to force them to do so); it is not good for people to devote themselves to pursuing wealth or individual self-aggrandisement. But it is good for them to acknowledge and value their cultural roots and live their lives accordingly.

Raz claims that groups where membership is a matter of belonging rather than achievement – groups whose membership is determined by non-voluntary criteria – are more 'suitable for their role as primary foci of identification. Identification is more secure, less liable to be threatened, if it does not depend on accomplishment' (1990: 447). It might be objected that this idea of what is central to a good life is not generally true; that what is important to many people is that they are committed to some project, ideal or community, that they have some relations to others which they regard as central to their lives – not necessarily that they value the community to which they belong because of birth or upbringing. But whatever the plausibility of the nationalist idea of how to live the good life, it is not something that can be laid down as a moral requirement on individuals. It does not create ethical obligations to a community. For what individuals count as a good life must be in the last analysis up to them; they are entitled to decide, and whatever choice they make, even if it is foolish, is their choice. They can be criticised for being irrational or for surrendering too lightly something they would have found valuable, but we have no entitlement for saying that they failed to do a duty. To say that people ought to be loyal to their national community because this is in their best interests as individuals is not the ethical 'ought' that nationalists are looking for. Moreover, even if it is generally accepted that people are better off being true to their cultural roots and native communities, what this means can be variously interpreted. What culture? What community? It does not follow that it is the nation that I should value (rather than the people and culture of my local community, my village, my family, etc.), let alone that it is the nation that I should value the most.

So even if we manage to define what a nation is, the problem of ethical justification still remains. If, for example, a nation is a group of people who speak the same native language, it remains a question why I should regard myself as having a special ethical relation to others just because they happen to speak the same language. If race is taken as a primary criterion of nationhood – as it often was in the nineteenth century – then this not only raises difficulties about what race is and whether it is meaningful to classify people according to race, but also why being a member of a particular race should give an individual any ethical obligations. If culture is taken as the criterion, this not only raises questions about what a national culture is and how cultures should be distinguished, but also why individuals should regard it as a duty to preserve and develop their native culture.

Nationalists have sometimes argued for the existence of such an ethical obligation by use of the common analogy between the family and the nation. Just as members of a family have a duty to their family and others in it, so do the people of a nation have a duty to their nation and the people in it. A person acquires these familial and national duties simply by being born into a family or a nation, not by choice. Duty to your nation, like duty to your family, is not a contractual obligation, not one you volunteer for, but real nevertheless. There can be good reasons for refusing it. Your family or your nation may be so corrupt and oppressive that you are perfectly justified in abandoning it. But you are not entitled to abandon it and refuse to honour your obligations to the people who are part of it just because you have acquired other commitments or would prefer to do other things with your life.

Even if we accept the idea that individuals can have commitments and duties that they do not choose, the question still remains what kind of commitments these are. The nationalist argument depends for a lot of its force upon the idea that duties to the nation and duties to the family are categorical, that they hold regardless of conditions. But this is questionable. The general nature of the society in which the family is embedded affects what familial duties it is reasonable to suppose that we have. In a welfare state where everyone gets a pension and free medical care children do not have the kind of obligation to their ageing parents that they would have in a society where old people have no one to rely on for support and care but their children. If children were in addition brought up communally and husbands and wives lived independent lives, people would have virtually no family duties as such. Thus we cannot appeal to our conception of family duties in order to argue for the preservation of the family as we know it. Similarly, even if we do have duties to the people of our nation, we cannot suppose that these duties are unconditional. In a different kind of world order – in a world state, for example – there might be no reason for their existence.

What the nationalist who uses the family analogy is perhaps supposing is that we are better off, more free in a true sense, if families and nations, and thus the duties these communities entail, continue to exist. As rational individuals we will recognise this and thus seek to preserve families and nations, for in doing so we will be reconciling our individual freedom with social order in the best possible way. But even if this communitarian ideal is accepted, nationalists still have to provide a reason for thinking that the nation is the community which most deserves to be the object of love and duty. Why not the local community in which I grew up? Why not the nation I choose to adopt rather than the one I happen to have been born in? And why should I be obligated to love and cherish my nation above all other communities that I belong to or could join? Nationalists have not adequately answered these questions. The analogy between individual and nation is sometimes employed to try to persuade us that loyalty to a nation is something that exists as a matter of course. Just as individuals do not need any justification for being concerned about their own well-being (being self-concerned is only natural), so it is equally natural for people to feel obligated to their own nation. But there is nothing natural about a nation, as the history of nationalist movements makes clear. In any case, the naturalness of an attachment is no reason for regarding it as rational or ethically desirable. Hegel is right to be suspicious of any commitment that is recommended simply because it is natural.

The conception of the nation which I have been criticising can be described as a 'closed' conception. It attempts to classify people and assign them duties according to the facts of their birth or upbringing. Being a member of a nation is something that happens to an individual; it is a matter of fate and not choice. It is the closed conception of a nation that makes the analogy between the nation and the family seem so apt. However, there is another conception of the nation which sometimes figures in nationalist writings, a conception which can by contrast be called 'open'. National identity so understood is a matter of choice, not fate; your nation is the community you choose to commit yourself to. In most cases people will commit themselves to the nation in which they were born, since they were brought up to be the sort of individuals who would be inclined to make this choice. But they can legitimately decide to adopt a different allegiance.

That a nation is something an individual can choose to belong to is suggested by most of the criteria that are used to identify nations. If a nation is distinguished by its culture or its spiritual ideals or its language, then it seems that any one who is willing to adopt its culture, learn its language, accept its spiritual ideals should count as belonging to the nation. Fichte sometimes treats being German as a matter of spirit, which, logically enough, can be appreciated by those who were born elsewhere. You don't necessarily have to be born a German in order to be in favour of what Germany stands for, he says:

> Whoever believes in spirituality and in the freedom of this spirituality, and who wills the eternal development of this spirituality by freedom, wherever he may have been born and whatever language he speaks, is of our blood; he is one of us and will come over to our side. Whoever believes in stagnation, retrogression . . . wherever he may have been born and whatever language he speaks, is not German and a stranger to us.
>
> (1807: 108)

If the nation is defined by the ideals it stands for or the way of life it promotes, or the relations with others which it makes possible, or some combination of these, and if individuals commit themselves to a national community according to their own understanding about what a good life consists of, then at least we can understand why being a member of a nation imposes obligations upon individuals. The reasons are much the same as the reasons why committing oneself to a democratic community entails obligations. [People who commit themselves to an ideal or a way of life, who take this good as their good, acquire at the same time duties to their chosen community and whatever responsibilities to other members of the community that the pursuit of these ideals or the living of that way of life entails.]

The question still remains whether it is rational or moral for people to make the commitments that they make. It might indeed be argued that people who are rational and moral ought to end up with the same ideals and way of life, and that therefore an attempt to defend national differences and national self-determination by an appeal to the entitlement of people to pursue ideals collectively is going to fail. Open nations will turn out to be one big nation. Fichte suggests this when he claims that Germany is not merely a nation, but the nation – the community which because of the purity of its language and cultural life is destined to be the spiritual leader of the world. But Fichte's position not only rests on questionable assumptions about language and culture; it also depends upon a transcendental perspective – an idea of what is good for humanity and what constitutes human progress. Neither in theory nor in practice have the differences of opinion about such matters ever been resolved, and there is no reason to think that they ever will be. Individuals have as a matter of fact different ideals, different ideas about how to live, and it does not seem that there is going to be any rational or moral argument, any appeal to what human beings really are or really need, which is capable of determining that a particular way of life or ideal is the one that everyone ought to accept. This does not mean that there is no such thing as an irrational or immoral commitment, or that there is no reason for thinking that some ideals are better than others, but merely that there probably is no conception of the good that can be defended by reasons that every rational person has to accept. If this is true (or at least until it is shown to be false), a respect for individuals means respecting their commitments and communities – providing these commitments are not obviously irrational or immoral.

The more defensible conception of a nation, then, seems to be one which defines a nation as a group of people who have in common a commitment to an ideal or a way of life. Since there are, and probably always will be, differences among people concerning ideals and ways of life, there are and always will be different nations, and providing there are no rational, moral reasons to the contrary, those who belong to them are justified in defending them from anything that threatens to destroy or undermine them, and they are entitled to pass on their ideals and way of life to their children. For these commitments, and resulting duties to past and future generations, are constitutive of the identities of the people who make up their nation.

There are, however, some serious problems with this definition of the nation. First of all, it doesn't fit the facts. At best it fits those nations of immigrants, like the United States, where people are drawn together by their allegiance to certain ideals and principles – though even in the case of the United States it would be difficult to specify exactly what ideals everyone is supposed to share, since there are many ideas of what the 'American way of life' is supposed to mean. For older, more traditional nations, it is even more implausible to suppose that people are united by any set of ideals or agreements about a culture and way of life. Existing nations, like the states that they are supposed to underwrite, are incurably pluralist in their ideals, way of life, etc. Earlier I suggested that this pluralism might be a virtue rather than a problem. But the open conception, at least as defined, does not allow for much plurality, let alone explain why it is a virtue. Until we can do this, nationalism as we know it remains a mystery, and its ethical basis unexplained and unjustified.

The second major problem with the open conception of the nation is that it has disturbing implications for domestic and international politics. If commitment to a nation is a matter of choice, then there is no reason why individuals are bound to be loyal to the nation in which they happen to live. Nor is there any reason why they should be prevented from having more than one national loyalty, providing these are not incompatible. Indeed since a nation is a group of people who share the same way of life or ideals, individuals will often have national ties to people outside their state. If membership in a nation is a matter of choice, then people ought to be able to change their commitments if they choose. But none of these possibilities is compatible with the requirements that states impose upon citizens: that individuals be and remain exclusively loyal to their own state. They are also not compatible with the ideal of international organisation which nationalists and others support: a world consisting of peacefully coexisting sovereign nation-states. For in this world people must be divided into stable and fixed political units according to their national allegiance. But if people are allowed to choose their allegiances according to their convictions, then national identities will tend to overlap, and they will not be fixed or stable. A nation as an open community is likely to have a fluid membership and not one that can easily be pinned down to a territory or contained within national borders. But this means that a nation so conceived is not compatible with a world of states, let alone a politically stable world.

It is not surprising then that the closed conception of a nation, and the analogy between nation and family, remain attractive. For the closed conception promises to do what the open conception cannot do: to divide up the population of the world once and for all into mutually exclusive national groups, and in doing so provide a stable basis for political authority in a world of sovereign states. Unfortunately the promise is not fulfilled, and the closed conception is in any case ethically unsatisfactory. It is therefore not surprising that philosophers and others are so often inclined to dismiss nationalism as an irrational and pernicious doctrine. Nevertheless, in the next chapter I will defend an open conception of the nation and attempt to show how it could be the basis of a just world order.

Chapter 9

Towards a just world order

The discussion of nationalism in the last chapter makes it clear that a satisfactory conception of the nation, if there is such a thing, must be explanatorily adequate. It must provide a characterisation of the nation which is useful in accounting for the national loyalties that people actually have, though it need not endorse everything that people believe about nations. But it must also be ethically adequate. It must provide the basis for an ethical justification of nationalist loyalties, both in terms of the needs and interests of free individuals and in terms of what is required for the international world to be just. If the nation turns out to be an incoherent, ambiguous concept or if the kind of loyalty which makes nationalism possible is likely to result in political oppression, irrationality, aggression or injustice, as critics of nationalism suppose, then we will have to reject the nation as a basis for a just world order. If, on the other hand, a satisfactory account of the nation brings into question a world order and conception of international justice based upon sovereign states, then we must determine what kind of world order and idea of international justice are compatible with the self-determination of nations.

One of the main problems in providing an adequate account of the nation, I have argued, is that nations, like states, are pluralist societies: they contain people of different classes, different neighbourhoods, often of different religions and with different political and social ideals, and, especially in immigrant nations, people with different ethnic backgrounds. But at the same time, what identifies a nation is supposed to be something different from what identifies a state, with its politically determined boundaries. The people of a nation are supposed to share something which not only gives them a sense of belonging together but is the basis for loyalty and an ethical life requiring service to the nation and to the people in it. But given the pluralism of a national society, the basis for this solidarity is bound to be elusive, and the failure of nationalist philosophers to provide a clear, consistent account of what a nation is also leaves its ethical foundations in doubt. On the other hand, Rawls' 'justification' (1987) of a pluralist society in terms of the consensus about justice which it promotes is not able to account for why individuals should regard it as important to be loyal to their particular nation – whether to this England or that Romania – and important to resist cosmopolitan tendencies which seem to threaten it.

I will tackle these problems by presenting, first of all, a model of social interaction which, I claim, can serve as the basis for explaining national identity. I will then say something about what is required to make people who have these kinds of relations into a nation and what this entails as far as their behaviour and conception of self are concerned. In doing this I do not claim to be giving a historical account of the genesis of nations, though if my account is to be true to what people understand a nation to be, it must have some explanatory value. My principal aim, however, is to make the notion of a nation intelligible in much the same way as Hobbes and Rawls attempt to make intelligible how a political consensus is possible among individuals who have contrary objectives and allegiances. Finally, I will describe what justice means in such a national society and the implications of the existence of nations for international relations.

To form the basis of a nation, I claim, what is needed is not simply an overlapping consensus, but overlapping communities, what I will call a society of interlocking communities. As the name indicates, it is a society which consists of groups, a society of individuals who have various community allegiances. The communities that individuals belong to, I assume, are relatively long-term features of a society, and not groups that people form just for a particular occasion (e.g. for organising a fête), and they are not groups created by the classifications of social theorists. People are aware of belonging to their communities and value their membership in them. They are communities of many different kinds, and individuals belong to them for a variety of reasons and have different levels of commitment to them. Some are united by common ideals or a common doctrine (for example, groups with particular social or religious ideals); some are organised to pursue particular economic interests; some are based on territory or residence (e.g. a village community); some are united by a shared heritage or way of life (ethnic groups, and sometimes racial groups); some come together to perform a definite task or function (a town council, a professional organisation); the purpose of some is primarily social (a sporting club). Some of the communities are formal: they have a definite organisation and charter of membership, meetings, etc. Others are much more informal, more a matter of people recognising that they have common attitudes or concerns, and thus being sometimes prepared to give each other support. What is important about all these communities, formal and informal, is that people in them recognise themselves to have common interests or concerns, and thus some kind of bond with each other.

Communitarians make a distinction between groups or communities which people join in order to further some predefined interest, groups which are properly described as 'contractual', and communities which contribute to defining a person's objectives, determining who he/she is and what his/her interests are. This distinction is important, but there is no easy way of distinguishing between the kind of groups which are merely contractual and those which contribute to defining a person's interests and objectives. Individuals may join a political organisation in order to pursue certain predefined objectives, as Rousseau's story of the social contract supposes; but as the result of working with other people, defining goals through collective participation, they may come to regard these collective aims as their aims, and achieving the political objectives of the group as an important goal of their lives. They may as a result become a different kind of person. The commitments that individuals can and do form are various, and they may be committed to their communities to a greater or lesser degree. We can assume that individuals will be committed to some organisations more than others. For example, they are likely to be committed to a religious or political group in a deeper, more constitutive way than they are committed to their sporting club (though the reverse is not unknown). There may be good reasons for saying that people ought to have certain kinds of commitments or are better off in some communities than in others. But I make no judgments here about what communities people ought to be attached to and how; nor do I make any prescriptions about how groups ought to conduct their affairs. I do assume in this model society that everyone is a member of communities and that for each individual some of their community commitments are important to them and contribute to defining who they are and determining how they ought to live their lives.

I also assume that these communities are generally self-interested. They are dedicated to pursuing their own collective goals and/or the interests of the individuals who make them up. They are not, in other words, communities formed to pursue the good of the society as a whole. People in them may have no conception of such a general good. My starting point is thus similar in many respects to the starting point of Hobbes, Rawls and others who begin with self-interested agents and consider what agreements with each other they may be prepared to make. The difference is that the individuals I start with are organised socially, and this social organisation has a complex form. The agreements they make, their ideas about justice, the kind of political relations they would be prepared to accept will be influenced by the kind of communities they have and the relationships between them.

Depending on the nature of a community and the extent of the commitment, individuals will regard themselves as having specific duties to the group and its members. In some cases they will be minimal, merely what is needed in order to co-operate for the sake of a common purpose. In other cases they will be extensive; they will require that individuals take some responsibility for satisfying the needs of other group members. Whether or not the nature of their activity or commitment requires this, people who participate in communities and develop relationships in them will be inclined to appreciate the desires and points of view of other members, and sometimes inclined to give them help and support.

The assumption that individuals belong to communities and are committed, sometimes deeply, to them, flies in the face of a common view about modern pluralist societies: that members of these societies have become increasingly autonomous and devoid of important social relations. Having been detached from the pre-modern communities which gave life a meaning, individuals are now said to exist as social atoms, belonging nowhere and to nothing.[1] I believe that this idea of modern life is an exaggeration. What is certainly true is that economic and political developments have tended to undermine or destroy those traditional communities in which most individuals were at one time totally immersed: the traditional village, the tribe, the clan, the family. But if we understand 'community' in a broader sense, then it is far from plausible that modern life has destroyed all of our allegiances or important associations. It has in fact generated new groups, new causes and new focuses for loyalty and group activities – political parties, unions, interest groups, social movements, etc. Those who complain that community has vanished from the modern world generally have as their ideal the kind of community which Hegel tried to show could exist in the state and some utopians think could exist in small democratic political societies: a community in which individuals are at one with their social world, and are not subject to conflicting demands.

I have argued that such communities are not a viable option and are, in any case, not all that desirable from an ethical point of view. There may, nevertheless, be some truth to the idea that an increasing number of people in modern societies have no significant relations with other people (except, perhaps, with family and friends). My model of society is not a reflection of how things actually are, but a starting point for understanding what social relations in a nation are like, or what they could become under certain conditions.

In this society made up of communities I am assuming that most groups are open. This means membership is not in most cases determined by birth, but by interests, ideals, occupation, social position – something an individual can acquire or aspire to. This means that people are generally free to choose their allegiances and affiliations, and they have a range of options to choose from. I also assume that most people belong to more than one community and have more than one commitment. For example, a person might at one and the same time be a member of a religious group, have an ethnic or neighbourhood allegiance, belong to an environmental pressure group, etc. Some of these groups are likely to be more important to an individual than others, but it is not generally the case in this society that one community attachment is of such importance to a person that he/she would give up all other commitments for its sake.

As the term 'interlocking communities' suggests, the society is woven out of a network of overlapping communities. These communities have overlapping objectives and concerns, and to accomplish their goals or pursue the interests of their members they need the co-operation or acquiescence of others. But more important, the communities interlock through their members, i.e. the membership of each group overlaps with the membership of others in such a way that each individual is linked directly or indirectly to all other individuals. For example, a person might be connected to one group of people through a church, another through membership in an ethnic community, and at the same time be associated with other people as a member of a political group. Each of the members of these groups will be affiliated with people in other communities, and so on through society. That everyone will be connected in this way is a likely result of the fact that everyone is a member of at least one community, that most will be members of more than one, and that most communities are open communities.

A society of interlocking communities, I claim, is predisposed to peaceful and co-operative relationships. This predisposition exists not simply because of the benefits of inter-group co-operation, for as we have seen, people are not always predisposed to be co-operative even when co-operation would benefit them. What is important is that in the interlocking society there is no community the members of which are excluded from other groups, and thus it is difficult to single out any category of people as the enemy, as a suitable object for hatred and aggression. Moreover, the interlocking nature of group relationships will tend to dampen down conflicts and prevent them from turning into hostilities. If some individuals in community A are also affiliated with people in community B and some people in community B have affiliations with people in community C, then A will hesitate to commit an aggressive act against C for fear of disruptions to relationships with people in B. In any case, people in community A are likely to regard people in community C as having an indirect connection with themselves – for some people who are Bs are at the same time Cs – and for this reason will not be inclined to regard C as an enemy.

In such a society people for the same reason will be inclined to establish and adhere to processes and practices which are generally agreed to be just. This doesn't mean that they will not need a government to maintain law and order and regulate their affairs, but it ensures that a government will be able to govern without use of extreme force and suppression. It can do this because people are motivated to act according to moral principles and can agree on, or at least make compromises concerning, processes and principles of justice. Thus this model of society can be regarded as filling one of the explanatory gaps left in Rawls' account of the achievement of an overlapping consensus in a pluralist society. It is able to explain how people with different objectives, who belong to communities with contrary ideals and interests, can not only manage to achieve a modus vivendi for the sake of peace, but will be motivated by moral requirements.

This account of how moral relations become possible suggests that the difference between a peaceful and just society and a society prone to civil war and the oppression of minorities is that in the latter people are divided into mutually exclusive communities along the lines of religion, race, ethnicity, ideology, etc. Since there is little or no overlap in community membership, co-operative relationships will easily be destroyed by real or imagined grievances or conflicting interests. It is less likely in such a society that a modus vivendi, even if this is achieved, will turn into relationships based upon justice. For those who have power will tend to use it to extract whatever concessions they can.

What principles or ideals of justice will people in a society of interlocking communities be likely to agree to? Basic to an interlocking society in which most groups are open is the presumption that individuals ought to have an equal freedom of association, an entitlement to form and maintain communities according to their interests, needs, achievements or sense of self. A general commitment to freedom of association is compatible, it should be said, with the existence of some communities which are not open to whoever wants to join. It would be unreasonable, for example, for people to demand to be admitted to an American Indian tribe on the grounds that they want to live in an Indian way. For such a community, like the family, is based upon kinship relations. What freedom of association means, above all, is that no authority will have the entitlement to insist that individuals remain exclusively members of any one community or prevent them from forming new relationships.

It will also be a basic principle of this society that communities should be able to conduct their relations and pursue their interests as their members please, providing they don't harm other communities or individuals. This principle assumes that it is generally up to a community to determine for itself the terms of co-operation between individuals, what entitlements they have, what resources should be regarded as common, what goods or services distributed among them and how. Intervention in the internal affairs of a community will usually not be justified, except to prevent great harm to individuals (especially if they request intervention), and in order to prevent violations of the freedom of individuals to associate. It might be justified, for example, to interfere in the affairs of a religious sect, if the education programme for its members' children prevents any contact with outsiders or the ideas of outsiders.

The third basic principle is that disputes between communities be decided according to procedures that the parties can all agree to (or are at least willing to compromise on). There is going to be no formula for resolving such disputes in the interlocking society. We cannot suppose that all communities are equal or have equal rights. Some are much more important to their members than others; some represent more people; some are concerned with more important interests than others. Communities change or disappear as individuals change their ideals or ideas of what they want. So what procedures or guidelines are appropriate will depend on the needs of the groups in question and the relationships of their members. In the interlocking society, for example, it will be accepted that trade unions are entitled to make demands upon the companies which employ their members, even though there is no agreement between the parties concerning what demands are justified. Nevertheless, we can expect that all will be inclined to accept certain procedures for settling disputes and will be prepared to make compromises with each other. Class warfare will be unlikely because people who belong to unions and employer groups have other allegiances in common and will thus be reluctant to create divisions which threaten these other relationships. Irreconcilable ideological, racial or ethnic conflict which makes compromise between groups difficult or impossible will also be absent. What is important is not a consensus about a particular principle for resolving conflicts – I am not assuming that there will be such a consensus – but social relations which encourage compromise and conciliation.

In a society of interlocking communities no group or individual is likely to use political power to dominate others. Those who rule are likely to depend upon the support of a number of communities, and therefore will hesitate to use power in a way that alienates some of these groups, and since each is connected to others in the web of social relationships, no community is likely to be singled out as the object of persecution. Moreover, political leaders themselves will be inclined to abide by the principles of justice which are basic to the society. This does not mean that there will be no injustice or suffering in the society of interlocking communities. We can expect that in this society, the powerful will sometimes attempt to take advantage of the weak, that there will be complaints about the administration of justice, disagreements about what that involves; there will be disputes, strikes, protests, boycotts. But at least it should be possible for injustice to be remedied and disputes to be settled to the satisfaction of most people.

There are two important differences between the society of interlocking communities and the societies which people think of as nations. One of them is that people in the former do not necessarily have any consciousness of the network of communities as such, let alone value its existence. They think of themselves as belonging to various communities but not necessarily as belonging to an overarching community to which they owe a special loyalty. The second is that their principles of justice do not require universal distribution of resources. Goods and services are supposed to be distributed within communities, depending upon the nature of the groups and the relation of the members, but there are no arrangements for distributing goods or services among all individuals. In this society communities may guard their autonomy jealously, and will tend to resist the suggestion that resources which they want to use for their own projects and purposes be taken away and given to others to whom they have no direct connection. The society of interlocking communities is thus not a nation as this is usually understood, but it satisfies the social preconditions for becoming one. A nation, as I define it, is a society of interlocking communities which has become conscious of itself – a society in which individuals are aware of the interconnections of their communities and value them. The history of the rise of nations is thus a history of how these interconnections came to exist and how people came to appreciate them.

There is probably no single correct account of what makes a society into a nation. Benedict Anderson (1983: Chs 2, 3) stresses the importance of shared communication in producing a national consciousness – the circulation in the common vernacular language of literature, newspapers, etc. This kind of contact, he claims, not only informs people about the existence of others and what they are doing, but gives them a sense of belonging to a society in which their activities coexist and interweave with the activities of countless others. Gellner and Walzer stress the role of shared political institutions in creating a national identity, the sense of having a 'common life'.[2] However national consciousness is created, what underlies its existence, I am suggesting, are interlocking social relations among those groups and communities that individuals value. Where this is missing and cannot easily be created, having a common language and common political institutions will probably not be sufficient to make a population into a nation.

Nationalist literature makes it clear that the formation of a nation goes along with a change of consciousness which is sometimes exhilarating and liberating. Becoming conscious of being part of an extensive network of communities and individuals enhances individuals' sense of who they are, encouraging them to look beyond the boundaries of their particular communities, enabling them to appreciate and even feel sympathy towards people who were before unknown and strange. From this broader perspective they are able to appreciate what is precious about their own communities and way of life, and at the same time are in a better position to be critical of aspects of their way of life. The widening of horizons gives them more choices about how they should live and what communities they should be part of. The development of a national consciousness thus increases the freedom of individuals and it is also a form of moral development: people are as a result more inclined to appreciate the interests and needs of those who belong to different, and sometimes remote, communities – more inclined to be concerned about the well-being of all members of the society. If individuals properly value the freedom which being a member of the nation promotes, and the association with others that it makes possible, then they will also come to value the nation itself. They will form groups and organisations dedicated to pursuing the national good as they perceive it, and they will try to ensure that the activities of their other communities are compatible with the survival of the nation. Given the interlocking relationships of communities, this should not be difficult.

One of the effects of this change in moral consciousness will be the development of a new sense of what justice means. People will now be more prepared to take responsibility for all members of their society, ensuring, at least, that everyone has sufficient resources for the proper exercise of their freedom of association. This means that individuals and groups will be prepared to accept some interference in their activities for the sake of justice. But it does not mean that they will necessarily agree on what distributive justice requires. There will be continual conflicts between those who want only minimal aid to go to the disadvantaged, those who are willing to accept Rawls' difference principle and those whose conception of justice is more egalitarian. People will sometimes resent the interference in their activities that a policy of distributive justice requires and will fear, sometimes justifiably, that their communities will as a result be weakened or even destroyed. But the existence of a national consciousness will encourage them to accept distributive justice in principle and their co-operative relations should make it possible for them to reach compromises in practice.

What this story is supposed to do is to fill up another explanatory gap in Rawls' account of the development of just relations in a pluralist society. It is not co-operative relations among communities that bring about the acceptance of some form of distributive justice, but the existence of a national consciousness that involves both the ideas that as members of a society we have something that unites us, and that our common association is of value. This account of the nation as a self-conscious community of interlocking communities also helps to explain why individuals in a pluralist society – a society in which there is no general agreement about ideals, principles, way of life – can nevertheless develop a strong sense of community. This unity, as I have presented it, arises out of their interlocking social relations and the value they find in them. Given that this is so, national symbols, slogans, historical traditions can mean different things to different groups of people in the nation without this difference becoming something that divides them. For the people of a nation can disagree, often radically, on political and social questions and yet be prepared to maintain and value the framework in which these disagreements occur.

By means of the conception of the nation as a community of interlocking communities we can also find a way, it seems, to justify loyalty to a particular state. If a state protects, enhances or makes possible the national life that people value, then they will also believe that it deserves their loyalty. It is their particular state to which they are obligated, because it is their nation, the particular communities, relationships and people in it, which are valued. Individuals who live in good states thus have a number of related reasons for being patriots: its institutions not only protect their freedom as individuals, their lives and their property, they protect the communities which individuals value, and in addition the network of community relationships which make up the nation. There may be no states in the world which do all these things well, but if the social basis for national unity exists in a state, then it seems reasonable to hope that an imperfect state can become a better one.

The fact that people value their nation and are loyal to their state doesn't mean that their nation or state deserves to be valued, or for that matter that the ethical life of the nation is a good ethical life or that the conception of justice made possible by the existence of nations is the idea of justice we ought to accept. It is a premise of this book that there is no metaphysical measuring stick, no 'original position' which we can use to determine what conception of justice we ought to accept for either national or international society. Nevertheless, the problems associated with other ideas of community give us some reasons for thinking that the ethical life of the nation is the better alternative. As a community of interlocking communities, the nation provides for individuals a form of liberty that is not adequately provided for in Hegel's state or in the small democratic community. In the nation individuals are not confined to a community which demands their total loyalty and makes it difficult for them to criticise or question their commitments. The ethical life of the nation therefore allows for dissent and for people to live according to their different conceptions of what a good life is.

It has to be acknowledged that this ethical life has costs as well as benefits. Individuals will have divided loyalties, be subject to competing ethical demands which they will have to reconcile as best they can, and in doing so they will never be free of doubt or guilt. They will never be in complete agreement about what their nation is, how it should develop, or what ethical duties commitment to it requires. This means that they will never achieve the kind of social life which Hegel wished to create in the state and utopians in the democratic community – a society in which consensus on values is universal, in which conflicts are resolved in a higher synthesis, and ethical requirements are clear. I have argued, however, that this kind of social life and the conception of freedom that goes with it are probably unrealisable and in any case not desirable. Conflict and diversity do exist and cannot be suppressed without injustice. Thus a pluralist society that allows individuals to choose their communities is a society that reconciles individual freedom with social existence in the most satisfactory way.

The life of the nation not only makes it possible for diverse individuals and groups to co-operate with each other but brings them together in a community which gives a greater meaning and value to their lives. Moreover, by doing this, it makes it more likely that individuals in this community of communities will take sufficient responsibility for each other to ensure that some of its resources are used to help individuals and groups who are the least well off. Thus the ethical life of the nation seems to make it possible to realise an ideal which, I argued, is implicit in the recognition of the importance of individual freedom: that each person should have what is required to exercise this freedom.

However, whether a view about justice or the ethical life is satisfactory depends not only on how it affects the individuals in communities where it is accepted. We also need to know what implications it has for relations between communities. In some respects my account of the nation seems to support the idea of nationalist thinkers that a world of nations is likely to be a peaceful and just world. It serves, at least, to counter some of the criticisms made of nationalism and to alleviate some of the fears about the propensities of nations. The nation is not intrinsically war-like or aggressive. Its formation does not require opposition to others or hatred of outsiders. Moreover, the nature of a nation's identity suggests that as a social entity it will be defensive rather than aggressive. The 'general will' of a nation expresses itself in international affairs as simply a will to survive, for this is all that the people in the nation can recognise as a legitimate collective aim. All rational people will regard the continuation of the nation as important, and will be prepared to defend it. But there is no further objective which they will recognise as being in accordance with the will of their nation – as opposed to the will of some particular group in it. This should mean that citizens of a nation will tend to oppose actions by their government which seem to favour sectional interests, and that they will tend to oppose any action by their state in international affairs which is not clearly required for the defence of the nation.

However, even if this is true, it does not follow that nations can be depended on to live in peace. In a world where resources are limited the possibility remains that nations in pursuit of the requirements of national survival may come into conflict with each other. The possibility also remains, as Freud feared (1933), that there are dark psychological forces associated with the behaviour of people in groups which can cause irrational outbursts of chauvinism. But a nation as a group does not seem to be in a worse position than other forms of community to resist aggressive and destructive impulses or find peaceful ways of resolving conflicts with others. Indeed by encouraging tolerance and co-operation among a diversity of communities it may be better able to do so than small democratic communities and Hegelian states. If people have learned to live according to principles and procedures of justice within their national society, if they get value and satisfaction out of participating in the life of their nation and the communities that make it up, then why can't we suppose, as did Kant, that the habit of being tolerant and law-abiding will come to predominate in international relationships?

On the other hand, some of the international problems associated with nationalism remain. If a world of nations is a world of autonomous nation-states, as many nationalists assume it should be, then it is reasonable to doubt whether a just world can be achieved peacefully or achieved at all. The formula 'one nation, one state' not only assumes that it is possible in an uncontroversial way to divide the world up into discrete nations, but it also ignores disputes among nations about territory, and the resulting dangers associated with the break-up of multi-nation states. Moreover, many of the nation-states which come into being are likely to be too small to be truly autonomous; and some because of geographical position or resources will be much richer than others. Being members of a caring, sharing nation won't help the least well-off people of the world if they don't have anything to share.

Problems associated with dependency and poverty might be alleviated if nation-states can join together in federations. These federations may, like Kant's, impose a minimal obligation on members, or they may be more similar to what I have called a regional state.

From a nationalist point of view, it should be said, there is nothing inherently wrong with the idea of a multi-nation state so long as the parties to the contract of federation consent and the government does not favour one nation at the expense of others. Since nations are made rather than born (in spite of nationalist mythology which asserts the contrary), there is no reason why a multi-national state should not eventually become a nation-state – perhaps as the result of a long, peaceful association in which individuals of the different nations form communities with each other and develop the interlocking relationships which are fundamental to national identity. Language differences are a barrier to close association of people from different nations, but not an insuperable one: people can learn each other's language, or sometimes find a common language to use for cross-national communication. It is not impossible, for example, to suppose that the people of Europe might someday come to think of themselves first and foremost as Europeans, and only secondarily as French or German or British. In this case, a united Europe will be in a true sense their nation.

However, the question of what kind of states are compatible with the existence of a world of nations raises a more fundamental difficulty about the relation between nations and states. For one thing, if nations can be made, if there is nothing inherently wrong with a multi-nation state, then we cannot justify an international status quo by reference to the inviolability or inalterability of existing nation-states. Nationalism thus does not provide an insuperable barrier to cosmopolitan schemes (some of them, at least) for reorganising the world – though it does put forward considerations which cosmopolitans usually ignore. There is nothing sacred about presently existing nation-states, and there are no borders which are unquestionable or simply natural.

More important, the conception of the nation which I have been defending, like the open conception of the nation discussed in the last chapter, is not easily made compatible with any particular idea about how the borders of states ought to be drawn. A nation as a community of interlocking communities is not an eternal, immutable, precisely delineated social entity which can be tied down to a particular territory or confined within borders. People within a state are indeed likely to have religious, ethnic, cultural, ideological, etc. affiliations with people living in other states. A system of interlocking communities does not naturally stop at the borders of states. This means, first of all, that the communities which make up the nation can present a challenge to the sovereignty of the state. The loyalty of citizens may be divided between their obligations to their state and their ties to people outside their country. It also means that the problem of defining what a nation is – who belongs to it and who does not – is not simply a problem of making distinctions in borderline cases. A nation is an inherently dynamic social entity. It depends upon the existence of social relations and people's attitudes towards them, and both of these factors are subject to change. People who belong to several nations can, as I suggested, come to think of themselves as belonging to one nation, or, more commonly in our world, people who belong to one nation can as the result of ideological divisions or persecution come to regard themselves as members of different nations.

The fluidity of nations poses a problem for a system of states, whatever form this system takes. For states, if they are to exercise sovereignty over a territory, must have fixed borders; they must divide up the world's territory and population into mutually exclusive entities. The tension between the dynamics of the nation and the requirements of states thus creates a problem for world order. It means there is never likely to be a status quo which is immune to nationalist challenges to existing borders, and thus the promise nationalists hold out of achieving a stable world order based upon nation-states turns out to be illusory. It also means that the attempt to justify the existence of any particular system of states by reference to the value of nations is going to fail. The defence of the nation-state as a body that protects and enhances the nation turns out to be much more limited than nationalists have supposed. Once again we have to conclude that nationalist considerations cannot defend the nation-state against all proposed changes to world order.

There are two ways in which the practical and moral problems associated with the relation of nations and states might be solved. The first is to make nation-states into closed societies in the way that Fichte (1800) suggested. Citizens will be discouraged from close contacts with communities outside their borders, either through restrictions on movement or by punishing 'treasonable' activities. Institutions of state will try to ensure through education and welfare policies that citizens develop and maintain co-operative relations with each other and are, above all, loyal to their nation-state. The nation will be sculpted to fit the state. This means that if the borders of nation-states can be fixed in a way that most people find satisfactory, the policies of states will ensure that they remain fixed and unchallenged.

Some of the problems with the idea of the closed society have already been discussed. It seems to require, as Fichte assumed, economic autonomy. For interdependent economic relations are likely to lead to the establishment of international communities of one sort or another. But most modern states would find it difficult, if not impossible, to become autonomous, and in any case, citizens will regard the measures that would have to be taken as a restriction of their freedom. And rightly so. For the achievement of a closed society would not only mean curtailing some of their economic activities, but it would also restrict their freedom of association. Since the freedom of people to form and maintain communities according to their needs, desires, convictions, or their sense of who they are, is basic to the ethical life of a nation, attempts by states to prevent them from doing so are illegitimate. The closed state and the open nation are not compatible with each other.

This incompatibility may help to explain some of the pathologies historically associated with nationalism and nation-states. In their efforts to preserve the integrity of the state from the dynamics of the nation, leaders may be tempted to engage in hostilities with other states as a way of forcing people to become patriots, to come to the defence of their state in order to preserve their nation. Under these circumstances hatred of an enemy will come to play an essential role in the national psyche, bringing citizens together behind their leaders when other measures fail. War, or acquiring the power to threaten others, will be the activity which defines and unites the nation-state. And given that there is no proper social basis for this unity, we cannot expect that there will be any rational bounds to conflict. If this is a correct account of the conflicts that sometimes occur, then the problem posed by nationalism is not the result of the nature of nations or the nature of states, considered by themselves, but is found in the relation between nation and state.

The second way in which the problems associated with the relation of nations and states might be solved is to try to work out a way in which the world could consist of nations without being a world of sovereign nation-states. What such a world would be like and whether it is feasible is difficult to determine, and I do not claim to be able to provide more than a rough sketch. Nevertheless, beginning from the conception of justice appropriate to the nation, it is worthwhile attempting to work out what political and social conditions would have to be like if justice in this sense were to prevail universally in a world where association is not limited by state boundaries.

In the world society I am imagining freedom of association will be the fundamental right of all individuals. There will be no limitations on the entitlement of individuals to form and maintain communities according to conviction or desire, except what is entailed by the equal right of others to do so. Inevitably this will mean that people will form associations with others across borders and some of these communities will be centrally important to the lives of individuals. People already have ethnic, religious and ideological ties with those who live in other countries, and these associations would no doubt play a much larger role in people's lives if the development of these communities were not curtailed or limited by the obligations imposed by states. In an increasingly interdependent world, people are likely to form new regional and international communities of various kinds. Some will exist only for the economic convenience of the members, but others have a potential to become the sort of communities in which people form their identity as persons – their sense of who they are and what duties they have to others.

We will assume that as these cross-national associations develop, institutions of state will become less able and inclined to impose their authority on them. This does not mean that states will wither away and cease to exist. There will continue to be a need for some political body to make laws for those who live in a territory, and states will probably continue to be the most appropriate political bodies for this purpose. But increasingly in making decisions and exercising political power, institutions of state will have to take into account the determinations of communities whose activities are not, at least entirely, within the scope of their authority. These communities, whether religious groups, ethnic groups, pressure groups, bodies of people who have similar economic interests, are likely to become more formally organised; they will engage in some kind of collective decision-making process and will make demands upon states as well as upon each other. Institutions of state will negotiate agreements with these communities; they will not be in a position to lay down the law.

As more and more individuals come to participate in communities that reach beyond their national borders the world will develop into a society of interlocking communities. This does not mean that nations will disappear or that the world will ever consist of one united nation. It will probably continue to be important to people that they are French rather than German or Mexican rather than Canadian. People will continue to speak different languages and continue to have a special sympathy for people they perceive as sharing their way of life or culture. They will form organisations to protect and develop this heritage. But nations as such will become more amorphous and indefinable. Being a member of a nation will become more obviously a matter of choice, of conviction and not birth. It will become possible, as Fichte sometimes imagined, for people to be members of a nation no matter where they happen to live. There is indeed no reason why they can't belong to more than one nation. But loyalty to the state or the nation will become for most individuals one loyalty among others, and not necessarily the most important one.

As the powers of states become more limited, we can expect that other communities will take over some of the tasks that governments are now expected to perform. Ethnic communities, religious bodies, even companies, co-operatives and trade unions will be increasingly able and willing to take on the responsibility for ensuring the welfare of individual members. They will now have the formal decision-making capacity for undertaking this task, and because of the nature of their association and their participation in decision-making individual members will be inclined to accept this responsibility. This means that communities through their formal institutions will distribute the resources they administer – or those they can obtain through their activities or levies on members – according to their customs, nature and the collective decisions of their members. Education, the circulation of information, activities which encourage personal development, will similarly come to be carried on within communities, according to the needs of individuals in them and the purpose of their association.

There are some obvious similarities between the nature and development of the world society of interlocking communities and the world state described in Chapter 5. As in the case of the world state we can assume that international associations of people will be encouraged by economic interdependence and the need to solve common world problems. We can also suppose that in the world society of interlocking communities there will be an increasing number of regional and international regulatory bodies for co-ordinating relations between communities and between communities and states, judicial bodies for arbitrating disputes etc., and even bodies for enforcing joint decisions. Nevertheless, there are significant differences between the world state and the society of interlocking communities. The society of interlocking communities is based upon communities and depends upon community relationships among individuals, some of which contribute to forming the very identity of these individuals, their attitudes, goals and values. This basis will be reflected in the ideas about justice which are appropriate to an interlocking society and in consequent ideas about what international political institutions should and should not do.

We can assume that the ideas of justice that will prevail in the world society of interlocking communities will be similar to ideas of justice appropriate for smaller-scale societies of interlocking communities. Freedom of association will be a fundamental right. Individuals will be entitled to form and maintain their communities as they choose. This does not mean that all communities will be open to everyone. There may sometimes be good reason for limiting the membership of a community to those who happen to be born in a particular place or of a particular clan, but we can reasonably assume that the membership of most communities depends on choice rather than birth. States will be another kind of community and their existence and nature will depend upon the desires and choices of the individuals and other communities attached to them. If a smaller community of people wants to secede and form their own political society, then this should be allowed, though compensation may have to be paid to those individuals and communities who are disadvantaged by this action. It is likely that states in the world of interlocking communities will become much smaller than they are now – but at the same time there will probably be regional and world bodies which play a role in co-ordinating economic and social activities and resolving disputes.

In world society there may not exist any political body whose responsibility it is to ensure that freedom of association is universally upheld. Obedience to this principle will thus depend on it being generally recognised as a fundamental requirement and on there being means for punishing violators. Since communities in this society will have many ways of putting pressure on other communities, this requirement should be enforceable. The system will not work perfectly, but so long as it is possible in world society to correct injustices, as long as communities are willing to accept procedures for settling disputes, freedom of association will be generally recognised and practised.

Justice in a world society of interlocking communities also requires that communities be able to carry on their affairs and pursue their interests as their members choose, providing they do not harm other individuals and communities and providing they do not interfere with the freedom of association of individuals. This means that what 'rights' individuals have, what they are entitled to, will be determined by the communities to which they belong. Outsiders will not be entitled to interfere in order to insist that every community recognises a tablet of human rights, a law of property, a particular idea of the good, or even to enforce a particular idea of fairness. In a world society based upon communities we are not entitled to assume that there are any ideas about individual rights, apart from the right of free association, or any views about what individuals are entitled to, that are universally accepted or acceptable.

On the other hand, the interlocking nature of world society, the right of free association, the open nature of most communities, means that individuals are not likely to be trapped in oppressive communities. If, for example, members of a minority group are persecuted within their state the other communities to which they belong are likely to put pressure on the government to change its policy. The interdependence of communities will ensure that such pressure can be successfully applied. Moreover, people who belong to a number of communities, who can make choices about what community they belong to, do not have to put up with oppressive or authoritarian relationships. They have ways of escaping them or ways of forcing them to change.

A just world society also requires that relations between communities be just. Once again we cannot assume that all communities are equal or have the same objectives or requirements. Thus we cannot expect to find any principles, no matter how general, appropriate for all interactions. But as in the case of the model of an interlocking society described earlier, we can reasonably suppose that disputes and conflicts will be settled by procedures which all parties will recognise as fair. This agreement will be encouraged not simply by co-operative relationships between communities but by the fact that they have overlapping membership.

In the interlocking world society there are likely to be procedures that a community can use to claim compensation from others for harm done; procedures that small communities can use to claim a share of resources from the larger, regional community to which they belong. But there are not likely to be any procedures for sharing goods and resources among individuals in the society as a whole. The kind of society in which such a distributive requirement is likely to be perceived as just, I have argued, is a community where people have a sense of belonging together and value this association more than the autonomy of their more particular communities. This may never happen in world society as a whole. The existence of the 'deep comradeship' which encourages people to take responsibility for each other's welfare may depend upon their having a limited community, an identity different from others. If this is so, then the world will remain a society of communities rather than a community of communities.

This means that the existence of a just world society is compatible with inequalities within communities and inequalities among communities – this is the price paid for valuing community autonomy and allowing difference. But in an interlocking society there are some reasons for thinking that individuals will not be persecuted or impoverished. International communities will include people from all parts of the world; they will have the means to distribute goods and services among members, and because of the importance of their association they will generally be inclined to regard doing so as a matter of justice. Communities in the interlocking society will be able to make legitimate demands on each other which will be taken seriously and judged according to just procedures. We can expect that the result will often be a redistribution of resources to exploited or disadvantaged groups.

The world society of interlocking communities will not be a 'utopia'. There will be conflict and struggle; some individuals will suffer and live unhappy lives. Some people and communities will have more resources and power than others and will try to use it to further their own ends. There will be selfishness, greed, competition. But there will also be a general respect for the communities which individuals want to form and maintain, a tolerance for their different values and ways of life, and a predisposition to settle conflicts peacefully through just procedures. This consensus about justice will no doubt be backed up by international judicial bodies and regulatory agencies, but how far the society of interlocking communities moves in the direction of world government is something for the people of the future to decide.

Conclusion

In my approach to a theory of international justice I have aimed to show how four important but difficult-to-reconcile moral objectives might be achieved in the international world: promotion of individual liberty, respect for the communities which individuals do or could value, a distribution of resources which would ensure that all individuals are able to exercise their liberty and maintain their community life, and peaceful relations among communities based upon principles or procedures which all can agree are fair. A just world order is a world in which all of these objectives are realised and made compatible to the extent that this is possible.

By emphasising the value of community my standpoint takes seriously the communitarian insistence that individuals form themselves and their ideas of the ethical in the framework of their social relations and through their commitments to their communities. Individual well-being and integrity are thus inseparable from the integrity and well-being of community. The world is as a matter of fact divided into communities, and most people regard the continued existence of their state, their nation, as extremely, even supremely, important. A theory of justice has to take these loyalties seriously, but at the same time it cannot avoid considering whether they are justified. The very existence of a theory of international justice requires that we be able to make moral judgments about the behaviour and nature of communities and the rationality of people's commitments to them. A theory of justice also has to make judgments about the different ideas that philosophers and others have put forward about what kind of communities the world ought to contain.

The desirability of a community or of a proposal for a world order can be judged, I have argued, in terms of how compatible it is with the realisation of the other moral objectives: with individual liberty, peaceful relations among communities, the well-being of all individuals. What it means to promote individual freedom depends in turn upon the social framework in which individuals form their conceptions of who they are and what they ought to do. In a world of communities freedom means, above all, freedom to associate, freedom of individuals to form and join communities, to maintain their community life according to their own ideas of what is good and in their interests. However, to be free in any real sense an individual has to be capable of making rational judgments about his/her community, making choices about commitments based upon knowledge of personal needs and of the opportunities available. The importance of realising the value of freedom has thus led me to reject a common communitarian ideal: the community in which members are so much at one with each other and the requirements of their ethical life that there is no real conflict possible between inclination and duty, and no divided loyalties. In the real world individuals do as a matter of fact have divided loyalties as well as goals of their own, and their identity as individuals, their goals and moral objectives, are formed not simply by being members of communities but in the course of having to reconcile the demands of different communities. This is a situation that makes modern life difficult, but it also helps to make us free. I argue that a world in which individuals have a number of community allegiances provides the best possible way of reconciling freedom with community.

By assuming individual freedom to be a value I will perhaps be accused of adopting a totalising, transcendental perspective from which to pontificate about the world. If so, many communitarians themselves can be similarly accused, for they too have generally assumed that individual autonomy is of value and have tried to show how freedom can be made compatible with, and can even be enhanced by, social life. Like the communitarians, I have tried to show how this project affects the conception of freedom itself and brings to the fore considerations which cosmopolitans generally ignore. And by finding the ground of individual freedom in social relations, I have tried to show how such an approach can eschew metaphysical or theological ideas of the self and the will.

Nevertheless, it has to be acknowledged that the idea that individuals have an equal entitlement to freedom, however freedom is interpreted, belongs to a particular philosophical tradition. This ideal is not universal and it has not always existed. It is, I have suggested, the product of particular political developments which took place first in the western world – above all, the creation of pluralist national societies in which religion and tradition could no longer be counted on to underwrite political authority or moral requirements. But if freedom as a value has a historical and cultural origin, whatever exactly this may be, how can we use it as a universal standard for judging societies present and future? On what basis can we say that a future world order in which freedom is realised is better than a world order that realises contrary values?

The only possible answer to this question is a practical one. Most people in the world do live in pluralist societies. The day of the traditional, exclusive, homogeneous community is over – except for those few people still living in tribal societies, and even they by choice or necessity have had to come to terms with plurality. To undo the developments of several hundred years would require wars, revolutions, the suppression and subjugation of populations, enormous suffering and destruction. But a theory of justice has to start from where we are, and not with a utopian or abstract ideal of how human beings should live, and therefore it has to reckon with social conditions as they exist and the interests, values, ideas of the self that arise out of them. A conception of justice and the values on which it is based is always relative, and this means that unanticipated historical developments can make them obsolete or unattractive. But given the historical developments that have occurred and the kind of societies we live in, there are good reasons for advocating certain values and rejecting others.

The fact remains that the philosophical tradition on which I have depended is a western tradition, and it is very likely that many of the assumptions it makes are not universally shared. There is no cure for the fate of being a creature of one's culture. The ideal of complete objectivity is not only unrealisable but it is based upon a conception of the self which communitarians and others rightly criticise. But the problematic nature of any pronouncements about international justice is not a reason for not making them, but rather a reason for recognising that they are only a contribution to an ongoing debate which ought not to be dominated by western concerns and interests.

The third moral objective I attempt to embody in the idea of the just international society can be regarded as a consequence of regarding individual freedom and community as valuable. If individuals are to exercise their freedom and maintain their communities, then they must have resources sufficient for these purposes. On the other hand, policies of distribution have often been seen as incompatible with both individual freedom and community. For the pursuit of individual interests and the maintenance of a community way of life seem to require that individuals and groups be able to pursue their own affairs and dispose of their resources as they see fit without outside interference. I have argued that there is no a priori way of determining what justice requires as far as distribution is concerned. Whether principles and procedures of distributive justice are applicable to a social order and what they require depend upon the nature of its communities and the relations between them. I have argued that communitarians are right to suppose that within certain kinds of community distribution of resources in a way that benefits the least well-off can be reconciled with individual self-determination. If ensuring the well-being of the community and others in it becomes an important objective for an individual, then he/she will be prepared to regard sharing as a duty of justice owed to other community members. In a community the well-being of each becomes bound up with the well-being of all. But one of the most difficult challenges facing a theory of international justice is to show how self-determination of communities can be made compatible with arrangements which will ensure that the least well-off people in the world have sufficient resources to enjoy the benefits of freedom and community.

I have attempted to solve this problem in two ways, first of all by supposing that new communities will be formed in the international world, communities which overstep national boundaries and include individuals from both wealthy and poor regions, and that within these groups there will be a distribution of goods and services according to principles which members collectively endorse. Second, I suppose that relationships between communities will make it more likely that the activities and relationships which in our world tend to cause or exacerbate poverty and oppression do not occur and that past injustices can be remedied. These arrangements may not solve all problems of poverty and exploitation but they provide, in my view, the best way of reconciling the moral desirability of ensuring the well-being of all individuals with individual freedom and self-determination of communities.

For relations between communities to count as just there must be ways of settling conflicts which all parties will regard as fair. I have not supposed that in international society there will ever be general agreement about who is in the right and who is in the wrong in a dispute, or any principle that can decide such a thing to everyone's satisfaction. This kind of agreement does not even exist in national societies. What I have tried to do is to specify the social conditions under which communities in the international world are likely both to respect the entitlements of other individuals and communities and to resolve their disputes by compromise and conciliation using procedures that all accept.

Central to my approach is the idea that a theory of international justice ought not only to show how moral objectives can be realised and how the problems of reconciling these objectives can be solved, but that it ought to do so in a practical way. Being practical involves satisfying a number of requirements. It means, first of all, that a theory of justice must take into account the values, allegiances, objectives, ideas about justice which individuals and communities now have. These values and objectives do not have to be taken as fixed or regarded as beyond criticism. However, if a theory of justice is to be satisfactory it must be possible to persuade rational moral individuals that they ought to accept it, that they ought to act according to its principles, or that they ought to try to create the social order in which these principles can prevail.

If the principles prescribed by a theory are to prevail, then it must also be reasonable to believe that the social order it prescribes is sustainable. This means not only that political and social arrangements must be reasonably stable, that it should not be likely that this new world order will dissolve into war or serious and irresolvable conflicts. It also means that it must be reasonable to suppose that individuals and communities in it will be able and generally motivated to act according to principles of justice. One of my primary objectives has been to show how relations in the international world can be ordered in a way that promotes respect for individuals and communities and a peaceful and just resolution of disputes.

For a theory of international justice to be practical it must also be reasonable to suppose that the world order it prescribes can actually be brought into existence. I have argued that there are good pragmatic and moral reasons for insisting that a just world order be achieved peacefully and without subjugation and use of force. This does not mean that we should accept Kant's prohibition against revolution or wars of liberation. There may in some cases be no other way in which people can defend themselves against persecution or exploitation. But what should be avoided is using violence or force in order to try to create world peace or a new international world order. If a theory is to satisfy this condition it must thus be plausible to suppose that through reforms, gradual development of new social relations, the world can peacefully and without the use of aggression and domination become a just world order.

I have tried to satisfy this requirement in two ways. First of all by attempting to show that realists and Marxists are wrong to believe that peaceful progress towards a just world order is impossible; and second, by trying to present a plausible story of how the international world could develop into a just world order. It must be admitted that there are obvious problems with this exercise. A story about the future invites one or both of the following complaints: that its account of progress or of the future world society is too schematic to give us a good idea of whether the development it describes is really feasible; or that the details that the story does contain are bound to be wrong in some important respects. Speculations about the future are notoriously inaccurate. I claim no more for my story about progress to a just world order than Kant claimed for his. It is supposed to give us hope that such a world is at least possible and it is supposed to give us some indication of what can be done to bring it about. Nevertheless, views about social possibilities depend upon assumptions and theories about social structures and forces, human motivations and desires, and these may turn out to be wrong. What this means is simply that my ideas about these matters are subject to refutation, as are the ideas of others.

It might be objected that my account of international justice fails to be practical in the most crucial respect. It does not seem to tell us how to resolve the disputes that actually occur in the world: it does not tell us who has justice on their side, the Palestinians or the Israelis, the IRA or the British, the Lebanese Christians or Muslims, the Greeks or the Turks, etc. If it cannot give us an answer to the question of what side of a dispute between communities is just, then what use can it possibly be?

However, nothing much would be accomplished by a theory which did give us a judgment about these disputes – except perhaps to fuel the sense of righteousness of one party or another. For those who are on the other side are unlikely to acquiesce. And why should they? There are very few international conflicts where the justice of one cause is clear. In most cases disputes involve not simply a difference of opinion about a particular issue – whether a territory or the right to rule belongs to one people or another. What divides opposing sides is generally a whole history of grievances and conflict which has resulted in opposing historical perspectives and contrary or incommensurable interpretations of events. There is no easy way of resolving such disputes – which is why war is such an inadequate tool for pursuing justice in international affairs. It generally addresses the wrong question and does nothing to resolve festering grievances.

This does not mean that individuals are not entitled to form an opinion about the justice of existing disputes; nor does it mean that we can't say that some of these opinions are more rational or better from a moral point of view than others. But it does mean that we should be suspicious about theories which claim to give rational, objective judgments about international disputes. Whose justice and whose rationality? Given the nature of these disputes and the fact that those who engage in them are often separated not just by different opinions but by a different world view, the only reasonable course is to attempt to envision the kind of social and political environment in which parties, in spite of their different perspectives, would be able and prepared to make concessions and compromises. This is what I have attempted to do in my approach to international justice.

Nevertheless, it is reasonable to require that a theory of justice give us some indication of how we should deal with the world as it is. If a theory of justice is valid, it must be applicable to our present situation, and not merely to a future world order which may never be realised. What does justice require us to do?

In an international context the moral objectives of promoting individual freedom, the value of community, general well-being, peaceful resolution of disputes, give rise, I have claimed, to three basic 'principles' of justice: that individuals should be free to associate according to their goals, interests, attachments and needs; that communities determine for themselves their political and social arrangements; that communities develop and support mutually acceptable structures and institutions for the resolution of disputes. Being just means acting according to these principles in so far as this is possible in our world.

Freedom of association in our world is limited both by prejudices of individuals and groups and by the requirements of states. Those who aim to make the world more just will do what they can to counter prejudices and to allow and encourage associations across borders, particularly those that include people from both wealthy and poor regions of the world. So long as our world is a world of states, individuals will be rightly reluctant to form associations which could prejudice the survival of their state. On the other hand, people are justified in resisting policies of governments and leaders which attempt to isolate them from outside influences, encourage them to regard outsiders as enemies, misinform them or attempt to confine them to their national communities. The entitlements of states are not sacred.

Encouraging people to associate across borders does not mean welcoming all developments which are making the people of the world more interdependent. For this interdependence not only creates dislocation, hardship and poverty in some areas of the world; it can also compromise the ability of people to form and maintain the communities which they value. Those who aim to make the world more just will thus take seriously and often support movements of people for self-determination and the attempts that communities make to control their own political and economic destiny – though this does not mean that everything that is done for the sake of self-determination is acceptable. In some cases, it may be necessary for the people of a state or nation first to establish their independence and their sense of community identity before entering into broader associations.

People who aim to make the world more just will also attempt to establish agreements, institutions, relationships which enable disputes to be resolved in a mutually acceptable way. This means, first of all, that everyone ought to make the associations to which they belong, whether countries, companies or political and religious groups, more just, both in their relations to other members and in their dealings with outsiders. And second, it means that existing international bodies and procedures for settling disputes should be strengthened, but in a way that does not allow them to be controlled by a few large powers. For most people of the world are not likely to regard as equitable institutions or procedures dominated by the USA, the USSR or the wealthy countries of Europe. To the extent that more acceptable procedures and agreements become common in our world it will also become more possible to promote and realise the other principles of justice.

If the world becomes more peaceful it is also likely to become more just, and if it becomes more just then it will undoubtedly be much more peaceful. On the other hand, the opposite development may occur. When I first began working on this project the world was frozen into the political configuration caused by the Cold War, and no radical change seemed possible – except the catastrophic consequences that would have resulted from nuclear war. Within an incredibly short time the situation changed: the Soviet Union embarked on a programme of reform, arms control and even disarmament were put on the agenda and the people of eastern Europe were freed from their long confinement. The possibility of peace and more just political arrangements seemed to become greater. Now as I finish, the prospect looks more ominous. Reforms in the Soviet Union and eastern Europe have bogged down and so have disarmament talks; crisis and war in the Middle East suggest that regional conflict will be endemic to the world of the immediate future, and that the new world order may be determined, as it often has been, by the interests of those who are willing and able to use force.

Providence appears in the background of Kant's history as a hope or faith that out of the conflict, cruelty and human suffering which form the everyday events of history will come progress to a perpetually peaceful world. By replacing Providence with the Angel of History, Walter Benjamin captures the feeling of helplessness and sometimes despair with which we view the unfolding of events:

> His face is turned toward the past. Where we perceive a chain of events, he sees one single catastrophe which keeps piling wreckage upon wreckage and hurls it in front of his feet. The angel would like to stay, awaken the dead, and make whole what has been smashed. But a storm is blowing from Paradise; it has got caught in his wings with such violence that the angel can no longer close them. The storm irresistibly propels him into the future to which his back is turned, while the pile of debris before him grows skyward. This storm is what we call progress.
>
> (1973: 259)

Whether we should look at the events of our world as a source of hope or a reason for despair is not something that is humanly possible to determine. Those who aim to bring about a just world must take what opportunities are offered with the acknowledgement that their efforts may be futile or even counter-productive, but also without abandoning the hope that their goal will eventually become the common cause of humankind.

Notes

Introduction – the problems of international justice

1. Well-known contemporary realists include Reinhold Niebuhr (1932), George Kennan (1951), Hans Morgenthau (1946, 1978), Raymond Aron (1966).
2. This realist prediction is discussed in relation to the future of Europe by T. Risse-Kappen (1990).
3. For a statement of this position, see C. Wright Mills (1958).
4. My position is similar to that presented in Rawls (1973, 1985).
5. Beitz presents two accounts of international justice in his book. The first is similar in some respects to the conception presented in Chapter 4. But the following is the one he thinks is most appropriate for an interdependent world.
6. Rawls' views about what kind of social relations are required as a basis for his conception of justice are most completely expressed in his later 'Idea of an overlapping consensus' (1987). I criticise his idea of what binds people together in a community in Chapter 5.
7. Simmons (1979) argues that neither social contract theory nor appeals to justice succeed in grounding political obligation. I explore this problem in relation to questions about international organisation.

1 Being realistic

1. An example of an advocate of the first type of realism is Kenneth Waltz (1959). An example of a realist who argues that leaders have an obligation to pursue national interest is Craig Carr (1986). Morgenthau (1978) is a well-known advocate of balance of power.
2. This is not an entirely accurate account of Hegel's position, for he too had a conception of world order and thought that the relations between states should be respectful, if not always peaceful. Nevertheless, the way in which he reaches this result is very different from the reasoning of cosmopolitans. See Chapter 6.
3. The page references are to the 'Head' edition and are included in most modern editions of the *Leviathan*. Hobbes' spelling has been modernised.

4. Women do in Hobbes' scheme of things generally end up in a subordinate position. But this is due to what happens in the state of nature rather than the natural right of men to rule. See Carole Pateman's discussion of Hobbes (1988). Since, however, the individuals which Hobbes has in mind are clearly men, I will use masculine pronouns to refer to them.

5. Two prisoners are accused of committing a crime and are interrogated separately by the police. Each is told that if he confesses and implicates the other, then he will receive a light sentence (two years), but that if he does not confess he will get twenty years. However, both of these prisoners know that if both of them refuse to confess, then they can only be convicted on a lesser charge and will each get five years. Both also know that if they both confess and implicate each other each will get ten years, and each knows that the same deal has been offered to the other. The case is such that the choice both prisoners are likely to make as rational, self-interested agents will result in a worse outcome for each than would probably have resulted if they had been less rational or self-interested.

6. Locke insists that the state of nature is not a state of war, and requirements of justice apply there and can be enforced, though imperfectly. See Paragraph 6ff.

7. Rawls (1987: 2) makes a similar suggestion about Hobbes' concerns.

8. Hobbes sometimes refers to conditions in his own society in order to persuade us that in a state of nature we would be at the mercy of aggressors:

> Let him therefore consider with himself, when taking a journey, he arms himself, and seeks to go well accompanied; when going to sleep, he locks his doors; when even in his house he locks his chests; and this when he knows there be laws and public officers, armed, to revenge all injuries shall be done him.
>
> (1651: 62)

2 Achieving perpetual peace

1. Kant himself seems to have favoured constitutional monarchy, and argues that the best way of achieving a republic is to begin with absolute monarchy and gradually reform it (Reiss 1977: 101).

2. Thomas Carson argues in ' "Perpetual peace": what Kant should have said' (1988) that a viable world federation must have sufficient military force to prevent states from arming and waging war.

3. Some commentators have seen a difficulty in reconciling Kant's emphasis on the role of law in 'Perpetual peace' and his insistence that morality depends on the unforced will of the individual. According to his conception of morality, ideally individuals ought to be living together in a 'kingdom of ends' where they act freely in accordance with the moral law. But Kant did not suppose that this ideal could be realised. The power of the state will always be needed in order to back up obedience to law. However his account of how even forced obedience can provide a moral education shows how in the imperfect human world, legal requirements and sanctions can serve a moral purpose. See Riley (1983).

4. Kant also rejects the idea that republican states are justified in intervening in

the affairs of non-republican states – even though republican states possess a legitimacy which despotic states lack. However, republican states are justified in defending themselves against aggression. Kant is not a pacifist.
5. This is the problem which Freud, whose idea of progress to peace is obviously influenced by Kant, draws attention to in 'Why war?' (1933) and elsewhere.

3 Marxism and international relations

1. The existence of political democracy in countries like America and England encouraged Marx to speculate that there might be a peaceful road to socialism (1872). However, he also believed that this road is not open in most countries; and his views about the nature of the capitalist state suggest that even in the most favourable environment class struggle is not likely to be peaceful.
2. This is suggested by his views on the Crimean War. Russia, he sometimes argued, is the fountainhead of political reaction and it is in the interests of both capitalists and workers to contain its influence by war if necessary. See the articles he wrote for the *New York Tribune* during the Crimean War (1853–6), reprinted in *The Eastern Question* (1969).
3. One of Marx's most explicit statements about the nature of the communist society is in the *Critique of the Gotha Programme*:

> In a higher phase of communist society, after the enslaving subordination of the individual to the division of labour, and therewith also the antithesis between mental and physical labour, has vanished; after labour has become not only a means of life but life's prime want; after the productive forces have also increased with the all-round development of the individual, and all the springs of co-operative wealth flow more abundantly – only then can the narrow horizon of bourgeois right be crossed in its entirety and society inscribe on its banners: From each according to his ability, to each according to his needs.
>
> (1875: 23ff)

4. The rate of profit has a tendency to fall, Marx argued in *Capital*, vol. 3, part III, because constant capital – what is invested in machinery and infrastructure – tends to increase over time in relation to variable capital – what is invested in living labour, the sole creator of surplus value and thus the source of profit.

4 Cosmopolitan justice in a federation of sovereign states

1. Beitz, who doubts whether the 'right of sovereignty' is always compatible with justice, argues that the claims of needy people can over-ride this right. A defensive war, he says, may not always be just: 'a war of self defence fought by an affluent nation against a poorer nation pressing legitimate claims under global principles (for example, for increased food aid) might be unjustifiable' (1979: 176).

2. For more extensive discussions of the pros and cons of intervention, see Jeff McMahan (1986), the reply by Neil MacCormick (1986), Walzer (1980a, 1980b), Beitz (1979).
3. This is, in effect, Freud's criticism of Kant's idea of perpetual peace in 'Why war?' (1933).

5 Cosmopolitan justice in a world state

1. One philosopher who does is Bertrand Russell in *Common Sense and Nuclear Warfare* (1959).
2. In his earlier book on the problem of nuclear war, *Fate of the Earth* (1982), Schell supports Einstein's idea that world government is the logical, and probably the only effective, solution to the problem of war. However, in *The Abolition*, he drops this idea as impractical and undesirable and looks elsewhere.
3. A number of constitutions have been written for world government. See Eaton *et al.* (1944), Clark and Sohn (1966).

6 The state as a community

1. It should be said that this is the starting point for his political philosophy but not for his philosophy as a whole. The *Phenomenology of Mind* (1807) contains an account of why individuals must come to recognise each other as free beings. It should also be said that 'all individuals' really means 'all male individuals'. Women, for Hegel, have a different social status and destiny. For this reason I use the pronoun 'he' to refer to individuals in the context of a discussion of Hegel's political philosophy.
2. I am assuming that Rawls still believes in his later works that the values and idea of justice of pluralist societies are or ought to be universal, and that in this respect his position is unlike Rorty's defence of 'bourgeois liberalism'. To claim that ideals arose in a particular political environment does not mean that they cannot be regarded, once found, as universally valid.
3. Marx is, in the section on bureaucracy, primarily concerned to criticise the 'spirit' of the bureau, and claims that it hinders rather than furthers anything that can be called real political ends: 'Avowed political spirit as also political-mindness therefore appear to the bureaucracy as *treason* against its mystery' (1843: 24).
4. Pelczynski (1984) criticises Hegel's dismissal of nationalism and suggests that the Marxist failure to develop a theory of the nation can be traced to this inadequacy in Hegel's view of social life.

7 Democratic communities

1. Rousseau also briefly refers to the idea of a federation in *Emile* (1762: 430). It is thought that Rousseau wrote more extensively on this topic, but the manuscript was unfortunately destroyed.

2. See Kirkpatrick Sale in *Human Scale* (1980), Part V, Ch. 1, for one extended critique of the politics of modern states.
3. This is how some theorists believe that participatory democracy can best be realised in a modern context. See, for example, Carole Pateman's *Participation and Democratic Theory* (1970).
4. For a discussion and criticism of such theories, see Pateman (1970, Ch. 1).
5. For examples, see Unger (1975), Michael Taylor (1982), Balbus (1982).
6. Kirkpatrick Sale suggests a development something like this in Part V of *Human Scale* (1980), though he doesn't go into details.
7. See Boris Frankel's criticism of utopian communities in *The Post-Industrial Utopians* (1987: pp. 87ff.).

8 The nation as a community

1. Not all nationalist thinkers have believed that it is necessary for each nation to have one state. Fichte, in fact, thought that there were advantages in the existence of more than one German state. Not all nationalist thinkers have thought it absolutely necessary that each nation have its own state. Otto Bauer (1927) argues that there is nothing wrong with a multi-nation state so long as it allows each nation in it sufficient autonomy to maintain its culture and way of life. Nevertheless the formula, 'One nation, one state', is widely accepted.
2. For discussions about the historical origin of nations, see Benedict Anderson (1983), Seton-Watson (1977), Smith (1971), Kohn (1944) and Nairn (1977).

9 Towards a just world order

1. This is a common complaint of modern social thinkers. It is found, for example, in Durkheim (1933).
2. Gellner (1983) argues that nationalism is a species of patriotism – something which is encouraged by states and their institutions. Walzer (1980a, 1983) does not talk about nations as such, but his idea that through sharing political and social institutions people develop a sense of having a common life can be taken as an account of what makes a nation. There are, in fact, some obvious similarities between my idea of a nation and Walzer's (1983) idea of a common life achieved by participation in various social spheres.

Bibliography

Amdur, Robert (1977) 'Rawls' theory of justice: domestic and international perspectives', *World Politics* 29, 3: 438–62.

Anderson, Benedict (1983) *Imagined Communities: Reflections on the Origin and Spread of Nationalism*, London: Verso.

Armstrong, A. C. (1931) 'Kant's philosophy of peace and war', *Journal of Philosophy* 28, 8: 197–204.

Aron, Raymond (1966) *Peace and War: A Theory of International Relations*, London: Weidenfeld & Nicolson.

Axelrod, Robert (1984) *Evolution of Cooperation*, New York: Basic Books.

Balbus, Isaac D. (1982) *Marxism and Domination*, Princeton, NJ: Princeton University Press.

Barone, Charles A. (1985) *Marxist Thoughts on Imperialism: Survey and Critique*, London: Macmillan.

Barry, Brian (1982) 'Humanity and justice in a global perspective', in J. Pennock and J. Chapman (eds) *Nomos XXIV: Ethics, Economics and the Law*, New York: New York University Press.

Barry, Brian (1986) 'Can states be moral? International morality and the compliance problem', in Anthony Ellis (ed.) *Ethics and International Relations*, Manchester: Manchester University Press.

Bauer, Otto (1927) *Die Nationalitätenfrage und die Sozialdemokratie*, Vienna: Wiener Volksbuchhandlung.

Beck, Lewis White (ed.) (1963) *Kant on History*, New York: Bobbs-Merrill.

Beitz, Charles (1979) *Political Theory and International Relations*, Princeton, NJ: Princeton University Press.

Benjamin, Walter (1973) *Illuminations*, London: Fontana.

Berlin, Isaiah (1979) 'Nationalism: past neglect and present power', *Partisan Review* 46, 3: 337–75.

Berns, Walter (1959) 'The case against world government', in R. A. Goldwin (ed.) *Readings in World Politics*, New York: Oxford University Press.

Boxill, Bernard R. (1987) 'Global equality of opportunity and national integrity', *Social Philosophy and Policy* 5, 1: 143–68.

Brown, Lester (1972) *World Without Borders*, New York: Random House.

Bukharin, Nicolai (1917) *Imperialism and World Economy*, New York: Howard Fertig, 1966.

Carr, Craig L. (1986) 'Are states moral agents?', *Social Theory and Practice* 12, 1: 75–102.

Carson, Thomas (1988) '*Perpetual Peace*: what Kant should have said', *Social Theory and Practice* 14, 2: 173–214.

Clark, G. and Sohn, L. B. (1966) *World Peace Through World Law: Two Alternative Plans*, 3rd edn, Cambridge, Mass.: Harvard University Press.

Cobban, Alfred (1964) *Rousseau and the Modern State*, 2nd edn, London: George Allen & Unwin.

Cohen, Marshall (1984) 'Moral skepticism and international relations', *Philosophy and Public Affairs* 13, 4: 299–346.

Cox, Richard H. (1960) *Locke on War and Peace*, Oxford: Clarendon Press.

Debray, Regis (1977) 'Marxism and the national question', *New Left Review* 105: 25–41.

Doyle, M. W. (1983) 'Kant, liberal legacies and foreign affairs', *Philosophy and Public Affairs* 12, 3: 205–35 (Part 1); 12, 4: 323–53 (Part 2).

Durkheim, Emile (1933) *Division of Labour in Society*, New York: Macmillan.

Eaton, Howard O. *et al.* (1944) *Federation, the Coming Structure of World Government*, Norman, Okla.: University of Oklahoma Press.

Eibl-Eibesfeldt, I. (1979) *Biology of Peace and War*, London: Thames & Hudson.

Fichte, Johann Gottlieb (1798) *Science of Rights*, trans A. E. Koreger, London: Routledge & Kegan Paul, 1907.

—— (1800) *Der geschlossne Handelstaat* ('Closed commercial state') in Werke I, 7, Stuttgart: Friedrich Frommann, 1988.

—— (1807) *Addresses to the German Nation*, ed. G. A. Kelly, New York and Evanston: Harper & Row, 1968.

Frankel, Boris (1987) *The Post-Industrial Utopians*, Cambridge: Polity.

French, Stanley and Gutman, Andres (1974) 'The principle of national self-determination', in V. Held, S. Morgenbesser and T. Nagel (eds) *Philosophy, Morality and International Affairs*, London, New York: Oxford University Press.

Freud, S. (1915) 'Thoughts for the times on war and death', in the Pelican Freud Library, 12, London, 1978.

—— (1930) 'Civilisation and its discontents', in the Pelican Freud Library, 12, 1978.

—— (1933) 'Why war?' in the Pelican Freud Library, 12, London, 1978.

Funke, Gerhard (1975) 'Concerning eternal peace – ethics and politics', in W. H. Werkmeister (ed.) *Reflections on Kant's Philosophy*, Gainsville, Fla: University of Florida Press.

Galbraith, J. K. (1963) *American Capitalism: The Concept of Countervailing Power*, Harmondsworth: Penguin.

Gellner, Ernest (1983) *Nations and Nationalism*, Oxford: Blackwell.

Gilbert, Alan (1978) 'Marx on internationalism and war', *Philosophy and Public Affairs* 7, 4: 346–69.

Hare, J. E. and Joynt, C. B. (1982) *Ethics and International Affairs*, New York: St Martin's Press.

Hegel, G. W. F. (1807) *Phenomenology of Mind*, trans. J. B. Baillie, 2nd edn, London: Allen & Unwin, 1931.

—— (1821) *Grundlinien der Philosophie des Rechts*, trans. T. M. Knox (1952) as

Hegel's Philosophy of Right, Oxford: Clarendon.

Hegel, G. W. F. (1840) *Vorlesungen über die Philosophie der Geschichte*, trans. R. S. Hartman (1953) as *Reason in History*, New York: Bobbs-Merrill.

Herder, J. G. (1791) *Outlines of a Philosophy of the History of Man*, trans. T. Churchill, New York: Bergman, 1966.

Hobbes, Thomas (1651) *Leviathan* ed. C. B. Macpherson, Harmondsworth: Penguin, 1968.

Hobson, J.A. (1902) *Imperialism: A Study*, 3rd edn, London: George Allen & Unwin.

Hoffmann, Stanley (1981) *Duties Beyond Borders*, Syracuse: Syracuse University Press.

Howard, Michael (1978) *War and the Liberal Conscience*, London: Temple-Smith.

Kant, Immanuel (1784) 'Idea for a universal history from a cosmopolitan point of view', in Lewis White Beck (ed.) (1963) *Kant on History*, New York: Bobbs-Merrill.

—— (1795) 'Perpetual peace', in Lewis White Beck (ed.) (1963) *Kant on History*, New York: Bobbs-Merrill.

—— (1797) *Metaphysical Elements of Justice*, New York: Bobbs-Merrill, 1974.

Kavka, Gregory S. (1986) *Hobbesian Moral and Political Theory*, Princeton, NJ: Princeton University Press.

—— (1987) *Moral Paradoxes of Nuclear Deterrence*, Cambridge: Cambridge University Press.

Kedourie, Elie (1961) *Nationalism*, 2nd edn, London: Hutchinson University Library.

Kennan, George (1951) *American Diplomacy 1900–1950*, Chicago: Chicago University Press.

Keohane, Robert O. and Nye, Joseph S. (1977) *Power and Interdependence: World Politics in Transition*, Boston, Mass.: Little, Brown & Co.

Klare, M. T. (1990) 'Growing firepower in the Third World', *Bulletin of the Atomic Scientists* 46, 8: 25–29.

Kohn, Hans (1944) *The Idea of Nationalism*, New York: Macmillan.

Kubalkova, V. and Cruickshank, A. A. (1985) *Marxism and International Relations*, Oxford: Clarendon Press.

Lenin, V. I. (1916) *Imperialism, the Highest Stage of Capitalism*.

Locke, John (1690) *Two Treatises of Government*.

Lorenz, Konrad (1966) *On Aggression*, London: Methuen.

Lyotard, Jean-François (1984) *The Postmodern Condition*, Manchester: Manchester University Press.

MacCormick, Neil (1986) 'Reply to Jeff McMahan's "The ethics of international intervention" ', in Anthony Ellis (ed.) *Ethics and International Relations*, Manchester: Manchester University Press.

MacIntyre, Alasdair (1988) *Whose Justice? Which Rationality?*, Notre Dame, Ind.: University of Notre Dame Press.

McMahan, Jeff (1986) 'The ethics of international intervention', in Anthony Ellis (ed.) *Ethics and International Relations*, Manchester: Manchester University Press.

McNeilly, F. S. (1968) *The Anatomy of Hobbes*, London: Macmillan.

Marx, Karl (1843) *Contribution to the Critique of Hegel's 'Philosophy of Right'* in R. C. Tucker (ed.), *Marx-Engels Reader*, 2nd edn, New York: W. W. Norton, 1978.

—— (1872) *Speech at Amsterdam* in *Marx, Engels Collected Works*, 23.

—— (1875) *Critique of the Gotha Programme* in *Marx, Engels Selected Works*, Moscow: Progress Press, 1968.

—— (1878) *Capital 3: A Critique of Political Economy*, trans. D. Fernbach, Harmondsworth: Penguin, 1981.

—— (1897) *The Eastern Question*, London: F. Cass, 1969.

Marx, Karl and Engels, Frederick (1848) *Communist Manifesto*, in *Marx, Engels Collected Works*, 5, London: Lawrence & Wishart, 1976.

Mazzini, Giuseppe (1860) *Duties of Man*, London: Dent and Sons, 1966.

Mill, John Stuart (1885) *Principles of Political Economy*, 9th edn, New York: Sentry Press, 1965.

Mills, C. Wright (1958) *The Causes of World War Three*, New York: Simon & Schuster.

Morgenthau, Hans (1946) *Scientific Man Versus Power Politics*, Chicago: University of Chicago Press.

—— (1978) *Politics Among Nations: The Struggle for Power and Peace*, 5th edn, New York: Knopf.

Nairn, Tom (1977) *The Break-up of Britain: Crisis and Neo-Nationalism*, London: New Left Books.

Niebuhr, Reinhold (1932) *Moral Man and Immoral Society*, New York: C. Scribner & Sons.

O'Conner, James (1974) *The Corporations and the State*, New York: Harper & Row.

Pateman, Carole (1970) *Participation and Democratic Theory*, Cambridge: Cambridge University Press.

—— (1988) *Sexual Contract*, Oxford: Blackwell.

Pelczynski, Z. A. (1984), 'Nation, civil society, state: Hegelian sources of the Marxian non-theory of nationality', in Z. A. Pelczynski (ed.) *The State and Civil Society in Hegel's Political Philosophy*, Cambridge: Cambridge University Press.

Raphael, D. D. (1977) *Hobbes: Morals and Politics*, London: George Allen & Unwin.

Rawls, John (1973) *A Theory of Justice*, Oxford: Oxford University Press.

Rawls, John (1985) 'Justice as fairness: political not metaphysical', *Philosophy and Public Affairs* 14, 3: 223–51.

—— (1987) 'The idea of an overlapping consensus', *The Oxford Journal of Legal Philosophy* 7, 1: 1–25.

—— (1988) 'Priority of right and ideas of the good', *Philosophy and Public Affairs* 17, 4: 251–76.

Raz, Joseph (1990) 'National self-determination', *Journal of Philosophy* 87, 9: 439–61.

Reich, Wilhelm (1970) *The Mass Psychology of Fascism*, New York: Farrar, Straus & Giroux.

Reiss, H. S. (1977) *Kant's Political Writings*, Cambridge: Cambridge University Press.

Riley, Patrick (1983) *Kant's Political Theory*, Totowa, NJ: Rowman &Littlefield.

Risse-Kappen, T. (1990) 'Predicting the new Europe', *Bulletin of the Atomic Scientists* 46, 4: 9–13.

Rorty, Richard (1983) 'Postmodern bourgeois liberalism', *Journal of Philosophy*

LXXX, 10: 583–9.

Rousseau, Jean-Jacques (1755) *Political Economy*, trans. Judith Masters, New York: St. Martin's Press, 1978.

—— (1761) *The Social Contract*, trans. G. D. H. Cole, New York: Prometheus Books, 1988.

—— (1762) *Emile*, trans. B. Foxley, London: J. M. Dent, 1969.

Russell, Bertrand (1959) *Commonsense and Nuclear Warfare*, London: Allen & Unwin.

Sachsteder, William (1954) 'Kant's analysis of international relations', *Journal of Philosophy* 51, 25: 848–55.

Sale, Kirkpatrick (1980) *Human Scale*, London: Secker and Warburg.

Sandel, Michael (1982) *Liberalism and the Limits of Justice*, Cambridge: Cambridge University Press.

Schell, Jonathan (1982) *Fate of the Earth*, London: Picador.

—— (1984) *The Abolition*, New York: Knopf.

Seton-Watson, Hugh (1977) *Nations and States*, London: Methuen.

Simmons, A. John (1979) *Moral Principles and Political Obligation*, Princeton, NJ: Princeton University Press.

Smith, Anthony D. (1971) *Theories of Nationalism*, London: Duckworth.

Taylor, Charles (1975) *Hegel*, Cambridge: Cambridge University Press.

Taylor, Michael (1982) *Community, Anarchy and Liberty*, Cambridge: Cambridge University Press.

Thompson, E. P. (1980) 'Notes on exterminism, the last stage of civilisation', *New Left Review* 121: 3–31.

Thompson, Janna (1986) 'States in the state of nature', *Critical Philosophy* 3, 1 & 2: 114–25.

—— (1990) 'Land rights and aboriginal sovereignty', *Australasian Journal of Philosophy* 68, 3: 313–29.

Unger, Roberto Mangabeira (1975) *Knowledge and Politics*, New York: Macmillan.

Waltz, Kenneth (1959) *Man, the State and War*, New York: Columbia University Press.

—— (1962) 'Kant, liberalism and war', *American Political Science Review*, 56, 2: 331–40.

Walzer, Michael (1977) 'World War Two: why was this war different?', *Philosophy and Public Affairs* 1, 1: 3–21.

—— (1980a) *Just and Unjust Wars*, Harmondsworth: Penguin.

—— (1980b) 'Moral standing of states: a response to four critics', *Philosophy and Public Affairs* 9, 3: 218–19.

—— (1983) *Spheres of Justice: A Defence of Pluralism and Equality*, Oxford: Blackwell.

Warren, Bill (1973) 'Imperialism and capitalist industrialisation', *New Left Review* 81: 3–46.

Williams, Howard (1983) *Kant's Political Philosophy*, Oxford: Blackwell.

Wilson, E. O. (1978), *On Human Nature*, Cambridge, Mass.: Harvard University Press.

Young, Iris Marion (1986) 'The ideal of community and the politics of difference', *Social Theory and Practice* 12, 1: 1–26.

Index